SAMANTHA WALTON is a Reader in Modern Literature
Bath Spa University, where the focus of her research
the link between nature and mental health. Previously,
she was a Writing Fellow at the prestigious Rachel
Carson Centre in Munich. She is also a poet and has
appeared on the BBC, and at a number of festivals
including Green Man and Wilderness to speak about
her research. She lives in Bristol.

amlwalton

Everybody

Needs

Beauty

In Search
of the
Nature
Cure

Samantha Walton

BLOOMSBURY PUBLISHING
LONDON · OXFORD · NEW YORK · NEW DELHI · SYDNEY

BLOOMSBURY PUBLISHING
Bloomsbury Publishing Plc
50 Bedford Square, London, WC1B 3DP, UK
29 Earlsfort Terrace, Dublin 2, Ireland

BLOOMSBURY, BLOOMSBURY PUBLISHING and the Diana logo are
trademarks of Bloomsbury Publishing Plc

First published in Great Britain 2021
This edition published 2022

A catalogue record for this book is available from the British Library

ISBN: HB: 978-1-5266-2072-9; TPB: 978-1-5266-2071-2; PB: 978-1-5266-2102-3;
EBOOK: 978-1-5266-2070-5; EPDF: 978-1-5266-4528-9

2 4 6 8 10 9 7 5 3 1

Typeset by Newgen KnowledgeWorks Pvt. Ltd., Chennai, India
Printed and bound in Great Britain by CPI Group (UK) Ltd, Croydon CR0 4YY

MIX
Paper from
responsible sources
FSC® C171272

To find out more about our authors and books visit www.bloomsbury.com
and sign up for our newsletters

Contents

Introduction
An Ancient Ritual

I set out at 7 a.m. Midsummer has just passed, so the sun rose hours ago and is blazing high in the sky above me as I wheel my bike out onto the road. I usually love the hot weather. Like many people living with a wet, changeable island climate, I rush outside at the first hint of sun. But we're currently in the middle of a long, lingering heatwave, the northern hemisphere's joint hottest summer on record. For six weeks daytime temperatures will soar above 30°C. Flowers in window boxes are withering. Clothes stick to the skin. The lawns of Castle Park, Bristol's favourite drinking spot, are rubbed to dust.

As I speed down the city's network of cycle paths, like arteries running from east to west, I try to ignore the wilted plants, smoke fumes, and rush-hour traffic crowding the streets for another day's work. Office

1

blocks and shopping centres whizz by, followed by flyovers and industrial estates. Finally I reach the city limits. The fields may be sun-bleached – more victims of the heatwave – but still, I'm grateful. I'm leaving the concrete and tarmac, putting the smell of petrol and hot tar behind me.

From the city limits, it will take me another hour to reach my destination. According to the map on my phone, the route will take me past farms, fields, along the banks of a river, before it follows snaking train tracks deep into north Somerset. I'm already soaked in sweat, but I can't turn back now. Escaping the city, I'm taking the first step in a ritual that's at once staggeringly ancient, and absolutely modern. I'm going to nature in search of health.

There's nothing exactly wrong with me, not at the moment. But recently, I've noticed an interest in nature cures emerging everywhere. Schools are taking their classrooms outdoors. Hospitals are being retrofitted with gardens and green spaces for patients to relax and unwind. Mental health charities advise us to get our 'daily dose of Vitamin N', to find ways to switch off in forests and nature reserves. Natural consultants sell wild excursions to businesses, promising that their workforce will become more productive, creative and resilient. In the tiny Scottish archipelago of Shetland, it is now possible to walk into a doctor's surgery with symptoms of depression, anxiety or stress, and walk out with a 'natural prescription', including advice on how to connect with the living world on Shetland's windswept shores.

As sudden as this fashion seems, the idea that nature might be healing is nothing new. Tales of people who find comfort, restoration and meaning in natural settings have been with us for a very long time. We can credit the Romantic poets for inventing gentle, healing Nature – a place of innocence that teaches us to be good, and where we can get in touch with our own best selves. But look further back, and our deepest cultural memories, the oldest myths and legends of Western cultures, tell us nature may be curative to mind and soul. The ancient Greeks and Romans had their bucolic poetry, tales of the farm and forest that enticed citizens outside the city walls, promising a purer, more sensuous and thrilling kind of life. The long shadow of their rural paradise, Arcadia, hangs over literature and art. It's not just another Eden. The pastoral is a golden place where people, animals, plants, and earth, air and water – the elemental forces of ancient medicine – all coexist in happy sympathy.

Like so many others, nature has been tempting me away from cities, offices and the comfort of my home for the best part of my life. I never used to think about these journeys as a quest for health, or even a medical cure. My early influences were literary, not scientific. I grew up reading books about nature: cheering on the Animals of Farthing Wood, adventuring with the Famous Five, then moving on to the desolate moors of the Brontës and the ecstatic woods and mountains of Shelley and Wordsworth. Stories taught me to crave wild, free places. I learned to see my moods mirrored in nature, and trained myself to be responsive to the subtle emotional influences of plants, animals and weather. Literary landscapes became part of my own psychological landscape, giving shape and name to the messy, complicated emotions of growing up. But growing up in the suburbs, within earshot of the M25, forests and mountains weren't part of my daily reality. I hunted for 'wild' places among the mosaic of intensively ploughed fields that make up London's precarious green belt as testing grounds for the emotions I'd read about in books. Could these grand feelings be for me too? Sometimes, the slivers of nature I was able to grasp at made me feel better. Sometimes, they gave me a place to be angry, lost and confused.

The recent explosion of interest in nature cures suggests that science is catching up with the old stories – or finally finding evidence to prove things that have long felt natural and commonsense. But it's more complicated than that. For a start, what does it mean 'to go to nature'? *Where* is it – at the end of the garden, beyond the tarmac fringes of the city, at the end of a road, the summit of a mountain, or muddy footpaths slipping between housing estates, road and fields? These questions matter, because more people – around 55 per cent of the world's population – live in cities, and this is only expected to rise. The old definition of 'nature' as a world separate from humanity may not mean much in a world of microplastics, urban sprawl and climate change.

Can the nature cure survive the loss of a pure, untouched green world? Maybe the idea of that luminous wilderness is just too hard to let go of, so we pretend to be more intimate with nature than ever, even as it is engulfed by crisis. Or maybe the return of the nature cure is a sign that a new, exciting form of environmentalism is emerging. The conservation movement has been accused, sometimes fairly, of prioritising nature over people: putting wildlife before transport links, or protecting charismatic species like elephants and lions, but not the communities who live dangerously close to them. But it shouldn't be a matter of choosing one over the other. The 'human vs. nature' conflict is a false dichotomy, and we urgently need to move beyond it. What if the nature cure could help? What if it could bring us closer to caring for that other world of oceans and vegetation, atmosphere and ice, wildlife and microorganisms with which we're bound together, with whose health and fate our own is absolutely entangled?

This entanglement takes us far from the shiny, self-help approach of the wellness movement, which has quickly exploited the revival of the nature cure. The companies that sell us beauty products, holidays and clothes know how susceptible we are to the charms of healing nature, and how much we're craving it. The glossy magazines and Instagram influencers who promise to make us happy with shopping and meditation are now selling rural retreats and wild excursions: phrases that evoke pristine wilderness, golden countryside, and soothing, lapping oceans.

The truth is that no one can buy happiness or sell a connection to nature, and the promises of wellness culture do more harm than good. While we're busy measuring ourselves against a stranger's dubious path to enlightenment, the things that give us value and meaning in our own lives can start to look tawdry, and somehow not good enough. Playing into our anxieties, 'wellness' can become just another stick to beat ourselves with, a way to weaponise wellbeing by blaming people for not being as healthy or happy as they should.

Something does happen when we 'go to nature', though, something that can't be bought or sold. Perhaps you are foraging in a forest, or lounging beside a loch. Perhaps you are walking to work along a leafy cycle path, or taking a shortcut through a peri-urban edgeland, where the seeds of decaying weeds are scattering across the concrete. You might notice your heart rate calm, your mind begin to wander, or the headache that's been pounding in your temples slowly ease off. When we talk about what nature does to us, we're probably thinking of this moment. This is when we relax, unwind, breathe deeply, and switch off. It's whimsical and historically dubious to use modern science to make sense of the beliefs of the past, but the ancient nature cure must surely have been inspired by similar feelings. The senses come to life again and the ratcheting adrenaline that has kept us on the edge of panic begins to disperse in the blood.

The simple question is – why? One of the first scientists to ask it was the American field biologist E. O. Wilson. From the 1950s, Wilson travelled the world to study plant and insect life. He was meant to be collecting data, but during these voyages the kernel of his 'biophilia hypothesis' was formed. Humanity's love for nature is innate, Wilson claimed, a product of millennia of evolution in which we lived in intimate relation with natural elements, creatures and habitats. Our instincts, physique and senses are perfectly attuned to perceiving natural threats, and to finding safety, refuge and life-giving nutrients in living environments. More than that, nature is the bedrock of our fantasies, threaded through our languages, its elements and animals recurring in our faiths and fables. 'Nature holds the key to our aesthetic, intellectual, cognitive and even spiritual satisfaction,' Wilson wrote. Biophilia is, put simply, our love for life. Not only our own life, but the vibrant, vital flourishing of organisms, species and wild places, with which, according to Wilson, we feel an innate 'urge to affiliate'.

Wilson gave a name and a psycho–evolutionary story to nature appreciation, then, from the 1990s, other scientists stepped in to work out the mechanics. Compiling data from blood samples, heart-rate monitors and patients' accounts, scientific studies are now lining up to try to prove that green and blue places, from parks to woods and coastlines, can soothe stress, restore attention, lower blood pressure and improve mood.

These findings are persuasive, and they've urged me to be a bit more honest about my own relationship with nature, particularly when I was younger. I wasn't just playing out every teenage stereotype as I stormed across what passed as moors in Metroland and pictured myself as a doomed Gothic heroine. I was experiencing what I now recognise as depression, though I didn't have the language to name or understand it then. My devotion to forest walking grew in a dance with my difficult moods, heightened by trauma and experiences of small-town prejudice. It's only with hindsight that I can fully appreciate how vital and sustaining the quiet, non-judgemental spaces of field and forest were.

I still experience regular bouts of insomnia, self-critical thinking and anxiety, and for these I depend heavily on natural environments to manage stress and keep me sane. Certain routes are guaranteed to calm me down and draw my thoughts out of their agitated little mazes. I've become intimately acquainted with the paths winding out towards the river from my house on the edges of Bristol, and the tracks that lead away from my university office into quiet green fields where my phone signal and the all-pervasive 4G can't penetrate.

I'm impressed with what science tells us about the nature cure, and instinctively identify with many of its findings. But I'm also sceptical about some of the bold claims made by researchers. There's a danger in assuming any one treatment will work for everyone, and that we all experience sickness and healing in the same way. When we get excited about the way light, colour or natural scent affects mood, we're guilty of treating people as little more than plants that need to be gardened: a drop of magnesium, eight hours of sun and two inches of water a week, and we will flourish as told. Surely our culture, our beliefs, the stories we share, as well as our personal traumas or desires, shape the way we feel and the kinds of connections we yearn for? And what about people with long-term, chronic or difficult to treat conditions, who may spend years experimenting with the right mix of medicines and treatment to help alleviate symptoms, achieve remission, or simply find a way of living with pain? Nature cures are often sold as an alternative medicine, or promoted as something that will help you taper off your medications. There are plenty of good reasons to be critical of the for-profit pharmaceutical industry, but at the same time, many medicines save lives. The language of the 'cure' can be alienating to those people who may never be 'cured' or want to end their prescriptions. Is there such a thing as a nature cure that isn't ableist, but is instead accessible to anyone who desires beauty and a connection with nature?

I set out hoping to explore these questions today. But right now, I'm lost. I've left the cycle path and must navigate the latticework of country lanes that will lead me to my destination. It's fiddly work, and twice already I've gone in the wrong direction and had to trace a path back down shadowy, hedge-lined roads. I'm getting more and more disorientated, and I don't want to be late. Eventually I turn the volume of my phone on full, switch on the satnav function, and secure the handset in my top pocket. I set off again, craning my ear down to my chest to hear the robotic voice bark out the directions. Finally the hedgerows fall away either side of me, and the country lane I've been following ends abruptly at a car park, with a view of woodland and fields beyond. I pull my phone from my pocket to check my location one more time. A look at the blinking blue dot on my map confirms it: I have reached my destination.

An hour later, I'm sitting in a clearing in the forest with twenty or so strangers. The woman leading the group has long grey hair, twisted into a plait. She's dressed in loose, neutral cotton, just right for the heat, and everything about her exudes calm and a sense of belonging.

We go around in a circle to introduce ourselves and tell everyone why we're here. When this awkward exercise is over, the group leader tells us to lie back and close our eyes. The people around me collapse onto the grass like fallen petals. It takes me a moment to realise I'm supposed to do the same. The leader catches my eye and smiles, and down I go. I came prepared to take notes, to observe and be critical. But already my bag is resting under my head, my notebook and phone abandoned.

A couple of moments pass, and then she starts speaking in an exaggeratedly soothing voice.

'Listen. What can you hear?'

Flies buzz around my ears. I can hear a very light wind agitating the leaves. Somewhere, a mile or so down the hill we climbed to get here, a lorry rattles by.

'What can you smell?'

I can smell fresh grass, earth, and the scent of pine. There's nothing else. The air is remarkably fresh. I lie quietly, drawing the breath deep into my lungs.

'What can you taste?'

I open my eyes a millimetre and peer at her through my lashes. Is it a trick question? She is smiling at me placidly. I shut my eyes at once. But after a moment passes, my breathing goes back to neutral. I let the moments pass unobserved, without worrying about her gaze on me, or whatever elusive taste I'm supposed to be enjoying.

'What do you feel?' she asks. What do I *feel*? I don't know. I press my hands down into the grass by my side. It's long and tangled, more like a meadow than a forest floor. When I first sat down, I saw a long earthworm writhing through the grass, and I hope it's not about to crawl on me now. It's thrilling, though, to imagine all the frenzied life pulsating beneath us.

After she asks her last question, the group leader goes silent. We're left alone with birdsong, the vivid scent of the forest, and, presumably, our thoughts. But I'm finding it hard to concentrate. The sun is like a bullseye in the sky above us and even with my eyes closed, the intensity of the light is dazzling. I can feel the skin on the right side of my face is burning, but there's nothing I can do about it. We lie there for five long minutes, and then the group leader speaks to us softly. 'You can get up now, as slowly as you like. We have time to talk about what you experienced, if you want.'

I've just taken part in my first mindfulness exercise, a guided meditation. I'm not sure it was successful, but it's meant to help me focus on the here and now, and to reconnect with nature. That's what this whole day is about – a one-day festival of nature and wellbeing held in a forest. More precisely, we're meeting in an activity area usually devoted to nature cures, or what the therapists call 'green care'. A simple outdoor kitchen, compost loo, tree-house meeting space and obligatory yurt are signs of human occupation. Other than that, all the outdoor therapies on offer here rely on the training of the counsellor, and the forest itself. What more could you need?

It's a good question. Whether they're quoting scientists or not, most of the people gathering in the wood believe in Wilson's biophilia. We are natural animals. Green spaces please us instinctively, beyond all reason. 'Nature is our home,' one woman answered when we introduced ourselves, and everyone nodded sympathetically. It's so self-evidently true that it trips off the tongue. Even our term for the study of natural systems – ecology, from the Greek *oikos*, meaning home – affirms humanity's heritage as evolutionary homemakers.

Although everyone shares some common values, there's not one typical 'nature seeker' here. One woman describes herself as a witch, and swears by natural magic. Another practices shamanic healing, inspired by her Caribbean heritage. Two sisters are here because they've just purchased a thin sliver of woodland

11

outside Birmingham. They plan to use it as a retreat for vulnerable children and young offenders from the inner city. There are speakers from mental health charities who have come to tell us about the outdoor therapies they offer, and conservation groups who've realised they can encourage people to visit their nature reserves by promoting the benefits to our health. There are community organisers, a refugee-run allotment group, and anti-globalisation protesters fighting for social justice. There's even a doctor from the Royal College of Psychiatrists, the most austere, no-nonsense body of mental health professionals in the UK, who announces in his talk that we need a *natural* health service, as well as a national one.

Some people are here because they have a story of their own, like the military veteran who shares how outdoor therapies helped him manage PTSD. His hands shake as he demonstrates a technique that he found helpful for coping with dissociative episodes. Holding a leaf between his fingers, he traces its web of veins, holding it up to the light to see the delicate matrix of green and yellow revealed by the sun. It is an exercise in paying attention, in becoming conscious of life beyond our own that carries on its processes of creation and destruction regardless, and in his most desperate states he found it both comforting and captivating.

Interest in nature and wellbeing unites people with many different ideas about sickness and health, and they are all on display in the forest today. Some people are interested in improving general wellbeing: helping people feel happier, more grounded and empowered in their day-to-day lives. Others work with people suffering from the most serious mental illnesses. Wellbeing is not exactly the same thing as mental health, and even the meaning of 'wellbeing', and how we might achieve it, is not set in stone. While objective measures of wellbeing tend to influence most research in this area (taking into account equality, access to education, and healthcare), theories of what wellbeing means existentially fall into two broad categories. The 'hedonic' concerns our personal sense of happiness and life satisfaction. The 'eudaimonic' focuses on how well an individual functions socially (for example, having the skills and resources necessary to live a purposeful, autonomous and flourishing 'good life'). The American psychologist Abraham Maslow's 'hierarchy of needs' also influences holistic, philosophical and person-centred accounts. In research spanning the 1940s to the 1970s, Maslow distinguished between our basic needs for sustenance and survival, our psychological needs for belonging and esteem, and our highest needs for self-actualisation and transcendence. A desire to connect with nature often falls into this last category, even though our basic survival obviously depends on the natural environment. But to experience 'transcendence' means to become the most creative, altruistic and wise version of ourselves possible, both in our behaviour towards others, and 'to other species, to nature, and to the cosmos'.

The 'nature cure' practitioners I meet in the forest tend to work with a blended understanding of wellbeing, and talk about it as something that is personal, social, spiritual and political, all at once. Many also define themselves as 'ecotherapists', drawing from ideas developed by the American pastoral counsellor Howard Clinebell in the mid-nineties. Ecotherapy, as its name suggests, urges people to become more respectful to and aware of nature as a path to holistic psychological recovery, and as a kind of hands-on, socially engaged environmentalism. It was vital to do this, Clinebell observed, because mainstream psychiatry failed to 'understand the complex interrelationships of personal health and sickness with the wholeness and brokenness of the biosphere, and all the people-serving institutions that impact our personal wellbeing day to day'. Looking at patients and their problems in sterile isolation meant clinicians focused 'only on maintaining personal health while ignoring the social causes of much illness in today's world'. But the health of nature and society couldn't be separated from the health of the individual. Therapeutic approaches that severed the person from the biosphere and society, and looked at them as simply a medical problem to be fixed, were being shown up as increasingly inadequate.

This way of thinking about health takes us beyond the simple 'nature cure', gesturing towards something more radical and intersectional – a real search for ecological recovery, for people, society and nature. Perhaps the revival of interest in natural healing, and the wider questions it raises, are a sign that we are waking up to the urgent need for such holistic thinking now. We are living through a crisis of mental health, social injustice and environmental devastation which are all terrible on their own, and inextricably entwined. Depression is one of the leading causes of disability worldwide, and suicide the second leading cause of death among all 15- to 29-year-olds globally, according to the World Health Organisation. The major determinants of mental illness are trauma and inequality, meaning rising cases of ill health have to be seen in their social aspects, and connected to the psychological violence of poverty, racism, sexism, homophobia and other forms of bigotry and marginalisation. Economic oppression is also at the root of so much global suffering and malaise. Most of the world lives under an economic system that concentrates wealth in the hands of a minority and denies the majority the means to live with health, dignity or a flourishing environment. Decades of warnings about climate change have gone unheeded, as economic growth and the demands of polluting industries have been put before the survival of people and the planet. Maybe the revival of the nature cure is another sign that people are pushing back against the narrative of business as usual, and confronting the crises at that intimate point of contact – where we meet the world, and where whatever happens to us might be a catalyst for change.

The people I meet in the forest are exploring these points of contact in the work they do every day. In workshops and over cups of tea, I listen in on conversations about health-service funding cuts and the social inequalities that make the people who seek their services unwell. Another big problem is finding safe, quiet places to run their projects. This reflects the fact that access to nature is desperately unequal in the UK. Spending a day in a forest is a pleasure not everyone can afford, and 'retreating' costs time, as well as money. In 2019, a report by Natural England found that 70 per cent of children from a white background spent time outside once a week, compared to 56 per cent of children from Black, Asian and ethnic minority backgrounds. A comparable report on nature engagement among adults showed that 25 per cent of

BAME adults over the age of sixteen never visited a park or other natural site, or did so less than once a month, compared to 18 per cent of the white population. In terms of the places people visited, urban green space dominated among young people from an Asian or Black background: 75 per cent of Black kids who were surveyed had recently visited a city park, while only 20 per cent had been to the countryside and 5 per cent to the coast (compared to 40 per cent and 19 per cent, respectively, for white children). These statistics, though rather blunt, reveal a lot about who feels they have a home in nature, and is empowered to seek it. They're a reminder that campaigning for the 'nature cure' needs to be intersectional: it needs to consider how factors such as race, wealth, social class, gender and disability intersect if it is going to really address the reasons people become unwell, and the contexts in which they might heal.

This has implications for what we mean by 'wellbeing' too. Wellbeing, in the hands of the wellness industry, can feel like an order to be happy, an obligatory command to cheer up. But nature may be somewhere to practise self-care in the most radical sense, as an act of self-preservation and 'political warfare', in the words of writer and Black rights activist Audre Lorde. Although the 'nature cure' has been recuperated and repackaged by business, behind the shiny facade of wellness culture I'm convinced there are more radical and hopeful stories, where people may find the strength to fight back and make a better world.

In this book, I'll tell the stories of people whose search for healing has been as socially and environmentally engaged as it has been personally transformative. People like Bessie Head, the writer and refugee who united psychological recovery with co-operative farming in Botswana; Robin Wall Kimmerer, the Indigenous American botanist exploring how gardening can awaken us to the animacy of the living world; and Beryl Gilroy, who led children on nature walks around the rubble and bomb sites of post-war London, teaching them empathy and compassion in a socially and ecologically fractured world. Their stories – and those of others who've fought for nature and championed mental health – open up radical possibilities for a nature and wellbeing movement that isn't just a fleeting trend, but might lead us towards a more just and radical way of life, getting to the roots of what it means to exist – and to coexist – well.

My search for the nature cure will also take me to places which, across time and across cultures, have been invested with a distinctive power to heal. The geographer Wilbert Gesler coined the term 'therapeutic landscapes' to describe these special sites – woods, parks, laboratories and farms – where the physical characteristics and the meanings attached to a place come together to create an effect that is curative, calming and transformative. I want to uncover how these places have achieved such enduring reputations for improving our mental health and wellbeing. And I want to understand if, and how, they work.

The best way to do that is experiencing them first-hand: plunging into sacred waters in Lourdes, 'bathing' at a *shinrin-yoku* forest in Finland, and – in a cramped room, in the heart of Bristol – immersing myself in an experimental virtual reality nature, now being pioneered as a brave new landscape of health. In each chapter I zoom in on one therapeutic environment, moving from water to mountains, forests, gardens, parks, farms and digital nature, before arriving on the shores of a 'lost place' in waiting to consider the impact of disappearing coasts and ecosystems on our mental health. Sometimes these journeys will be free and uninhibited. At other times (although I didn't know it on that first morning when I rode my bike out of the city), they would take place under conditions of coronavirus lockdown.

Either way, the goal remains the same: to discover if 'eco-recovery' can work both ways, not just using nature as a medicine, but forming mutual relationships of healing and care between people and ecosystems. I'll consider scientific explanations of the nature cure, and also ask challenging questions about the toxic cultures that harm us – looking at overwork in my visit to the therapeutic farm, and asking if urban green space is good enough. From the medicinal herb garden at Chelsea to the 'little wellbeing machine' of the landscaped park in eighteenth-century Bath and contemporary New York, this book will tell the long and global story of the nature cure. It will also look to the future, trying to find a new, healthier and more radical paradigm – a search for real wellbeing for people and nature.

Water
A Medium of Transformation

I still remember my first lake swim. It was evening, in a reservoir surrounded by pine forest. It had been hot all day and now the sun was going down. The surface of the lake shimmered in midnight blue and smoky rose pink. It looked so warm and alluring, but when I stepped into the shallows, the water was so cold, I couldn't believe I'd ever get in. Our bodies are used to warm showers, hot baths and the 'perfect' swimming-pool temperature (which is set between 25 and 28°C). In June in much of northern Europe, lakes reach little more than 16°C. Getting in was a slow process. Inching my body down, I had to calm my breathing and close my eyes, resisting the urge to pull away. It took everything to force my body to go against its impulses and take the first plunge. But once I was submerged, I seemed to grow a second skin. The further I swam from the bank and the colder the water, the more I wanted to shout and laugh. Afterwards, drying off on the grass, my body seemed to quiver with pleasure and a tingling, electric sensation that would stay with me for hours.

I'd swum in pools before and paddled in the murky waters of the English south coast, but a swim in a lake is a very different thing. There's no current, and if you're the only person swimming or the first to cut across into still water, the surface ripples apart as your hands pass through it. The sensation on the skin is always changing, too. Warm water is inviting, but on a hot day, it can feel as thick as soup. In early summer, heat may penetrate the upper surface, but as you push out further you often find the water around your feet is thrillingly cold. On those days, it's tempting to float on your back on the balmy water, knowing that there's a sharp, cool surprise in store as you begin to sink down.

That first plunge captivated me. Now I swim outdoors every chance I get, and when it's too cold, I squeeze into a wetsuit and bob around. Any expanse of water – aquamarine, teal, grey, blue-black – calls to me. It's hard to pass by a body of water or feel like I've really been in a place unless I swim. I don't mind going in alone, but I'm lucky I've found friends who feel the same way. In rushing streams, bottle-green lakes or in steel-black reservoirs bordered with frantic signs that scream NO SWIMMING, we've paddled in wetsuits or taken fast, shocking dives, emerging moments later with wet hair and stinging skin. It's more than just a dare, a way of proving something to each other. A swim braids together physical sensation, collective experience and the personal, often intensely private meaning it holds for each of us. It's about body feeling, but it's also about the ritual. A walk or journey that has a swim at the end of it offers a sense of completion, of purpose, that is all its own.

There's something so appealing and at the same time totally mysterious about water. It captivates the imagination and beguiles the senses, enveloping the skin when we are immersed in it and flickering on the edges of thought when we are far away. I divide the year into two seasons: the swimming season, and the dreaming-about-swimming season. The truth is, I'm not even very good. The only style I've really mastered is breaststroke. This means I'm competent enough not to endanger myself, but weak enough to find trouble occasionally, like the time I misjudged the height of a pontoon and had to doggy-paddle against the current and scramble out of the freezing water up a filthy, slippery bank.

But even when swimming leaves me cold, breathless, covered in mud or tangled in weeds, there's something about it that punctures the banalities of everyday life, and I find myself craving it. I've been told the experience of birth is like this: pain and discomfort are forgotten and the 'halo effect' leaves you convinced that labour was some kind of transcendent euphoria. I don't buy it at all (I've met parents), but if it's anything like swimming, then I can see why you might push the bad bits to the edges of thought and remember only bliss.

I'm not the first person to connect open-water swimming with wellbeing. It's daunting to skim through the shelves and see how many books have been written about wild water and their effects on the swimmer. 'Once in the water, you are immersed in an intensely private world, as you were in the womb,' writes Roger Deakin in *Waterlog: A Swimmer's Journey through Britain*

(1999). So too Tessa Wardley in *The Mindful Art of Wild Swimming* (2017): 'Our minds are no longer as turbulent as we swim … with this calmer mood, our bodies are becoming absorbed in soothing waters.' Now more research is being conducted on the psychological effects of wild swimming, exploring its value as a treatment for depression and anxiety, and as a practice that may improve wellbeing. This confluence of literary and scientific interest fascinates me, and it makes me want to test some of the claims that so many writers, doctors and self-styled 'health gurus' make about water. It's tempting to see water as a medium of transformation, and the plunge as a process of purification, rebirth or healing. I'm also guilty of treating water as a kind of cure-all for stress and anxiety, knowing that the minute my head is submerged in cold water, my thoughts and worries will be wiped away. But is this too easy, too idealistic? Is there any logic to it? Or are we just looking for an easy answer, the promise of magical transformation and instant health that flows in the undercurrents of the water cure?

To find out, I've travelled by overnight train from Paris to the edge of the Pyrenees to dip my hands into water that is famous around the world for its alleged healing properties. Pilgrims have been visiting the holy shrines at Lourdes since the mid-nineteenth century, when a fourteen-year-old Occitan girl reported visions of a lady in white emerging from a rocky outcrop next to the banks of the River Ousse. The girl, Bernadette Soubirous, returned day after day to speak with the mysterious woman. At first she was terrified. She threw stones and holy water into the niche in the rock, making the white figure disappear. But soon Bernadette began to speak to the woman and trust her (or so the story goes). After a fortnight, the girl's visions became the talk of the town. Some people thought she was mad and should be put in an asylum. Others were convinced she had witnessed a vision of the Virgin Mary, and on this conviction, the legend of Lourdes grew.

Now around 25,000 visitors come to Lourdes every day, following the instructions Bernadette received from the white lady 'to drink of the water of the spring, to wash in it'. Lourdes water is reputed to heal the sick, so pilgrims looking for comfort and renewal arrive with empty Evian bottles, three-litre plastic containers, or kitsch glass chalices moulded in the shape of the Madonna. With patience, they stand by a wall of taps to collect this slow-flowing holy relic. Then, if they have time, they join the long line leading to the rectangular stone baths built on the course of the stream that Soubirous uncovered, which, according to legend, has run clear since that day.

I'm not a religious person. I'm irreligious, in all honesty, impervious to spirituality and organised faith of any kind. But I've come to Lourdes because I want to understand the promise of water as a medium of transformation, and this is the most powerfully curative water in the Christian imagination. It's also within a day and a half's travel each way from my home in South West England, and I'm trying to avoid planes, totting up the carbon footprint of each of my journeys on a website called EcoPassenger. I dithered for a while before I booked the tickets. Even set against the bloated CO_2 emissions of the plane, the environmental impact and cost of the train seemed excessive considering I live by the city of Bath, one of the most famous spa towns in Britain. But Bath's waters have long since shed any spiritual associations. The rooftop pool is filtered and chlorinated, and you're more likely to share it with tipsy hen parties than worshippers of Sulis Minerva, the Romano-British goddess to whom the baths were once dedicated. There are holiday spas just like it all over Europe, hot springs worshipped since ancient times, whose mineral content is optimistically associated with all kinds of cures. I've been to a couple of these spas and emerged feeling sleepy and delirious, my skin soft. But to find out why water is so powerfully affecting, I needed to come here, where the spiritual power of the water is still a living legend.

The actual, physical water of Lourdes has nothing special going for it. According to scientific analysis conducted in the mid-nineteenth century, it's a harmlessly inert concoction with the usual traces of iron, potassium, sodium and carbonic acid. Immersing yourself in the waters at Lourdes is not an act of science, but of faith. Nineteenth-century records overflow with stories that match the 'perfect' Lourdes cure: instantaneous recovery from conditions like tuberculosis, fractures, tumours and weeping wounds, which are healed soon after submersion. Reliable medical evidence for these cures is dubious and scant. After a 'golden age' in the early twentieth century, with nearly 140 cures a year reported between 1890 and 1915, cases have dwindled to insignificance today. That doesn't stop people coming here. Lourdes is still a place where contact with water promises to effect a powerful alteration, and for some this can feel like a matter of life and death.

Does it work? Perhaps that's the wrong question. 'What does it actually do?' might be a better one. Scientists studying the 'Lourdes cure' speculate about the neuropsychological experience of visiting the baths and the effects it might have on healing and recovery. What they say they're witnessing is not so much a placebo, but a potent emotional stew of expectation and hope, faith and conviction, excitement and ecstasy. Could that rush of emotion itself be curative? The interconnection between brain and body is still so little understood. Perhaps at Lourdes it's the massive weight of spiritual expectation alone that so profoundly affects people when their bodies hit the water.

As I join the end of the queue on a hot late-August day, I hope there's more to it than that. I've been told the waiting time can be anything up to five hours. On my way to the covered area where we wait, I saw people with walking sticks and wheelchairs. One man was pushed past on a stretcher, while heartbreakingly frail children were supported by their families. This all makes me fairly uncomfortable. Critical disability activists point out that it is society itself, not physical ailments, that is most disabling. In a fully accessible society, where disabled people are not always coming up against physical and bureaucratic obstacles, I wonder how many of the people I see around me would still seek the Lourdes cure?

Not everyone here is looking for a physical transformation. Before I came here, I watched YouTube videos about the Lourdes shrine, clips of tearful Americans and bewildered Brits describing the experience of immersion: how it opened up a sense of 'space' in them, and left them with a profound and perfect sense of peace. What struck me most about the videos is that none of the people seem to be sick, or to talk about the experience as anything to do with medical treatment. The pilgrims staring dreamily beyond the iPhone lens came here looking for a personal transformation, a sense of acceptance and wellbeing, and they seemed to have found it. The old Christian tradition of purification by water had washed over them, and they felt cleansed, renewed.

This makes an elemental sense, as well as an evolutionary one. Our bodies are up to 60 per cent water, with the greatest quantities pooling in our organs, head and heart. Water regulates our temperature, carries oxygen around the body, lubricates joints, digestion and the nervous system. It is the first building block of all our cells. Beholden to water, we are barely conscious of all it does for us until we're deprived of it. Without water, human beings last little longer than three days before our vital functions begin to shut down.

It's fitting that the concept of wellbeing, in English, sprung from water. 'To be well' can be translated as 'to flourish', to be like or *with* water. In Old English and Norse, *wel* meant abundance. From West Saxon comes the word *wiellan*, meaning to bubble up, spring and rise. It's from *wiellan* we get the name for the subterranean source of fresh water we know as a well, but by the sixteenth century 'well' had undergone a sea change. It came to mean the height of good health, a holistic sense of comfort, satisfaction and soundness, where the body, mind and situation of life all converge in peaceful accord.

The act of immersion in this life-giving substance has so many ancient associations. It's hard to find a culture or religion, ancient or modern, without its own water deity, a health-bringing spirit of the spring, river or coast. Rain and life-saving waters run through the Qur'an, while the act of giving water to another is one of the most profound displays of charity. 'We are made from water every living thing,' Islam teaches, establishing the body as a watery entity, rather than one crafted from earth, as in the Greek and Christian creation myths. In Mecca, pilgrims on the Hajj visit the Zamzam Well to wash and collect water whose medicinal and spiritual properties are as hotly debated as those of Lourdes. According to tradition, water has flowed from this miraculous spring since Hājar and her son Ismā'īl were desperately thirsty in the desert. Coming into contact with the Zamzam Well now, visitors describe the purity of the water, filling canisters to share with those who couldn't make the long and often prohibitively expensive journey that pilgrimage month.

As a primal metaphor of cleansing, nourishment and renewal, water surfaces in so many faiths and cosmologies. It marks the entryways of the Shinto shrines dotted across Japan, where *temizu* basins provide the matter for spiritual and physical cleansing. In Judaism, *mikveh* pools are used for ritual bathing after childbirth, sex, and as part of conversion. The rules around the flow of water in a *mikveh* are complex and meticulous. Water must flow in from a natural source – rain, springs, taps or wells – and run out again to ensure the bath has purifying properties. Ancient in origin, the meanings of *mikveh* and its uses continue to change and transform. 'For a long time before I transitioned, I had this dream of being in my body, as myself, in a beautiful clean and light and open space filled with water,' says Mel King, a transgender Jew who now volunteers at the inclusive ImmerseNYC *mikveh* in Manhattan's Upper West Side. '*Mikveh* is a place where ritual and meaning can be made in new ways.'

The belief that running water is especially sacred is widespread across the world, investing places with special meaning and elevating some waterways to the level of the Divine. For Indigenous water defenders of unceded Coast Salish territory in North America, pollution and disturbance caused by tar sands expansion and oil pipelines don't just infringe Indigenous rights. They are acts of violence: violence against water, the community and life itself. As Will George, watch-house guardian of the Indigenous Canadian Tsleil-Waututh First Nation explains, 'We are people of the inlet and these waters flow through us.'

In other waterways, religious beliefs can, paradoxically, work against environmental messaging. In the Ganges in India, Hindus bathe, cast flowers and light *diya* lamps on flowing water that symbolises purity, although it is one of the most polluted river systems on earth. Does this pollution make the waters less hallowed or healing? Environmental sociologist Sonya Sachdeva has done extensive fieldwork around the Ganges, and suggests it may be the opposite: that 'sacred beliefs may inure participants to the harmful effects of pollution in the Ganges River'. Some of the worshippers she interviewed believed the river could clean itself, while others felt that 'a sacred space, by virtue of its sacred status, is seen as the epitome of purity,' and 'may be seen as protected from pollutants'. In spite of the filth, it was simply not possible for the river to be unclean.

I don't know what it is like to swim in the Ganges, either spiritually or physically. But I do know what it feels like to take a dip in water I know to be churning with chemicals, sewage discharge and the run-off from agriculture. I know every river in England to be polluted – with only 14 per cent of a good ecological standard, and none free of chemicals as of 2020. Does this stop me? Not exactly. When a swimmer friend sends me a link to a detailed, interactive map showing where drains overflow and water companies discharge filth as a cheap way of disposing of their waste, I see my favourite spots highlighted, and quickly close the screen. I have no faith to base it on, but my belief in pure and healing waters, untouched nature, a living sacred realm, is stubborn and hard to do without, even though there's a reality to face, and I don't want to get sick. Keeping my head dry, I return again, immersing my vulnerable body in the vulnerable water.

Of course, immersion in water isn't always a pleasure, and lakes and rivers don't always beckon us in without a struggle. The body, or the water, may resist. Across Central, Western and Southern Africa, people have long celebrated a pantheon of water divinities called Mami Wata. Notorious for pulling passing sailors under the river surface and showing them flickering glimpses of paradise, Mami Wata offer insight, beauty, protection and seduction, with a demand for sacrifice as the price for entry into their watery realm. The streams and rivers they occupy may be sacred, a vital source of life, but their waters are also shifting and slippery substances, equally creative and destructive.

Looking at these many faiths with the detachment of an atheist, I feel a kind of visceral yearning to experience the transformations they describe – the same yearning that brought me to Lourdes, and keeps me going as I wait hour after hour on the hard wooden benches for my promised submersion. Secretly I suspect these experiences are defined by belief, meaning they may be closed off to me for good. But isn't the cult of nature – the yearning to connect – its own kind of secular spiritualism? Why should the transformative experience of water have to fit within frameworks of religion and faith?

Already I hold many different stories in me when I swim. As a teenager I was fascinated by ancient Greek and Roman myths, especially as they are told in Ovid's *Metamorphoses* (8 CE). Water nymphs slip and splash through these stories: sea nereids or naiads, who offer gods and mortals an encounter with beauty as exquisite as it is threatening and vulnerable. These pretty, hyper-sexualised girls drip and seep into water in paintings by the Pre-Raphaelites, whose mythical, ornate canvases formed another of my teenage obsessions. I Blu-Tacked postcards of John William Waterhouse's *Hylas and the Nymphs* (1896) and John Everett Millais's *Ophelia* (1852) to my bedroom wall and would try to sketch them for hours. I was tracing the outlines of seduction, learning how to experience sexuality and the pull and tug between nature, the body and the self. But I was also yearning for water, the cold green cling of it to naked skin, the touch of lily pads, water weeds and the silver thrill of passing, darting fish.

Why did the water attract me? The bodies of the women in paintings, the doomed goddesses and mortals

I was reading about, disturbed categories that we like to keep in opposition: nature and the human, place and person, self and world. At the moment when my body was growing and changing, immersion in the absolute otherness of water offered an elemental attraction: the chance of obliteration, followed by something else, some promise of difference. I didn't stop to think about how many of these stories, these images, were created and controlled by men, and how pessimistic and fraught with danger they were. I felt my body reaching for water as an element of transformation, invested with the power to remake me in a form that I could choose myself.

What has this got to do with wellbeing? Everything, I think. So much of the great writing about mental health, particularly by women, is about the urgent need for autonomy: the necessity that is as personal as it is political to come into yourself, according to your own design. Rhiannon Lucy Cosslett – a writer who is critical of the over-representation of middle-class, white women in swimming literature – also notes that as 'young women's bodies are ... among the most surveilled by capitalism ... to remove one's body from its place as a perceived site of transaction and to dunk it in freezing cold water can feel rebellious and freeing.' Unlike swimming in the neatly divided lanes of a pool, being alone in open water answers an immediate desire for physical self-determination: the interplay between body and place that unfolds with each stroke, each decision about direction, depth and speed made in private conversation with water.

Simone de Beauvoir captures the particular elation women experience in nature in *The Second Sex* (1949). 'At home, mother, law, customs, routine hold sway ...

31

among plants and animals she is a human being; she is freed at once from her family and from the males – a subject, a free being.' This freedom resembles, but does not perfectly match, the experience of 'transcendence' usually reserved for men on the tops of their mountains. Women, according to de Beauvoir, don't experience the transcendent leaping above the self and world; the pleasure comes from the slipping of boundaries between the self and the place, and the escape (even if it's momentary) from social being. It's the achievement of a sense of 'liberty through a continuous reaching out to other liberties' – the smooth passage of clouds, the free-flowing exuberance of water.

In Kate Chopin's novel *The Awakening* (1899), her character Edna experiences rapturous communion with the sea each time she swims. 'She was becoming herself and daily casting aside that fictitious self which we assume like a garment with which to appear before the world.' Written at the end of the nineteenth century, it's a small masterpiece of feminist fiction with a sting in its tail. At the book's end, Edna plunges herself into the ocean, aware that society isn't ready for her new, transformed state. I still read it as a celebration of how water can change us, even though I know it ends with Edna drifting out into the wide empty ocean alone.

The idea of the 'false garment of the self' fascinates me too. It's true that swimming leaves us nowhere to hide. But does that mean the 'true self' emerges, and if so, what does it feel and look like? One of the psychologists who has most thoughtfully articulated the difference between the 'true' and the 'false' self is Donald Winnicott. Winnicott was a psychoanalyst who wanted to understand why some people feel grounded and happy, while others feel uncertain about their place in the world and desperate for answers. He considered that this difference was caused by a split between the 'true' and the 'false' self. The true self gives us feelings of purpose and authenticity. It's this true self that acts spontaneously, making us feel fully alive and 'real'. The false self is its opposite. It's the facade we live behind to fit in and to meet others' expectations of us. This false self might project a convincing mask of realness, but living with it leaves us feeling hollow, unreal, and never absolutely alive.

I've slipped, sometimes, into this sensation of unreality. Certain situations can slowly drain away my sense of who I am, what I value, and take away my power to change or challenge them. A friend, living through depression, once described the way she was feeling as 'life behind the glass'. 'I've forgotten who I am and what I like,' she told me. When I swim, I feel like I'm 'casting aside the fictitious self' and living vividly in my own skin. It's like something's tapping hard against the glass of the false self, and might even shatter it.

In fiction and in memoir, water is often a medium of liberation, an environment in which women grasp towards a sense of freedom and reality. In Tsitsi Dangarembga's *Nervous Conditions* (1988), a novel about growing up in 1960s Zimbabwe, her teenage heroine Tambu connects swimming in the river with freedom from the violence of colonialism and gender roles:

> when I was feeling brave, which was before my breasts grew too large, I would listen from the top of the ravine and, when I was sure I had felt no one coming, run down to the river, slip off my frock,

which was usually all that I was wearing, and swim
blissfully for as long as I dared in the old deep places.

This pleasure is one that's short-lived: soon Tambu's
too old to undress without being made to feel ashamed,
or worse. After years away at school, she returns to find
the riverbank developed and the water polluted. But
the memory remains, a site of lost freedom.

Childhood swimming often symbolises innocence, but
the non-judgemental quality of water also appeals to adults
who've survived things that should have never happened
to them. 'In water, like in books – you can leave your
life,' writes Lidia Yuknavitch in *The Chronology of Water*
(2011). Yuknavitch was once a competitive swimmer, and
in her memoir she weaves these experiences together
with an excavation of the long-term trauma of familial
abuse. Water can't possibly make these experiences go
away, but she comes to feel it as a vehicle of love, a site
of acceptance. 'Come in. The water will hold you,' she
writes, beckoning us into a text that swims with love and
is open to the possibilities of recovery.

When we have these experiences, we grasp for
language to name them, often settling on the word
'transcendent', meaning to rise above. Freud described
transcendence as an 'oceanic feeling of oneness', and
speculated about whether his patients were recalling a
primal womb-state, before the ego separated itself off
from the world in what we call 'the self'. Transcendence
seems to be the wrong word, though: it's much more
about being immanent, sensing our bodies become part
of it on a level that's not just emotional, but biological
too. The philosopher Stacy Alaimo coined the term
'transcorporeality' to describe how the human body is

34

part of its environment, quite literally, as flows of water, minerals and air pass between us and the world. It's easy to imagine transcorporeality, but hard to feel like we're really part of life in such an immediate, physical way. Most of the time we exist closed off from the world, separate in our own little spheres.

Is it possible to break out and feel that oceanic sensation again? The poet Elizabeth-Jane Burnett conducted a series of swimming rituals, diving into lakes, rivers and seas as a way of connecting with water. In her poems collected in *Swims* (2017), the experience of immersion seems to smudge the boundaries between the body and nature. The noun 'swimming' didn't quite do it justice, so she invented the verb 'rivering' to better describe this watery transformation:

> Not that   *the river is like* the body
> or   *the river is* the body
> but   both have gone
> and what is left is something else.

Rivering: it is a thrilling word, poised somewhere between *revelling* and *quivering* and suggesting self-abandonment, tumult, immersion bliss. Could experiences of this loss of self, this watery becoming, be what is so therapeutic about swimming? Perhaps. When I wade into the water now, I try to be conscious of my body as just one part of a much bigger ecosystem. There's a comfort in this: a feeling of openness and acceptance, of getting beyond ourselves, even just for a moment, to become something radically different.

For many, this transformative experience is connected to the shock of the plunge into cold water. But how can an experience that is so profoundly disturbing to the senses be therapeutic? Is it the emptying and flooding of the mind, or the way the senses are closed down, and then brought back to vivid intensity, that acts on the mind like a drug? Amy Liptrot explores this overlap between swimming and chemical highs in her memoir *The Outrun* (2015), written while she was recovering from alcoholism on the remote North Sea island of Papa Westray. Dives from the island's weather-beaten beaches prove 'cathartic' and 'refreshing'. At points, she attributes her successful sobriety to these swims. They sate, in ways alcohol or drugs never could, her deeper thirst for intensity, for extreme experience.

Most of the major swimming charities and organisations now boast the health benefits of swimming, and this includes its use to support people living with mental ill health. According to one poll commissioned by Swim England in 2018, 1.4 million adults who were surveyed believe that swimming has significantly reduced symptoms of their anxiety and depression. Polls like this don't contain evidence to explain exactly why this might be the case, but that hasn't stopped experts proposing plenty of explanations for water's supposedly curative properties. Swimming is said to improve our concentration and help us regain control of our breathing and thoughts, producing an effect akin to meditation. Others propose that blood flow to the brain is improved by swimming, or that cold water helps the brain generate new cells, which in the long run may help us process stress more easily. Even the colour blue has been claimed to have a soothing effect, an aquatic version of E. O. Wilson's biophilia hypothesis that sees us reaching for blue as well as green places. In the 1960s an outlandish hypothesis even claimed that we had evolved as 'aquatic apes'. The distribution of our hair, and our distinctive layer of subcutaneous fat, were taken as signs that our primate forebears were meant to be in water.

As fascinating as this is, much of this scientific writing lacks nuance and depth. Huge sample sizes are interviewed or surveyed online, but follow-up meetings are not always held to determine whether swimming really did achieve the wonderful things people claimed it had. Many of the theories about how swimming affects the brain have still to be tested. I do like the idea of my body and mind responding in such dramatic, physical ways to their environment: *rivering*, at the level of neurobiology and in the chemistry of the blood. But most of these accounts are hypothetical; stories as much as science.

In 2018, a study conducted in the UK brought some much-needed precision to current understanding of wild swimming's effect on mind and mood. It only focused on one woman, though, the subject of an innovative open-water trial. While this tiny focus means it's not possible to draw too many big conclusions, it offers something valuable that the massive surveys do not: a more personal insight into how cold-water swimming might help in the treatment of depression.

At the centre of the study was a woman who was diagnosed with major depressive disorder at the age of seventeen. At the start of the study she was been being treated with talking therapies and the antidepressant fluoxetine. She also had past experience with the drug citalopram, but nothing so far had helped alleviate her symptoms of anger, anxiety, low mood, despair and self-harm. In fact, the drugs were causing her unwanted side effects, making her feel she existed in a 'chemical fog' with no end in sight. Aged twenty-four, she had recently given birth to a daughter and now aspired to be symptom- and medication-free. With this ambitious goal in mind, she began a series of weekly swims in cold water. She was nervous and anxious when she began, and needed support to help her gain confidence and become acclimated to cold open water. But she desperately wanted to take part in the experiment, and persisted even when swimming was a struggle. After one month of guided swimming, she was able to reduce her medication. Four months later, she was no longer being treated with drugs at all.

How did this happen? Writers who reflect on the healing properties of water are often bold in their claims, but the scientist behind the study, Christoffer van Tulleken, is characteristically cautious. There are so many factors to consider: exercise, social contact, physiological response, and the effect of being out of doors – all must be taken into account. An extensive body of literature already backs up the theory that exercise can be helpful in the treatment of depression. Companionship with other swimmers and the teachers who guided her into the water are also likely to have had an impact on her new feelings of belonging and self-worth. Then there was the change to daily routines, the 'multiple lifestyle modifications', which will be intensely personal and possibly unquantifiable. But these are all transformations that could have been brought about by any kind of exercise: an aerobics club could have done it. So why swimming? What special effects did it produce?

Van Tulleken offers two key explanations of why open-water swimming is therapeutic. The first lies in the sense of achievement and empowerment. Getting into a lake in such forbidding circumstances is no small feat, and the fact the psychologists highlight its importance makes immediate sense. It's one of the reasons I often feel like my own swims are rituals. There's the moment on the bank or beach when you think that immersion is impossible, a superhuman achievement. And then, moments later, you're *in*, gasping in breathless wonder at the power in yourself.

Of course, the same could be true of any extreme sport or superficially uncomfortable activity. The second element, then, must be the water itself. Psychologists have yet to perfectly explain why cold water can make us feel euphoric. One hypothesis is that it produces a stress reaction, and by being exposed to stress and adapting to it, we become more adept at responding to other stressors in our lives. This cross-adaptation response, they propose, is also supported by changes taking place at the level of neurobiology. Studies have suggested that some people suffering with depression also experience brain inflammation. In one trial, a man who had been unresponsive to medical treatment experienced almost immediate relief from his depressive fog when given an anti-inflammatory drug. The scientists conducting the experiment proposed that the medicine, usually used to treat Crohn's disease, which causes bowel inflammation, helped by attacking the cytokine proteins his brain was releasing. Just like in Crohn's, where the body's own immune system ends up attacking the gut, the cytokines were thought to be producing damaging inflammation in the brain, contributing to disturbing dips in mood.

Similar experiments conducted on wild swimmers help to back up the hypothesis that swimming in cold water might stop inflammatory responses and reduce cytokine release without the need for drugs. In 2000 in Finland a study of experienced ice-water swimmers found that their cytokine responses were significantly lower than that of a test group who were unaccustomed to cold waters: a typically Nordic experiment, which adds medical legitimacy to the health claims of Finland's wood-sauna and lake-diving culture.

There's one more relationship to consider: the relationship between cold-water immersion and brain chemicals connected to experiences of elation, contentment and wellbeing. After a cold swim many people report feelings of euphoria, a lot like the high experienced by marathon runners at the close of a race. This rush of emotion coincides with the release of dopamine, serotonin and beta-endorphins – all of which are associated with elevated mood, motivation and interest in the world. Most drugs that are meant to treat depression and anxiety either target or simulate these chemicals in the hope of reproducing their effects: SSRIs (selective serotonin reuptake inhibitors) attempt to limit the brain's reabsorption of the body's natural serotonin secretions, while opioids – from prescribed medicines to drugs like cocaine – stimulate the production of dopamine, with therapeutic or addictive consequences. But cold-water immersion stimulates these reactions by itself, adding weight to the theory that it can be therapeutic for some and helpful in the treatment of depression and addiction. Research also suggests that serotonin release can be inhibited by inflammatory cytokine levels, meaning that by reducing inflammation and increasing serotonin release, cold waters have multidimensional, beneficial effects, taking the body from shock to euphoria in moments.

Reading the study of the wild swimmer and her incredible medical transformation, I'm almost convinced to end my search for the nature cure right here, in cool and healing waters. But something is worrying me. The fact that this is a single-subject study means that we can't draw too many conclusions from it. But a bigger question hangs over the study, and it concerns the resources used to support the woman through the month of wild swimming. She wasn't simply thrown into the deep end: she trained at a specialist 'extreme environment' research centre to prepare her for outdoor swimming, and when she experienced panic attacks in the water, a coach was called in to support her. Even van Tulleken himself got in the lake in his Speedos to boost her resolve. Regular Skype meetings between her and the doctor tided her over between swim sessions.

Was this support excessive? Absolutely not. Depression is worsened by social isolation and inability to access treatment, and this level of support is the very least that people suffering deserve as they struggle to overcome or live with the illness. What worries me about the study is way the story of 'healing water' is being celebrated, while the reality of time-intensive, compassionate, personalised support is receding into the background. People who've seen the nature-cure advice and want to try out open-water swimming would probably benefit from supervision and help building confidence and stamina. But when funding for health services is at an all-time low, or where health insurance is prohibitively expensive, such extensive encouragement is unlikely to be available to people who aren't wealthy enough to access private care. Swimming as a treatment for depression is 'more time-intensive than medication', as van Tulleken admits in his study, and this is one of the reasons it's unlikely to be widely prescribed.

Even so, the promise of transformation is so absolute and enticing, I found myself buzzing with excitement and optimism for the patient. I'm also impressed by the idea that medication can be tapered off in such a dramatic way after so many years of use. It's a laudable goal. As van Tulleken explains, there's been a 50 per cent rise in antidepressant prescription rates in the UK since he trained as a medic fifteen years ago, and the side effects of some of the most generously prescribed drugs can be punishing. Many also have the downside of not actually curing the illness they're prescribed for. But what works for one person might not work for others, and while it's inspiring to see someone experience such radical transformation from a relatively short intervention, there's an implicit danger to telling depressed people to cure themselves with water, or that they should be trying to phase out medicine that might be working for them. I love swimming, but I'm wary of the dream that it will only take a plunge into cold water to be transformed.

It's a dream that's worryingly familiar. Stories of watery transformations in mythology reinforce it, and it crops up in so many accounts of medical therapies, some of them old, others disturbingly recent. One short, sharp shock, and we emerge better, new.

Might we be living through a revival of dangerous wellness culture – a twenty-first century water cure? Water cures have an ancient inheritance, but in their modern form, they emerge out of the medical culture of the seventeenth century. The Flemish chemist and physician Jean Baptist van Helmont popularised the notion that water could heal physical and mental disorders in his book *Ortus medicinae*, published in 1643 and translated into English in the 1660s. 'Madness', in Helmont's day, was associated with an imbalance of humours and an excess of heat. In consequence, cool water seemed to be an obvious physical application to restore medical and mental order: a simple mechanical solution for a purely physical complaint.

Eighteenth- and nineteenth-century hydrotherapies were sold on Helmont's promise. Treatments that look horrific on paper and must have been hellish in practice were justified on the principle that differences in temperature and sudden immersion in water could shock the patient out of a disturbed mental state. Trying to cure the mind by way of the body, mechanical devices helped facilitate easy immersion of 'melancholic' or manic patients. An illustration from 1826 shows a *bain d'immersion* used in Belgium: a delicate arched bridge that leads to an ornamental pagoda whose platform floor could be lowered, patient inside, into the water below.

Another contraption, this time in use over a century later, is displayed in the Glore Psychiatric Museum, Missouri, US. The mid-twentieth century 'Bath of Surprise' incorporates a stretcher, which lies suspended by a chain over a raised metallic pool. At the flick of a button, the prone patient could be plunged into the water below. There were other treatments too: cold compresses, wet sheets, showers where patients were washed down with jets like animals, baths where they sat waiting to be doused with buckets of cold water by orderlies hiding behind wooden screens. Whatever therapeutic value cold water might have had, the punishing qualities of these regimes, the obvious terror they must have induced, and their dangers and discomforts mean they look so much like the 'ordeals by water' – an early modern method of persecuting women accused of witchcraft, from which later water cures evolved.

I don't think cold-water swimming feels much like these appalling 'treatments'. But now that it's being put forward as a cure for depression, I can't help but notice all the traits that new hydro and cold 'cryo' therapies share with the old practices. Common to both is the assumption that by strengthening our constitution, and submitting to demanding physical regimes, we might heal ourselves.

Why must we offer ourselves up to the cure, volunteer for sacrifice and purging, in order to be whole? There's a rugged Victorian sense of morality underlying it all: cold baths, salted porridge, ritual purging, and a demand for frugality, for 'doing without'. Innovators of nineteenth-century water medicine, like Bavarian naturopath Sebastian Kneipp, put patients on restricted, wholesome diets, courses of herbs and exercise, and regular plunges in cold waters and rivers. More extreme was the *Wasserkur* clinic established by Vincenz Priessnitz in Gräfenberg, Bavaria, where patients were subjected to intensive courses of sweating, cold wraps and immersion. By 1840 around 1,600 health-seekers travelled to the clinic each year, hoping that Priessnitz's demanding regimes would restore them to emotional and physical health. But the idea that pain and self-punishment have a part to play in recovery is disturbing.

Among its many cruelties, mental illness can produce a sense of guilt in the sufferer, a nagging suspicion that you don't deserve to feel better. What if we've internalised all the centuries of stigma, and are pushing ourselves to extremes as a means of ritual purging when we take that fast, shocking plunge? And underlying it all, I'm suspicious of the sense (another older, unwelcome inheritance) that mental illness might just be a weakness, caused by overheated humours, an inflamed brain, lack of exercise, cosseting, which we could fix for ourselves if we only pulled ourselves together and submitted ourselves to more extreme treatment.

Research is already being done into the value of cold-water exposure in indoor conditions – freezing showers, head immersions, plunges into metal pools that look disturbingly like the psychiatric Baths of Surprise. But what will be lost if we focus only on the benefits of the cold water itself, and not the meaning and the sensory richness of the lake, river or sea? What about the ritual of the swim, the sense of freedom and empowerment, and the relationships we form with other swimmers, with the people who lead us to the water, and the more-than-human lives we encounter there, with whom we are *rivering*? What about the people for whom the water cure will never 'work', who love to swim, but who still want to take their medication?

I'm getting close to the front of the queue for the baths at Lourdes. As each new group is called in, we rise from the wooden benches where we wait, walk one row forward, and sit down again. As my row completes our penultimate circuit, I'm picturing the deep rectangular stone baths I've seen in images, and feeling my heart begin to thump as I anticipate the coolness of the water. I've read countless guides to the baths, heard people's accounts on their YouTube videos, even read their reviews on TripAdvisor. I know that inside I will be asked to change behind a curtain before volunteers step forward to wrap me in a long white robe. Then, with their help, I will be submerged in water no warmer than 12°C (exactly the temperature often used in psychiatric testing of cold-water therapies). I watch the woman next to me, alone just like I am, as she runs a rosary through her hands in fast, practised loops. Sensing my gaze, she looks up and we exchange a brief, nervous smile before we turn back to our private worlds.

Some sceptical scientific research into the Lourdes cure side with the psychiatric studies, and propose that the constant stream of cold water – like the flowing baths once used in hydropathic treatments – lowers the body's temperature, producing shock, euphoria, and making our brain chemistry crackle and buzz. But the idea that such a powerful, life-transforming moment could be a side effect of a purely physical encounter is too depressingly disenchanting, too mundanely mechanical. For the people who emerge shaking with gratitude, there must be something special that separates the Lourdes experience from a cold shower, a spray of water from a jet, or a dousing from an ice bucket. Whatever that something special is, it is happening already to the woman next to me, and the women next to her, and to the women snaking away behind me to the far reaches of the queue. This act of supplication, this prayer for perfect grace, will have been acquiring potency and purpose for these women since they arrived in Lourdes, or since they boarded their train or plane to get here, probably ever since they planned the journey months or years ago. This is the difference – the element of choice, love and faith that transforms a plunge in cold water from a punishment into the highest pleasure.

The row of women in front of me is called through the stone doorway, and I rise with the others to make my way to the front of the queue. I know I will be invited through in moments, to take part in a ritual that means nothing to me. I have a premonition of the disappointment I will feel when I'm plunged into the water and emerge feeling just the same. Same worries, same anxiety and doubt, same old me.

But is that sameness such a problem? We've all been taught to believe we're broken, that only a dramatic transformation will save us. The wellness movement has long flourished by cultivating a sense of lack. But there's nothing wrong with me that this water can cure, I realise. There is no reason for me to be here at all. I rise and walk away from the line. There's a small murmur among the women around me, but I don't turn to see their surprised expressions, or to explain myself.

An hour later, I'm standing on the edge of a lake. I took the long route to get here, following the map on my phone through a field of cows and into someone's garden by mistake before I was pointed in the right direction by a woman speaking soft, southern French. There are end-of-season holidaymakers on the beach around me and what I guess are local families, cooling down after a day at work. You'd hardly know we were so close to one of the most famous religious shrines in the world in this bright place with its plastic boats, fold-out chairs and ice cream. Taking one quick last look at my bag, wrapped with its precious cargo of passport, money and phone in my towel, I head off down the beach.

I guess the woman I was waiting next to has finished her immersion in the baths by now and is sitting somewhere, maybe drying out in the sun by the riverbank. I hope that she experienced the rush of love and grace that she was waiting for.

Expecting nothing, I plunge into the lake knowing I will be accepted just as I am.

Mountains
A Way In

By the time I reach the path that will take me into the mountains, the frost is softening on the grass and the sun is just visible over the low hills to the east. I slept in this morning, and now it's 9.45 a.m. on a late winter's day and I am taking the long route into the Cairngorm Mountains. The Linn o' Dee, which has wound down from the high peaks, twists through a steep gully in the rocks here, and on either side of the park where I left my car there is pine forest. It's not exactly ancient. These are regenerated woodlands, where deer numbers are being managed and trees planted by Victorian landowners being replaced by older varieties. In time, and with careful rewilding, the montane forest of juniper, dwarf birch and willow will return, along with the rare species whose numbers dwindled when the mountains were given over to hunting and forestry. As

I walk further into the mountain following a sprawling stream, this pine forest will thin out, revealing rocks, heather, the crumbling stones of old dwelling places, and eventually the distant peaks of the mountain.

If water is a medium of transformation, then mountains are the heights on which we hope to reach the limits of ourselves, to rise above them, and transcend. This is where we experience the glory of the summit and the sublime. After a gruelling climb, an encounter with challenge and danger, we prove our worth as we touch the sky, high as a god, our arms outstretched. Imagine euphoria, and you might imagine standing on a mountaintop. Imagine numinous experience – that feeling of spiritual ecstasy, vibrant tranquillity and mysterious rapture that comes on us in rare moments – and you may think of yourself looking out on a scene like this.

That's what we've been taught, anyway. But today I'm taking the easy way in. The path I'll walk is circular and only promises the slightest elevation. To a mountaineer it would look practically flat. But I'm walking alone, with a stinking cold, and I don't want any challenges. I want to go into the mountains without scaling them. The landscape of the Cairngorms – their relatively low peaks and sinuous, looping passes – allows this. I'll still be walking all day on a 20 km–plus stretch. Dosed up with caffeine and paracetamol, I'm sure I can handle it. But if anything goes wrong, the path is straight and well marked, so I can just turn back.

It's taken me a long time to realise that is as legitimate a way of being in the mountains as any other. From European and North American cultures, I inherited the sense that seeking the summit was the only real 'way in'. This legacy makes mountains a contradictory pleasure.

Their silent regions of snow and ice entice me, their otherworldly terrains of crevices and peaks make me feel astonished to live on this world, where such hard-to-grasp beauty dominates vast regions I may never traverse or even witness first-hand.

At the same time, they incite a strange anxiety. I want to grasp them, to know them, to penetrate their mysteries. No other natural environment makes me feel this way – not the depths of rainforests, or the lowest regions of the sea. It's a kind of FOMO – the fear of missing out – blended with imposter syndrome – the sense that I'm not prepared physically or emotionally to reach the top.

In the past, I've beaten myself up about this. When I was living in Munich, within easy reach of the Tyrolean Alps, I had to excuse myself from the challenging climbs suggested by my friends. Zugspitze, Germany's highest elevation, is scalable using a marked climbing route of ladders and clips called a *Klettersteig*. Part of me was desperate to try it. I wanted the challenge, and was convinced that this way I could experience the mountain 'authentically'. But, thanks to the annoyance of vertigo, even thinking about it made me feel nauseous. Googling the Zugspitze route, I scrolled through pictures of *Klettersteigers* smiling as miles of empty space fell away beneath them. It was enough to twist my stomach into knots. Those kinds of heights set off a whirling in my head, which cycles through my body and runs right down to my feet. I had to look away from the screen and close my eyes, imagining flat earth, the embrace of solid ground, whatever I could to still the ripples of physical vulnerability running through me like an electric charge.

It wasn't easy to admit that I'd feel more comfortable taking the easier route. It was annoying to have to tell my friends – two men – that I was too frightened to do something that they went about breezily. It felt like a betrayal of my gender, and myself. In technique and strength, emotional preparedness and an animal head for heights, I felt like I had fallen short. The mountains would not reveal their mysteries to me after all.

My friends were understanding. When we went out together, we took different routes, snaking through the high passes along wide, marked paths. But above us, the shattered, snow-covered peak of Zugspitze was always visible. As we walked, I tipped my head back to look up at it and imagine how I'd feel if I was up there. What euphoric experiences was I missing out on? How would I have felt if I was exposed to the elements on that highest peak?

The story of mountains as healing places has long been bound up with fear and danger. Exploring the history of climbing in *Mountains of the Mind: A History of Fascination* (2003), Robert Macfarlane describes the daredevil approach to risk and reward that characterised nineteenth-century alpinism: 'Life, it frequently seems in the mountains, is more intensely lived the closer one gets to its extinction: we never feel so alive as when we have nearly died.' To transcend, to connect with these places fully, the message was that you needed to come perilously close to the edge.

It began with a fashion for vertigo – the horror brought on by height. This queasy sensation tempted travellers, poets and philosophers into the mountains in their hundreds, later their hundreds of thousands.

They would make arduous, expensive, dangerous journeys to experience it, scaling summits and peering over crevasses to bring on a rushing, stomach-churning sensation of terror, mingled with delight.

One of the first writers to give a name to this feeling and pinpoint it as a source of pleasure was the English playwright John Dennis. Dennis came of age in the 1680s, when rich young men were packed off on a character-building Grand Tour around southern Europe. Getting to the classical sites of Italy meant crossing the Alps, but the idea of lingering in these unconformable, unfashionable places didn't occur to most of the cosmopolitan types who traversed them. Dennis was drawn to them, though, and fascinated by the perverse pleasure of teetering on a precipice's edge: 'we walk'd upon the very brink, in a literal sense, of Destruction,' Dennis rhapsodised. 'The sense of all this produc'd different motions in me, viz., a delightful Horror, a terrible Joy, and at the same time, that I was infinitely pleas'd, I trembled.'

A century later the Irish philosopher Edmund Burke would define mountains as the ultimate sublime landscape. Burke was interested in the nature of beauty, asking psychological questions about how the mind reacts to the world. The mountains were an obvious testing ground for his ideas. Impending, dreadful, amazing, horrid, beautiful, terrible, stupendous: mountains produced delightful contradictions. In their barren expanses, without the distractions of culture and society, the relationship between the mind and the world could be observed as in a laboratory.

Standing on the edge of a precipice, hearing the booming echo of cataracts or gazing up at the terrible crevices of mountains, the soul and 'all its motions are suspended', Burke observed. We are overawed, astonished, reason is stopped dead in its tracks. But still, we survive. The attraction of the sublime lay in this blend of horror and safety. Bring a threat just close enough, and it worked a strange magic in the mind, turning the shocking sensation into deep reverence, awe that overpowered and could become addictive.

Burke's ideas ran like a charge through European culture. After reading his 1757 *Philosophical Treatise*, writers, artists and philosophers had a new lens through which to look at the natural world, and they started heading to the mountains with nervous anticipation. The artist James Barry took a Grand Tour in 1766, and reported back fulsomely on the 'horrid ridges', 'gloomy vales', 'horribly grand' tumbles, cascades, cliffs and, mysteriously, a view of the moon five times its normal size. This unrestrained language would infiltrate letters, travelogues, poetry, philosophy and Gothic novels, adding deep layers to the sublime imagery of the Alps. Wealthy travellers from across northern Europe headed south with a new hunger for extreme sensation – for an encounter with scenery that threatened doom, providing a thrill that was breathtaking. Writing in 1836 of the Mer de Glace in Chamonix, travel writer Mariana Starke advised her readers to 'pause a full half hour, to listen to the noises of distant and near avalanches', and to contemplate the glacier, so like a 'narrow and tempestuous ocean, whose towering waves have been suddenly rendered motionless by an all-powerful hand'. Not only in their epic proportions, but in their giddying compression of vast temporal scales were the mountains awful and inspiring. In their presence, emotions that were usually kept under control could be released. Subject to sublime forces, people would be purified and elevated.

What we now call 'the nature cure' owes a lot to this impulse. If people were sensitive to stimulation by nature, then it meant that we must in some way be nature-*like*. Gazing on the 'Dizzy Ravine!' of Arve by Mont Blanc, Shelley felt the mind 'holding an unremitting interchange/With the clear universe of things around'. In Byron's *Childe Harold's Pilgrimage* (1812–18), his speaker realises he lives

> … not in myself, but I become
> Portion of that around me …
> with the sky, the peak, the heaving plain
> Of ocean, or the stars, mingle, and not in vain.

It's this intermingling with the vast – and the promise that the human would be made vast in return – that confirmed mountains as places of transcendence. It was best to climb them alone to feel their full effects. Caspar David Friedrich's *Wanderer Above the Sea of Fog*, painted in 1817, is the poster boy for the Alpine sublime. With his frock coat, walking stick and woefully inadequate boots, he stands looking across a tumultuous cloudscape punctured by the jagged summits. The scale is vast, but there's power in his stance. This man has overcome nature and is looking down from what the literary critic Gillian Carter calls the '"Monarch-of-all-I-survey" scene typical of European Romanticism'. We can't see his face, but there's no doubt that something wonderful must be taking place in that mind – something extraordinary, that elevates him above all.

It's not clear why high places can make us feel euphoric. Scientists working on negative ions have suggested that higher altitudes might affect us because of the unusually high count of these ions in the atmosphere. Better known as the particles supposed to flow out of the salt-crystal lamps glowing in the corners of yoga studios, these are the electrified atoms that fizzle in the air after storms, smash from churning waves, and float in the air of mountains. Some research seems to suggest they can change our mood, making us feel briefly elated.

Were they why Dennis went into such rhapsodies in the Alps? Were they buzzing in the air around Friedrich's *Wanderer Above the Sea of Fog*? If that is the explanation, then I wonder if the thrill might have worn off. There's a thriving industry across the Alps catering to people who want to stare, from a point of relative safety, into the abyss. Above the Dachstein Glacier in Austria, a glass-bottomed suspension bridge stretches between two jutting peaks. At its end, the Stairway to Nothingness hangs like a forgotten relic of an abandoned mountain infrastructure, promising an uninhibited view of the Alps and the 1,300-foot drop below. Then there's the AlpspiX Viewing Platform atop Zugspitze in Germany, two criss-crossed metal walkways hanging forlornly over ice and rock. At its end, tourists pose as they shoot their own Instagram-worthy brushes with death at high altitudes. If ions were all it took, then no one would need to tiptoe to the edge of the platform. Just breathing in the air at the gondola's top station would be enough.

It can be a lot of fun to peer into the abyss, but there's also something quite banal about our thirst for the rush of sensation brought on by height, a desire to get the most extreme sensations we can from nature. When I see climbers queuing to reach summits, or waiting in the 'death zone' of Everest so they can have their own precious moment of elation in the clear, too-thin air, I'm grateful not to feel the need to push myself to such extremes. There's a pungently masculine aspect to it: a worship of the strength and prowess of the impossibly fit male body – what Sarah Jaquette Ray calls the 'wilderness body ideal' – which is often both colonial and sexist, as well as being ableist and perversely *anti*-nature.

An editorial from a 1907 edition of the *Scottish Ski Club* journal captures the yearning for thrills and dominance over nature that took people to the mountains. 'Man is alone, gloriously alone against the inanimate universe … He alone is Man, for whose enjoyment and use Nature exists.' And it wasn't just domination of nature. R. L. G. Irving, a mountaineer, writer and member of the Alpine Club, who scaled peaks all across the world, suggested that mountaineering became popular in Britain in the nineteenth century because young men weren't being sent off to war. As he wrote in 1939, 'when a period of peace allowed men, especially in Britain, to look for adventures in other ways than in war on land or sea, mountains began to offer a use of leisure in which body and spirit were refreshed and stimulated together'. Instead of proving themselves on the battlefield, men came to the mountains to satisfy 'the desire for dominance … the motive power behind the gospel of force'. The mountains are a series of obstacles, the wilderness ideal says. Overcoming them, you *conquer* nature, leaving your footprints in *virgin* snow.

More interesting is the work being done by neuroscientists to try to better understand what repeated encounters with fear might do to the brain. Much of this speculation focuses on one man: Alex Honnold, a 'free-soloist' who climbs alone without ropes or safety equipment. In 2018 Honnold became the first climber to make a death-defying near-four-hour ascent up all 3,000 feet of El Capitan in Yosemite National Park. The route he followed had to be completed with impeccable precision. There are no second chances in a climb like this. In some places, he progressed by 'smearing' his feet against the rock face to gain purchase, and at the same time slipping his fingers into shallow crevices that run like seams up the granite massif. The more about climbing you know, the more outrageous this sounds. Humans simply do not climb in this way. It's wildly physically demanding, even for climbers in peak shape. But more than that, the fear is too much for most people to handle. Hanging by chalked fingertips thousands of feet above the ground, with a fatal drop just a mishap away, is too cognitively overwhelming for any but this most fear-seasoned climber to attempt.

What is going on in the brain of a man who seems not to feel fear? In 2016 Honnold volunteered to be scanned in an MRI machine to help scientists find out. The cognitive neuroscientist running the scan was Jane Joseph of the Medical University of South Carolina. Joseph had heard Alex speak about his peculiar ability to control fear, and wondered how his search for extreme experience might relate to the psychology of the thrill seekers she usually works with: people living with alcohol and drug addiction, or drawn to the high-risk kicks of gambling. What she particularly wanted to know was, what was happening in his amygdalae? This is the site in the brain where we process fear: the threat-response system that produces instinctive expressions of terror and anxiety – like a racing heart and sweaty palms. Two small nodules buried at the brain's core, the amygdalae are part of our primordial limbic system, firing up before they pass information on to the frontal cortex, where the brain decides whether to turn generalised anxiety into the more concrete emotion of fear. The amygdalae have been implicated in a whole range of mental health issues, with researchers currently exploring whether activity in the amygdalae might affect people suffering from clinical anxiety, bipolar disorder and PTSD. Jane Joseph and her team wanted to know whether Alex's amygdalae were firing as normal, or whether some kind of malfunction might be behind his incredible ability to sail through feats that would incapacitate others.

What they found was surprising. Honnold's amygdalae were practically sedentary. But there was nothing technically *wrong* with Alex. In the astonishing documentary *Free Solo* (2018), Alex opens up about all the times he has experienced anxiety in his climbing career, proving that he's not immune to fear at all. Through meticulous preparations, he has somehow managed to train himself to overcome it: 'I work to expand my comfort zone until there is no fear there,' Alex reflects. This has had the effect not only of suppressing messages from the amygdalae, but inadvertently, stopping them firing at all. 'I think it could teach us a lot about potentially treating substance-abuse disorder, anxiety disorders, and coming up with strategies that people can use,' says Joseph.

A key point is that Alex is a compulsive journaler. Not only does he plan each step of each route before attempting it, he has gone over the same memories of climbs again and again to work out what he could have done differently. For those experiencing anxiety or PTSD, could Alex's approach to 'reconsolidating' fearful memories be helpful? Marie Monfils at the University of Texas at Austin has speculated on this. For a long time, the medical wisdom was that traumatic and fearful memories became 'consolidated' in the mind, and were hard to shift. Now behavioural neurologists like Monfils are exploring ways to target and attenuate fearful memories, decreasing their power over us, helping people to rewrite their emotional past and confront the things that make them afraid. Alex's journaling might help him reconsolidate fear. It's not just exposure therapy – a common behaviour treatment in which people are exposed to the thing that frightens them until the stress response is diminished. It's a way of reshaping the emotional charge of bad memories, and projecting yourself into a future moment in which a fear response is not triggered: training your prefrontal cortex to quench 'this amygdala-on-fire', as Monfils puts it. Alex's undeniable physical prowess means few will ever climb like him. But the calm and methodical practices he adopts to manage anxiety could be tried by anyone who experiences panic attacks, or faces personal challenges that seem insurmountable.

In the Cairngorms, I'm encountering no fear or challenges of any kind. The hills around me are high, but not towering, and it'll be another hour or two before I'm far in enough to see the peaks of the true mountain rising beyond them. The frost has gone completely now and the sun is cool and brilliant, turning the crushed meadow on either side of me golden. A rare, thin tree shoots up from heather and rock, and down in the valley the water flows uninhibited, splitting apart and rejoining, half bog and half stony, sunken burn.

There's something gloriously non-linear about walking in the mountains without climbing them. It scrambles our regular ways of thinking – the triangular path of base to summit is stretched and elongated to become something multiple and strange. It reminds me of my favourite moment in *The Prelude*, the long autobiographical poem that William Wordsworth started in the 1790s, then rewrote and edited throughout his life. The mountaineering episode took place in the late 1780s, when Wordsworth had set out with a friend to 'conquer' the Alps. What happened has become a classic anti-sublime moment, and a parable about not asking for too much from nature. Mont Blanc was underwhelming, and without intending to, they crossed from one side of the Alps to the other without even noticing it. Nothing special had happened to them. The sublime hadn't worked. They hadn't transcended anything. All that was left was to follow the path downhill.

I'm not setting myself up for disappointment today, or trying to prove anything. I stop repeatedly to take photos, unwrap a snack, or blow my nose. At Bob Scott's bothy, I'm distracted by a tree trunk that's tipped over the water. I want to know if I can climb it, and I can only find out by trying. I get a little way over before I slip, and must slither back to the right side. The sky is electric blue, and it feels like the sun will be up all day, but I know I need to keep moving. It's hard to resist the desire to stop and explore.

The book that opened up this way of being in the mountain to me is *The Living Mountain* (1977) by Aberdeenshire author Nan Shepherd. It's full of moments when the senses meet the life of nature, experiences of touch, scent and sight that flip everyday perception, urging her to see, feel and explore the landscape of the Cairngorms in inventive new ways. This leads her to poke fun at the machismo of hikers and their desire to experience elevation on the mountaintop. 'They want the startling view, the horrid pinnacle – sips of beer and tea instead of milk.' Sometimes they find what they're looking for, but at the same time they risk putting a rather restrictive box around the mountains, 'turning what is essentially an experience into a race'. They might be let down, like young Wordsworth, if the view is clouded, the pinnacle modest, if the moment passes without them feeling anything, and all that's left to do is turn back down. This is particularly true of the Cairngorms, where Shepherd walked all her life. Even on the high summits, the 'Monarch-of-all-I-survey' view – the climber's 'moment of glory' – is thwarted by the sinuous plateau formation of the Cairngorm massif. After a gruelling hike to the top, one is often greeted not with 'spaciousness for reward, but an interior'.

Shepherd doesn't focus on a single do-or-die climb, or talk up the heroism of mountaineering. Instead, she layers experiences of encounters that took place over many years all across the Cairngorm range – in the low valleys, as well as on the peaks and plateau. As Robert Macfarlane puts it, there 'is an implicit humility to her repeated acts of traverse, which stands as a corrective to the self-exaltation of the mountaineer's hunger for an utmost point.' Hanging her head over a precipice before falling asleep, or spending a morning tracking ice flows down mountain streams, are all ways of being attentive and experiencing the mountain. But these things don't happen at once. Her journey into the mountain's life is slow. It takes time to learn how to be present, to pay attention, and to simply *be*.

What if we were to follow Shepherd, and think about the psychological benefits of spending time with mountains less in terms of conquest and transcendence, and more about the experience as an elongated event, or an experiment in finding a new perspective on a place, which may never be complete?

This commitment to slowness and dedication isn't exactly common in mountaineering culture. Climbing is usually represented as a tough, high-octane struggle, with the videos climbers upload to YouTube accompanied by fast electronic music and sped up so an hours-long ascent takes place in a matter of minutes. This makes for good viewing, but it doesn't do much to reveal what's going on inside the minds of the people who dedicate so much time to preparing themselves to attempt the climb. Trusting yourself, and the mountain, enough to step into the void must call on intense resources of strength, perseverance and concentration. It can't be something that happens all at once.

Some climbers are now challenging the bravado of the sport, changing the face of mountaineering from a brute struggle against the elements into a more collaborative, thoughtful, even mindful enterprise. Anna Fleming, an author and climber based in Scotland, writes of how in bouldering (a rope-free form of scaling low-lying rock formations) 'we create our own routes, following chalk smears, linking features. A crack leads to a bowl; a ledge appears; here is a scoop for my foot; deep runnels welcome hands at the top.' It is a blend of precision and playfulness, the intricacies of the rock in close embrace with eye and hand.

Such experiences of fascination and absorption may be what makes climbing a potentially therapeutic activity. Christine Belk, founder of Vertigirls, a climbing club for women with mental health issues in Brighton, set up the club after benefiting from climbing herself. 'I have had fewer extreme episodes, which means I can be more involved in living and not so isolated and withdrawn,' Christine explains. The camaraderie and support of women in the group is clearly a big part of Vertigirls' success, as is its non-judgemental, non-competitive approach to climbing. A lot of their first climbs take place indoors, on climbing walls. But outdoor climbing also has the benefit of opening up the vertical, more-than-human landscape of rock. A combination of exercise, challenge, collaboration and adventure, it reveals an environment of novel wonders: an alien ecology of granite, lichen, moss and sky. The slow, thoughtful process of cutting a path across rock is a way of being with the hill, bringing mind and body into purposeful alignment with place.

When we ask mountains to shock us and test us, to take us to the limits of ourselves, we might take pleasure in rising to the challenge. Or we might simply be playing into the narrative that we're not good enough to be there – or not good enough yet. I've been susceptible to this in the past, striking out on the longest walk I can, and beating myself up for turning things down if they make me feel scared or unsafe. Resisting this demand for conquest, I release myself. It's an act of compassion, as much to the mountain as myself. Because, when seen as landscapes of pleasure and immersion, rather than places of fear and struggle, the mountains change. They're not terrifying obstacles to be overcome any more. They start to look more like complex, entangled ecosystems that we're a part of, and that invite us in. Even climbing seems less intense the more we approach it as a slow, devotional practice, something that can be an aesthetic and physical joy rather than a trial or test. And like reaching the summit, or walking as far as we possibly can, climbing starts to look like just one more way of being in the mountains, and not necessarily the best or only way in.

It's surprising that it should have taken me so long to discover this. The American mountaineering tradition is full of esoteric speculation – spiritual philosophising on the meaning and value of mountains – which drew from Buddhist and Taoist ideas about the sacredness of heights.

It began on a rainy August night in the White Mountains of the northern Appalachians, 1826. The Willey family had shut up their inn for the night. As the downpour intensified, rocks and mud began to dislodge from the mountainside. Hearing the rumbling and fearing disaster, they fled. With a tragic irony, the whole family was killed by the landslide that engulfed them, but their wooden inn remained intact.

Dark tourism to this deadly spot would be the origin story of North American mountain worship. The terrible event became the subject of morbid philosophical speculation, presenting 'an unfathomable mystery' as historian Gregg Mitman puts it, 'a reminder of man's mortality and of God's untold power'. Tourists came to see the site of the accident, and also to climb the fatal mountain – which was hastily renamed Mount Willey.

Henry David Thoreau is best known for his retreat to the woodlands of Concord. It was there he wrote his manifesto on the value of wilderness, *Walden*, in 1854. But years before he took to his cabin in the woods, Thoreau was scaling mountains. He first climbed Mount Washington – a few miles away from Mount Willey – in 1839, then sought summits all across the USA. For Thoreau, mountains were the ideal spiritualiser, places where one could find one's higher latitudes, and with the land be elevated and etherealised. In mountains, people could intuit divine truths, feel their way into knowledge of the world. Thoreau admitted that he felt 'the same awe when on their summits that many do on entering a church'. Not in books, in religious teachings or temples, but in nature at its most rare and lofty, could you find revelation.

Thoreau's fascination was infused with surprising ingredients. He was part of the Transcendentalist Club, a group of writers and intellectuals connected to Harvard University, who started meeting in the late 1830s. The Transcendentalists imbibed European Romanticism – sharing the hunch that people were their best selves in wild places – but they were also drawn to Indian and East Asian philosophy. Thoreau claimed to be the first American to practice yoga, and his ideas about identity were inspired by Hindu and Buddhist sacred texts. In *The Dial*, the Transcendentalist Club's magazine, the first English translation of the Lotus Sutra (undertaken by the writer and educationalist Elizabeth Palmer Peabody) was published in 1844. The Sutra is a foundational text in Buddhist thinking. It insists upon the unity of all things, and promises that the Buddhist ideal of enlightenment may be attainable to all. The path of the Buddha is one of compassion, meditation, and abandonment of the self. In this philosophy, the idea of the 'self' is inherently suspect. Buddhahood can only be achieved when this spectral entity – a tissue of memories, postures, shallow desires and falsehood – is relinquished, and the world is experienced in all the intensity of the unfiltered present.

Ralph Waldo Emerson – a friend and collaborator of Thoreau – was exploring similar esoteric territory, seizing translated ideas and applying them to the American landscape with gusto. In his 1836 essay, *Nature*, he considered how being among all that is 'not us' affects us for the better. Emerson slotted human health into the palm of nature, claiming that 'to the body and mind which have been cramped by noxious work or company, nature is medicinal and restores their tone'. Gazing at the sky, alone in the woods, or immersed in the sublime beauty of the mountains, humanity would become 'whole' again. To achieve this soul-affirming connection, we should go to the mountains alone. Only alone are we really open to nature's influences, to the power of nature to transform our mood, as 'every hour and change corresponds to and authorizes a different state of the mind'. With the self, the ego in abeyance, Emerson writes, 'I become a transparent eyeball; I am nothing; I see all; the currents of the Universal Being circulate through me.'

In reality, very little of the great American mountain writing really achieves the abandonment of the ego. What emerges, instead, is a new kind of individualism. Self-reliant and facing nature alone, the enlightened individual stands out against the rugged landscape of the North American ranges, elevated and ecstatic, transcendent and transfixed. Occasionally, though, the mountains resisted. After climbing Mount Katahdin, a stony, inhuman 'Titanic' mass in Maine, Thoreau wrote up his experience with grave concern. On 'Ktaadn', as he called it, he felt 'more lone than you can imagine', as if some vital part of him was escaping, 'grating of his ribs' with each step. Not every wild place answered the human striving for meaning and correspondence, or could be imaginatively overcome. On these stony limits Thoreau came to the edges of himself in the most disturbing way possible. He was no longer able to find beauty in a place, and to feel its welcome in return. Nature seemed to repel him, to ask, *Why did you come here? What do you want?*

The limitation of this philosophy wasn't just the Transcendentalists' expectations about what would happen to them in the mountains, but the ideal of the mountain as a 'wilderness' itself. Mountains became the quintessential American landscape of healing, 'a pristine sanctuary where the last remnant of an untouched, endangered, but still transcendent nature can for at least a little while longer be encountered without the contaminating taint of civilization', as environmental historian William Cronon puts it.

This transcendental wilderness ideal still shapes our perceptions of mountains, and influences the way ranges across the USA and the world are protected and managed. Much of this is the legacy of nature writer and conservationist John Muir. Muir was born in Dunbar, a fishing village on the east coast of Scotland, though his family emigrated to rural Wisconsin in 1849. A lifelong lover of nature, who described himself as a 'poetico-trampo-geologist-botanist and ornithologist-naturalist', Muir abandoned university in order to hike and camp instead. After travelling around Canada, the southern States and Cuba, in 1868, Muir found himself in the Sierra Nevada, the Californian segment of the vast American Cordillera mountain range. His first glimpse of Yosemite – a deep valley carved by glaciers – hit him as a vision of the Divine. From then on, the Sierra would become a site of ecstasy to Muir, where 'the whole body seems to feel beauty when exposed to it as it feels the campfire or sunshine, entering not by the eyes alone, but equally through all one's flesh like radiant heat, making a passionate ecstatic pleasure-glow not explainable'. Gazing at the soaring granite formations of Half Dome and El Capitan or the striking pinnacles of the Cathedral Range, Muir worshipped in a natural cathedral. Overwhelming the senses, striking him quiescent with awe, the mountains seemed to refine and elevate all who saw them: 'These blessed mountains are so compactly filled with God's beauty, no petty personal hope or experience has room to be.'

In spite of Muir's rhapsodies, the mountains weren't peaceful. When he arrived, the Ahwahnechee were being brutally forced from their land as the valleys were opened up for sheep grazing and gold mining. The Ahwahnechee had populated the area for over 6,000 years, but as Muir noted in *My First Summer in the Sierra* (1911), the subtle line of trails they had left were so slight, the valleys could easily be mistaken for untouched wilderness. How had these communities managed to 'walk softly and hurt the landscape hardly more than the birds and squirrels'? There's a patronising quality to Muir's description. Native people are reduced to what anthropologist Shepard Krech calls 'Ecological Indians': simplistic figures concocted by the European imagination, living in harmony with nature in a kind of timeless wonder. But Muir was right to notice the disparity between how white colonisers used and abused the land in contrast to the more sustainable and reciprocal ways of living with the land established over centuries by the Ahwahnechee. A few decades of capitalist land management had already made dramatic marks on the mountainsides: 'roads blasted in the solid rock, wild streams dammed and tamed and turned out of their channels and led along the sides of canyons and valleys to work in mines like slaves'.

This careless development seemed to Muir an insult against God, nature and humanity. Because, Muir realised, the mountains were becoming a lifeline for workers from the cities. Along with the miners and the farmers and the prospectors came the tourists, people who travelled to camp and hike in the valleys from their homes in San Francisco and Sacramento. Watching them, he felt he was seeing people return to their natural element.

'Thousands of tired, nerve-shaken, over-civilized people are beginning to find out that going to the mountains is going home; that wildness is a necessity; and that mountain parks and reservations are useful not only as fountains of timber and irrigating rivers, but as fountains of life,' Muir wrote in a scathing critique of modern labour and city living published in 1901. 'Few in these hot, dim, strenuous times are quite sane or free.' But in the majesties of Yosemite, people recovered from 'dust and disease'. He called these people 'nerve-shaken', tapping into medical understandings of psychological collapse as nervous overstimulation. Deep in the fleshy matrix of the nerves, so the theory went, people were shattered by the conditions of modern life, their natural vigour, health and humour sapped. Heading into the mountains, they weren't just untangling themselves from the neurosis of the city. They were getting in touch with the nerves of 'Mother Earth' herself.

When Muir stood up to defend the mountains, he spoke of their power as restorative places. His three-day camping excursion to Yosemite in 1903 with President Theodore Roosevelt is now legendary. Roosevelt returned from this excursion transformed, and willing to extend robust conservation laws into the Sierra, in order to preserve them 'for their children and their children's children forever, with their majestic beauty all unmarred'. The model of national parks that Muir created has cemented a certain understanding of mountains, and wilderness, in the American imagination, with repercussions around the world.

In his attempt to save the mountains of the US from development, John Muir proclaimed that 'everybody needs beauty as well as bread, places to play in and pray in, where nature may heal and give strength to body and soul'. Nature, and natural beauty, should never be thought of as some kind of luxury, something we can afford to set aside when the going gets tough. It is something basic, something 'everybody' needs, as much as everybody needs food to eat.

It is a fine sentiment. But the wilderness ideal hasn't lived up to that egalitarian promise. Instead, as Rebecca Solnit writes in *Wanderlust* (2001), 'walking in the landscape can be a demonstration of a specific heritage', with some people invited in, and others excluded. Beauty, to Muir, wasn't really for everyone.

'He made derogatory comments about Black people and Indigenous peoples that drew on deeply harmful racist stereotypes, though his views evolved later in his life.' These are the words of Michael Brune, the executive director of the Sierra Club, the conservation organisation founded by Muir in 1892. In the wake of Black Lives Matter protests after the murder of George Floyd in July 2020, the Sierra Club finally went public to apologise for Muir's racist comments and his association with white supremacists and eugenicists. But 'there is a dark underside here that will not be erased by just saying Muir was a racist', cautions Stanford history professor, Richard White. It 'is not just Muir who was racist. The way we created the wilderness areas we now rightly prize was racist' too.

Muir's ideas about the wilderness, and its relationship to wellbeing, still resonate today. Weary city dwellers head for refuges and spiritual retreats tucked into the mountains, seeking vast spaces where they can expand their inner latitudes. But the narratives that such experiences trade on – from Transcendentalism, to westerns old and new – are often stories about white people.

The 'white wilderness' ideal means that racist stereotypes about who belongs in mountains, forests and national parks persist. In *Black Faces, White Spaces*, Carolyn Finney documents the ways in which

Black people have been othered in nature, and mountain space racialised. A 'nonessentialized black environmental identity that is grounded in the legacy of African American experiences in the United States' only exists on the margins, or has been entirely erased from dominant Euro-American perspectives on the mountains. The right to wander, the right to dream, the right to rest or expand your horizons: these are the pleasures and gifts that so many people have taken from mountains. When these rights are denied or seen as not essential to Black people, the result is real psychological violence and a painful compression of the imagination, as Finney explains. Mountaineering remains a privileged pursuit – worsened by racialised wealth inequalities and reinforced by other forms of oppression.

This is not just an American problem. I learned more about how this manifests in the UK from Pammy Johal, founder of the outdoor organisation Backbone. We were both invited to give a presentation at a gathering of women mountain enthusiasts in Glasgow in 2018. The previous speakers (myself included) had already congratulated ourselves on the fact that so many women – a hundred or more – were there to celebrate mountains. This must have been some kind of record? But when Pammy got up to speak, she asked us to look around the room. 'What do you notice?' she asked. It was obvious as soon as she'd said it. Everyone in the audience was white.

'Why do you think that is?' Pammy asked. What made it possible for everyone there to get to know the mountains? 'Familiarity,' one woman shouted out. Plenty of people there were from rural places, where the moors and mountains were on their doorstep.

'Upbringing,' said another. She was taken on camping holidays by her nature-mad parents. And then a slew of voices piped up. Cars. The right clothes. Training in map reading. Scouts, Guides, Duke of Edinburgh Awards. Speaking the language. Money. Privilege. A feeling that you belong.

Such access is not guaranteed for the people Pammy's organisation works with – predominantly Black and Asian women who have often recently settled in the UK, who Backbone guides on mountain adventures. Their presence and their pleasure disrupt the assumed whiteness of Scotland's national parks, creating new stories and possibilities for representation and leadership in the outdoors.

Another significant problem with the 'white wilderness' heritage of mountaineering, particularly in the USA, is its tendency to simultaneously erase and appropriate from Indigenous cultures. In the Adirondack Mountains, one mountain retreat serves as an egregiously embarrassing example. It markets itself on the history of the area: Emerson led a group of writers, scientists and luminaries into the nearby hills in 1858 to experience a wilderness adventure of hunting, swimming, hiking and philosophising. Now, for $3,395, you can spend five days with like-minded health-seekers contemplating the power of mountains, becoming 'infused with the powerful energies of untouched wilderness' (never mind the fact the land is privately owned). Guided meditations, group ceremonies, trekking and fire councils are part of the transformative voyage on offer, inspired by the Transcendentalists, with a dab of shamanism pinched from wholly distinct Native cultures. Inca, Algonquin and Mohawk people are all name-checked, though Indigenous representatives are not part of the organising team. For the business leaders, healers and coaches who take up spots at the camp, activities culminate in a 'sacred' mountaintop ceremony where, it's promised: 'your shoulders drop, your heart opens, the sun warms you. Your energy merges into the vortex where "Condor and Eagle" meet. Energy spirals, stretching and soaring into the sky as your heart thrums with joy. You exhale… and let go.' Whatever that is supposed to mean.

Karen Ramos is a Ñuu Savi Indigenous activist from Oaxaca, Mexico, who is working to change things. As NatureChola on Instagram, she encourages people of colour, particularly women, to visit the national parks of California and the American South for the benefit of their mental health, and as acts of resistance and decolonisation. She documents her treks in mountain parks, often juxtaposing smiling, sunny photographs with accounts of racist microaggressions she's experienced on her walks, facts about healthcare inequalities faced by disenfranchised communities, and reflections on her struggles with depression and the feeling of imposter syndrome which makes her worry she's not 'outdoorsy' enough. As an Indigenous and Latinx ambassador, she challenges the stereotype that mountains are somehow 'for white people' only, and that the only way of experiencing mountains is by replaying old sublime and Transcendentalist stereotypes, or stepping into white people's fantasy of the Ecological Indian. This means talking about the histories – and the future – of Indigenous nations on trail walks, calling out racism and exclusion, and guiding people to approach natural places with respect and understanding.

Ramos's work is a powerful reminder that the wilderness narrative has long erased the voices of Indigenous people from mountain ranges in the USA, and all around the world. A place that is 'wild' is, by definition, somewhere people don't live. Stripped of their meaning, stories and identity, mountains are reduced to landscapes of sport, retreat and self-realisation, their cultural significance and connection to community identity disrespected and forgotten. In Aṉangu land in Central Australia, hikers have long flocked to Uluṟu, wanting to see the stunning desert landscape from the summit and challenge themselves to climb its steep red faces, often in intense heat. But in 2019, after years of protest by its Aboriginal owners, climbing Uluṟu was finally banned. Instead, the mountain has been restored as a sacred site of ritual and reflection. The late Aṉangu elder Tony Tjamiwa explains: 'You shouldn't climb. It is not the real thing about this place. The real thing is listening to everything. Listening and understanding everything.' In the Aṉangu creation story, Uluṟu is the site of a fatal battle between Kuniya – a mother python – and Liru, a poisonous snake. The scars of their fight mark the rock around all its sides, and now a signposted walk leads visitors around the base of the rock, taking in its waterfalls, rock art and wildlife, while carefully avoiding sensitive sites. This is the right 'way in' to experience the mountain. 'The tourist comes here with the camera taking pictures all over. What has he got?' Tjamiwa asks. 'Another photo to take home, keep part of Uluṟu. He should get another lens – see straight inside. Wouldn't see big rock then. He would see that Kuniya living right inside there as from the beginning. He might throw his camera away then.'

So many other ways of being in the mountains open up when we move beyond the old stories and reject exclusionary narratives – fighting back against racism, sexism and homophobia in national parks. On Instagram I follow Pattie Gonia, the American hiker and drag queen who's been taking to the national parks to promote the visibility of queer hikers, and to fight for access for marginalised communities in nature. Watching videos of Pattie dance on perilous peaks in platform heels, a rainbow Pride flag flapping behind her, is a lesson in how narrow the visual repertoire of normalised bodies in the mountains is, how restrictive our inherited sense of the 'right' ways of being in the 'great American wilderness'. In place of the clichéd image of the Gore-Tex-clad hiker gazing in wonder at the landscape from a cliff edge, we have Pattie spinning and dipping as she kicks away words that have been superimposed on the screen. 'Self-doubt', 'stress', 'hate', 'homophobia', 'toxic masculinity', 'pollution', 'global warming'. The celebration of queer beauty in the mountains is a powerful assertion of identity, of the right to exist and flourish with pride, without which wellbeing is impossible. Pattie's statement of visibility is also an attack on inequalities and oppressions. No longer just an individual journey for meaning or restoration, being visibly queer in the mountains is an act of transgression that reaches out to connected struggles, helping to create new communities ready to fight for environmental and social justice.

Finally, I have reached the other side of Lui Water, and come to the pass that will give me access to the mountain – by sight, at least. The black lump of Bod an

Deamhain – Gaelic for the Devil's Penis, but politely translated for Queen Victoria as the Devil's Point – now stands proudly erect in front of me. These histories of naming, and the fragments of cleared villages I have walked past, are a reminder that these mountains aren't 'wild' land either, and that the solitude and quietness of the Highlands have been dearly bought. To my right, the snow-covered peak of Ben Macdui is just visible, soaring white and impenetrable. Its danger and its distance, its serenity and silence, would have taunted me once. Now I know I don't need to climb it to experience what those old-school mountaineers called transcendence – elevation above the earth – to feel a sense of ecstasy and to know that I am whole.

Finding other 'ways in' has been a relief from these pressures. But the walk I've taken has, in its own way, been long and arduous. My physical ability to go on this long hike is something I haven't thought to reflect on, until now. I may have escaped the masculine sublime, but I've still contributed to the wilderness body ideal – assuming that physical prowess and feats of endurance are the only way to access the mountains authentically.

The rise of paraclimbing at world-championship level, and the record-breaking first ascents of routes in the Arctic by Jesse Dufton, a blind member of the GB Paraclimbing Team, are signs that things are changing, and that rock climbing and mountaineering are not only reserved for the narrow conception of wilderness body ideals. Adaptive climbing has the potential to open up experiences of vertical exploration to people with diverse physical abilities, creating new stories of encounter where the eye does not dominate, and where safety is prioritised over the old lust for danger.

But these are still demanding physical encounters, and potentially alienating to disabled people who may not want or be able to traverse mountains in that way. To really open up the mountains, it will take more. Physical barriers must be addressed, and so must conceptual ones. As the organisers of Kendal Mountain Festival's 'Open Mountain' events series (launched in 2019) explain, it also involves 'redefining mountain literatures and cultures to include voices and experiences often excluded or invalidated'.

In her essay, 'Walking' (2018), the author Alice Tarbuck reflects on how reduced mobility and living with chronic illness changed her relationship with mountains. The 'exhilarating eight-hour journey, from base to summit', was now out of reach, and with it, 'a significant way of engaging with the natural world'. Living with pain, she worried that she would be 'confined to a life without truly experiencing landscape, without participating in these natural spaces which … seem so crucial in forming identity and bonds with our world'. Like so many others living with chronic illness or long-term disability, access was either denied or the kinds of experiences available to her invalidated and deemed 'inauthentic'.

But reading Shepherd's *The Living Mountain* changed things, revealing other ways into the mountain than the hike or climb. The heat of the sun, the cold sting of water, the press of the wind against the cheek, or details rendered through the lens of a pair of binoculars: these are all sensory encounters with the world that can't be measured in miles or feet, but play out across the landscape of the skin and in the mind. These are experiences that can be had on the viewing platform by the visitor centre, or along trails where wheelchairs pass with ease. As Alice puts it, learning to accept that these experiences are real and valuable, that they are *enough*, has changed her relationship with nature and the hills. They let her 'dwell happily in this strange body, and let me shape myself in relation to the natural world'.

If the 'nature cure' is to be anything other than an ableist, classist hobby, it needs to start from a position of access and openness. Mountains, more than any other natural environment, show us the failures of the past, and how these can, and must, be changed. It's not simply about transplanting everyone into the mountains, but removing obstacles that stop people experiencing these places first-hand in ways that are pleasurable and meaningful to them. For the mountain snobs who worry that increased access might damage these precious environments, you need only look again at those crowds queuing to reach the summit of Snowdon, or dying as they wait to mount Everest, to see that existing cultures of mountaineering are not sensitive to wildlife's need for peace and quiet, or even necessarily humane to those attempting the summit.

I've discovered the importance of being kind to myself. In therapy, I've learned not to beat myself up about not doing enough or missing out. Using compassion-focused approaches developed by the clinical psychologist Paul Gilbert, I've worked at my tendency to dwell somewhere between the systems he calls 'drive' and 'threat'. Resisting the intense, hyper-focused ambition of the drive system and the anxiety and self-criticism of threat, I repeat little mantras to reach a 'soothing state': you're doing fine; this is enough; you can be content.

It doesn't work for everyone, but I've found it helpful. And as a useful side effect, it's helped resolve my difficult relationships with mountains. I don't feel bad about never having tried the *Klettersteig*, or turning up late at the mountain because a serious hiker would have been here at dawn. I'm happy to gaze at Ben Macdui from afar. I no longer think any of these things make me a failure.

I am even ready to accept that I am exhausted. I can't make the full circuit today. It's time to find a quiet spot to sit on the heather and eat lunch. Maybe I will lie down in the sun for what's left of the day, in the light that is almost as warm as spring. Ben Macdui is a hint of white on the rim of the horizon, Devil's Point a pinprick of black granite. Watching them from a slow, glacial distance, I feel that I have finally been invited into the mountain – I have found my own way in.

Forest
Embracing Darkness

The light slipping around the edges of the floral curtains wakes us. It makes the room glow, brightening the spaces that were dark and strange when we arrived late last night. I get up from the sagging bed, stretch, and pull the curtains open so I can look outside. On the GPS map we used to navigate our way here last night, the surrounding landscape seemed to be half underwater, a blue and green digital patchwork of forest and lake. But from the window, there's no glint of water visible. We're surrounded by deep forest. Pine, birch and dense green undergrowth as far as the eye can see.

I'm staying with my partner Jo in Savonia, colloquially known in English as Finland's Lakeland. This cottage was built by a forester in the 1920s, and this summer their great-grandkids have started renting it on the cheap to help pay for refurbishments. The insides are pure mid-century kitsch, almost unchanged since it was abandoned in the late 1970s. The floors are wooden, the windows a thin, smudged glass, and rooms are organised around a network of stoves and fires that cluster at the house's core like a heart. When I press my hands against the brick of the built-in wood burner buried deep into the wall, it's always warm. In the forest, resources must be used carefully. Water has to be collected in a bucket from the well, and one electric plug socket serves both fridge and cooker in turn. Piled up eight feet high around the outside walls, logs have been chopped and stored for winter. Everything is in order. But beyond the house, the land is a tangle of weeds, trees and outbuildings, blurring into forest. Bold young pines shoot up between sheds and the grass of the yard gives way to a thick undergrowth of wild bilberries, now bursting with a glut of fruit.

After a breakfast of dark sour bread, I set out into the forest to pick them, a basket hung over my arm. Walking slowly, my eyes tracking the ground, I look for bilberries, tiny wild strawberries and rare cloudberries, as colourful and luminous as amber. Summer so close to the Arctic Circle is short and intense: a month and a half of white nights, ripening fruit, camping, fishing and partying before the snow comes and the sun sinks down, becoming a silver smudge on the horizon. The fruit is fresh, the forest is wild and alive, and the sun glows through the trees. Winter may be coming, but for the moment there's release and joy to being in this easy, giving world.

It's easy to see why this landscape became synonymous with health. Trees and woodlands have sustained Finns and Sámi – the reindeer-herding communities of the

Arctic and Fennoscandia – for millennia, giving fuel, shelter and sustenance. Over the course of this long, symbiotic relationship, they've become sites of powerful meaning and attraction, of fascination and *glamourie* on white summer nights and dark winter days. In Finnish mythology, the Milky Way was once called the path of the birds, because in the dark days of winter they were believed to travel along this celestial route to *lintukoto*, a place of warmth, happiness and peace. Picking fruit in the forest is as close to *lintukoto* as I can imagine. The birds that have followed the star-path (or more likely, sensory cues from the sun's light and the earth's magnetic fields) seem to agree.

The forest still permeates Finnish culture in all kinds of ways. It can be comically banal, like in the airport at Helsinki, where the walls are adorned with photo-murals of trees, stuffed pine martens glare at you from above the baggage carousel, and you visit the loo accompanied by recorded birdsong and the synthetic scent of pine. Infinitely less tacky is the presence of the sauna. These heated wooden huts were originally used by families to wash and warm up on frosty nights. Now they're an obligatory communal activity. Within an hour of arriving in Helsinki, I had located the public sauna in the city centre and found myself naked in a room full of women of all ages, sweating contentedly on wooden beams arranged around a crackling orange pit. This was a world away from the grim electric or infrared versions I've experienced in the UK. The traditional sauna, fired by a wood-burning, coal-topped stove and supplied with a bucket of water and a bundle of fresh birch to revive the skin, is a source of intense pride and limitless speculation on its health-giving properties.

When we arrived at one of our B&Bs feeling under the weather, our host ran off to pack wood into the sauna that he was proud to remind us he had built himself. While it warmed, he rummaged around in his garage for a bottle of liquid tar, collected in a vast bonfire at last year's Midsummer festival. 'If booze, tar or sauna can't cure you, you're dead,' he explained, before giving me a whiff of the smoky brown liquid. The same tar concoction, as we discovered on our own visit to the Midsummer fire site, turns up in sweets and ice cream, a taste of the forest as crisp and comforting as a campfire.

Forests are often thought of as places of retreat and restoration, somewhere to get away from ourselves – or to find ourselves, depending on your needs. I came to Finland because I wanted to seek light and darkness in the forest, to understand the fables and scientific stories of woodland 'cures'. Watching the view flash past the window of the overnight train that took us north, almost to the Arctic Circle, I knew I wouldn't be disappointed. Forest, then lake, then little red house, forest, lake, little red house: the same scenery flicking past the Plexiglas for hundreds of miles before dusk finally fell. In dramatic contrast to most of its European neighbours, Finland is still around 78 per cent forested. With a population of 5.5 million, that's around eighteen people per square kilometre. The forests here aren't exactly untouched: the marks of the logging industry and the fire pits built along well-marked hiking trails reveal a pervasive human presence. The right to roam and camp is enshrined in law here: the *jokamiehenoikeus*, based on ancient Nordic principles of outdoor living, which guarantee the forests are free of fences and restrictive by-laws. But for this citizen of a high-density, largely deforested archipelago on Europe's western fringes, even in summer the Finnish forest is a place of disarming solitude, noisy only with birdsong and the flow of water. In moments like this, I can trick myself into believing the place is somehow primaeval. These acres of unbroken greenery seem to have escaped the ravages of modernity and the last two centuries of intense, ravenous, global tree felling. But there's something futuristic, almost utopian about it too. Taking a low-cost, high-speed train through the forest, or cycling on paths through Finnish cities like Oulu, where houses bleed into the forest's edges, I squint and get a vision of what the world could look like if we listened to scientists' pleas to undertake urgent, unprecedented tree planting as a way of capturing CO_2 and reversing current global warming trends.

Of course, forests are almost never primal sites, devoid of human occupation and meaning. In any land where trees flourish, people have found a way to worship them, to make groves sacred or to select special trees as wardens for protection. Germanic, Scandinavian, Greek and Celtic cultures revered forests as sites of transformation, the haunts of gods, elves and fairy folk, home of enchanted fruits and waters. In Nigerian Yoruba cosmology, Aja is a deity of the forest, a powerful Orisha, or spirit, who carries people into the depths of the woods to teach them the arts of botanical medicine, before returning them to their communities as powerful healers. Igbo culture worships Alusi, spirits who influence human fate and – a little like Shinto *kami* or Filipino *anito* – gather around trees and forests. Many cultures associate trees with knowledge and creation, from the Māori forest god

Tāne, who brings knowledge down from the heavens, to the Tree of Knowledge in Christianity's Eden and the Nordic Yggdrasil, the cosmic tree that connects the nine worlds of gods and humanity.

Often the old faiths have been forgotten, consigned to the realm of fantasy and myth. But in some places beliefs have been turned into something new, like sacred groves in Ghana, Estonia, Nigeria and India, which have been granted protections as wildlife sanctuaries. As forests around the world are continually burned and razed for pasture and logging, and local communities experience dispossession and violence, there is some hope in these urgent acts of legislation. Captured in the imperfect language of modern law, they struggle to recognise the intrinsic value of these places, to celebrate their social and ecological significance and protect them from imminent destruction.

The same is true in Australia, where Indigenous fire practices are being revived. Since British colonisation in the 1780s, traditional practices of culturally and ecologically sensitive control burns were suppressed, along with so much Indigenous knowledge. This meant forests hadn't been cleared of flammable debris at the right moments in the seasonal cycle, making them vulnerable to the kinds of catastrophic bushfires that now characterise summer heatwaves and lead to terrible loss of life. Unlike controlled burns practised in North America and Australia, Aboriginal cultural burns are shaped by principles of respect, responsibility and recognition – based on shared perceptions of Country as a holistic entity uniting community with the land and all living things. The Firesticks Alliance – a corporation of Indigenous communities committed to reinvigorating cultural burning – explains:

> cultural burning is based on an understanding that a reciprocal arrangement exists between people and Country. This is often summarised in 'healthy people healthy Country'. That is, healthy people with knowledge, authority and capacity are required to manage the Country. In return a healthy landscape is required to support the physical, mental and spiritual needs of the people who are the managers.

As the climate crisis creates longer, drier and hotter summers, these ancient and reciprocal practices challenge assumptions that humanity's health has become somehow disentangled from nature's. They also show up the complacency of colonial and capitalist land-use practice. The forest isn't simply a resource to be exploited or a dangerous environment to be controlled. It has needs too, and to ignore them is to hasten both our and the forest's destruction.

In Western Europe and the USA, at the same time as the Industrial Revolution began to strip nature of all meaning beyond its commodity value, ancient beliefs about forest were also revived and transformed as a kind of embryonic literary activism. The young William Wordsworth met 'Nature' in the forest, 'the spirit in the woods' who taught him 'gentleness of heart'. Thoreau took his 'tonic of wildness' in Walden forest, while John Muir thought 'the clearest way into the Universe' was through a wood. In Finland, Romantics like Johan Ludvig Runeberg helped to fix the forest as the nation's landscape, a place to redress the balance between our inner nature and the world. In Runeberg's 1848 poem 'Vårt Land', which would become the Finnish national anthem, summers are happy and bright and 'the hummings of eternal pines' accompany us on each step we take through the endless forest. In their first editions, pamphlets of Runeberg's poetry were adorned with lithograph prints of those forests, intercut by the waters of serene lakes. The same imagery haunts Finnish art galleries, with their portraits of cheerful foresters in sun-spangled woodlands, or night-time scenes of the moon shimmering through a canopy of pine and birch.

Over the course of the nineteenth century, Europeans and Americans fired up by Romanticism began turning to the sun, air and water in order to cleanse the heart and soul. 'Naturopath' culture, with its spas and clinics, health rituals and 'back to nature' holidaymaking, often took place close to the forest. When Swiss naturopath Arnold Rikli established a 'helio-hydroscopic' clinic by Lake Bled in Slovenia in the 1850s, health-seekers were encouraged to imbibe the air, swim in the lake, sunbathe naked, go vegetarian, and strike out on treks through alpine forests towards the distant hills. In the USA, Emerson's Philosophers' Camp drew its health-giving properties as much from the forest as from its mountain locations, with hearty hikes, botanising and wood-chopping part of participants' daily therapeutic schedule. Under the influence of the Transcendentalists, the surgeon-turned-health-guru John George Gehring established an inn in the White Mountains, Maine, in the 1890s. Offering unpretentious accommodation for nerve-shattered and exhausted intellectuals and academics, Gehring's guests (never patients) were given the chance to grow vegetables, chop wood, and hike into the forests and mountains to breathe the clear air. The retreat was popular. In the thirty-five years Gehring's inn was open, so many academics took the train north to Bethel that it became known as Harvard University's 'resting place', the Cambridge of the north.

What drove these people to the forest was the desire to rediscover a way of being in the world – a lost 'human nature'. Modernity, as well as literally felling forests, was severing humanity from influences that connected us to each other and the living world. This was more than an inconvenience: it was a terrible psychological schism, and thought to have led to the rise of new 'diseases of modernity' – nervous collapse, exhaustion and ennui.

D. H. Lawrence's short story 'Sun' (1928), captures this mood of yearning for a restored intimacy with 'nature'. It begins in New York, as a wealthy man is advised by a doctor to take his languishing wife away and into the sun to aid her recovery. Juliet, the nervous woman at the centre of things, is shipped to Sicily, where she slips into the forest by day to lie naked in the heat and light of the sun. Juliet is sceptical of the treatment at first, but soon the sun begins to envelop and penetrate her, flowing 'into her bones; nay, further, even into her emotions and her thoughts'. In Lawrence's universe, his characters – usually women – experience rapturous sexual and emotional awakenings in wild places, beyond the influence of stultifying civilisation and weak, sex- and sun-starved men. Under the eye of the sun, Juliet experiences a kind of carnal enlightenment as the chains that attach her to her husband, to society, and even to her child, begin to melt away. 'She herself, her conscious self, was secondary, a secondary person, almost an onlooker. The true Juliet was this dark flow from her deep body to the sun.' Sex, nature and death are all intertwined, and Juliet's nude forest wandering is a step towards killing the social self and recovering the fuller, wilder, and ultimately more peaceful animal nature she had reluctantly learned to repress.

Lawrence's hyper-sexual sun worship is many miles apart from modern forest therapies. Now we have forest schools and mindfulness centres, guided walks and wellness advice, where people are encouraged to get outdoors, supported by qualified nature therapists. I've had the chance to speak with the therapists who run sessions offering everything from meditation to tree climbing in areas of public woodland from Somerset to Scotland. For the most vulnerable people they work with – including those who've had referrals from their GP – getting into forests can be tricky. There are issues with transport and costs, and forests are places with bad associations for some, alien environments they may never have visited or explored. But with proper funding and support from carers, people make it to the site, and as the woodland leaders tell me, for some this is both the highlight of their week, and one of the few activities that can give them the strength to get out of doors.

This is a story I've heard from others too, anecdotal evidence that for people experiencing anxiety, depression and compulsive thoughts, the forest can be soothing if approached in the right way. I remember meeting a woman at a wellbeing festival in Bristol, who spoke of how the scent, colours and strange, spontaneous sounds of crackles and animal cries cut through the cycling anguish of her obsessive negative thoughts, clearing the mind for a moment of pure, uninhibited pleasure.

In the last decade, dedicated forest-bathing centres have started popping up across Europe and the US. Based on the Japanese *shinrin-yoku* trend, these retreats are usually led by guides who take people along special routes in the forest to help them experience the restorative benefits of the wood in meticulously planned and crafted ways. Soon after we arrived in Finland, we visited one of these centres and joined one of the most popular tours: a three-hour jaunt around a 2.5 km stretch of woodland with a group of other 'bathers'. Our guide was an experienced hiker who also leads groups on caving and cross-country skiing excursions in the winter. Before taking us into the forest, he gave a quick introduction to forest bathing, outlining what we could expect it to do for us. It was important to walk slowly, he explained, to take time to breathe in the scent of the place and to listen to the forest sounds.

'No one expects anything from you in the forest,' he explained, in softly accented English. 'It's not a judgemental place. This is why the forest can make us so calm and free.'

I know what he means. The freedom of the forest for me has always rested in a sense of being out of time, away from observation, obligation and scrutiny. There's more to forest bathing than this, though. Our instructor hints at it when he tells us that the health-giving power of the wood comes from 'the chemistry of the air'. You will see the same thing boasted on many forest-bathing sites – where 'volatile compounds' supposed to be coming from the trees and leaf mulch are said to penetrate the skin and reinvigorate breath, and where participants are promised any number of benefits, from 'deeper and clearer intuition', to increased 'flow of energy', *eros*, and a renewed ability to 'communicate with the land and its species'.

These are bold claims, muddling the realm of the spiritual with science and medicine. In recent studies, forest baths are spoken of in the same breath as mainstream medicines and treatments for diagnosable ailments. Conditions like ADHD, anxiety and depression are said to be improved by exposure to the forest. It's even raised as a preventative medicine for cancers, heart disease, type 2 diabetes and a range of serious mental health concerns. It's not that forest bathing is meant to cure cancer, or any other psychological or physical illness. Rather, its promoters boost its worth by connecting the beneficial chemistry of trees in reducing stress with the negative effect that stress plays in the development of many serious conditions. What the studies are really suggesting is that by cutting down on stress, you lower your risk of suffering from something worse.

On one hand, it's an optimistic exercise in joining the dots, and can lead people who don't actually read the studies into making some far-fetched and damaging claims about the forest's healing properties. On the other, there is certainly something going on in the biochemistry of the forest, which affects the human body in surprising ways. The secret lies in phytoncides: the antimicrobial essence produced by plants. Many trees – pine, oak and cedar in particular – release phytoncides as a way to combat insect and animal attacks and to prevent their bark from mouldering. What scientists working on forest bathing now suggest is that exposure to phytoncides, in both living forests and the essential oils used in traditional Asian aromatherapies, boosts the activity of what are known as natural killer (NK) cells. These cells are a subtype of our white blood cells and are responsible for protecting us from illness and disease. Some white blood cells are responsible for attacking fungus and bacteria. Others release histamine to provoke an inflammatory response or attack parasites. NK cells have a special function in suppressing the activity that leads to tumour formation, and repairing virus-infected cells.

Forest bathing is supposed to bring us into contact with these compounds in the wild. Even a forty-minute immersion in the forest is claimed to increase NK cell count, reduce hypertension (abnormally high blood pressure), boost immune functioning, decrease blood cortisol, and lower heart rate. In a 2008 study conducted in Japan, scientists tested twelve male subjects after a three-day forest excursion, revealing that their NK activity and number had increased, along with their levels of intracellular anti-cancer proteins. Similar changes also took place in a group of thirteen women tested under the same circumstances, and even a four-hour exposure to a forest park produced comparable results, lasting up to seven days. These sample groups are, of course, tiny, raising all sorts of questions about the reproducibility of these findings. We can also ask whether raising NK cell count is a good thing. One psychologist I spoke to at a conference told me that a high NK cell count might actually demonstrate that the immune system is overworked, and that it's possible we're fighting pathogens in the forest rather than experiencing their health-boosting effect.

In spite of doubts like these, the practice of forest bathing has spread rapidly from its home in Japan, with devotees now in the USA, Europe, and the rainforests of Costa Rica. Though relatively new, it has become a kind of 'classic' nature cure. No exception: it's the first thing people mention to me whenever I tell them I'm exploring these kinds of therapies. It does make me wonder if one of the reasons the practice is so appealing in Europe and the US is because it blends Romantic nature worship with ideals about the ancient wisdom of 'the East'. A slow walk through a forest, led by *shinrin-yoku* guides, incorporates practices of breathing, mindfulness and attentiveness to our surroundings that have a long heritage in Buddhist and Shinto cultures, but are recent imports into Western psychology and medicine. Traditions of Zen meditation and yoga have long been concerned with restoring mind–body equilibrium – calming and controlling the mind through methodical actions and consciously focused attention. Inspired by practices like *zazen* meditation and *takigyo* purification rituals – achieved through a plunge under fast-flowing mountain waterfalls – forest bathing is about clearing the mind and resetting the body's chemistry. When transported to the forests of Europe and the USA, these somatic practices are infused with reverence for the spiritual qualities of Nature with a capital 'N'. These are aspects of healing that Western psychology, obsessed with the clinical diagnosis and chemical treatment of illness, has often dismissed as irrelevant.

But celebration of the traditions that come together in *shinrin-yoku* can also encourage an idealised, even orientalist depiction of the 'East'. The Finnish forest bath was definitely sold to me, and my fellow walkers, as an authentic importation from a healing culture whose wisdom and penchant for holistic wellness stretches back centuries. Without any disrespect to Zen and

Shinto cultures – with which forest bathing claims only a tenuous link – the way forest bathing is spoken about and promoted in the West doesn't exactly match up with the realities of life in modern Japan. Just as nature therapies have become popular in Europe and the US as tonics for chronically stressed workers, *shinrin-yoku* retreats have popped up around Tokyo as micro-spas to de-stress workers and return them to industries that are just as hectic and unhealthy as any global financial centre.

It was a trend that began in the 1980s, as so many *shinrin-yoku* sites proudly announce. What they're less likely to mention was that forest bathing was invented by the Japanese Ministry of Agriculture, Forestry and Fisheries as part of a response to soaring rates of workplace stress and death. Offices were criticised for pushing people to work to extremes and for valorising overwork, so much so that a 1988 Labour Force Survey revealed that one in four male employees were working sixty-hour weeks. One in four Japanese people consider suicide over the course of a lifetime, while deaths caused by overwork – including strokes and suicide – have been given a medically and legally recognised name: *karoshi*. A *karoshi* hotline was set up in 1988 to help raise awareness, while educational efforts were launched to destigmatise mental illness and encourage workers to seek help. Combined with legal actions taken against companies whose workers died from stroke and heart failure, these responses helped to slowly improve conditions. But rates of illness and death remain worryingly high: according to the mental health charity Tell, around 21,000 people take their own life in Japan each year: that's nearly sixty people a day.

Now, there are sixty-two recognised forest-bathing sites around Japan, granted the title by the Association of Therapeutic Effects of Forests. To qualify, a site must have at least two fully accessible 'Therapy Roads' for people to follow, a rest centre, car park, insurance, pollution checks and forest-maintenance services. Some of these requirements are fairly standard for any national park, and ensure accessibility for all. What distinguishes these sites from the more feel-good forest baths found in Europe and the US are the extreme lengths centres have to go to prove they are medically therapeutic. At least three days must be set aside for investigators to conduct physiological field experiments, testing the heart-rate variability, blood pressure, pulse rate and salivary cortisol level of the forest bathers as they complete circuits around the site. Activity in the sympathetic and parasympathetic nervous system is also monitored, adding weight to the claim that forest bathing decreases activity in the sympathetic nervous system – responsible for the fight-or-flight reaction – and increases restorative parasympathetic nervous activity. Psychological measurements are also taken, testing stress and relaxation levels, semantic differentials (a rating scale designed to determine a person's attitude towards something) and mood with a sixty-five-point 'profile of mood states'. Researchers testing these things are trying to understand what the place means to the people who use it. What feelings does it inspire? Is it beautiful or ugly, good or evil, interesting or dull? Forest bathing, the testing shows, increases scores of positive feelings and decreases scores of negative feelings when compared to the answers given by subjects taken on walks in urban settings. So certification doesn't just prove that the centre has good facilities. It's there to test whether the site itself is specifically, verifiably, therapeutic. 'We have discovered that a body relaxes physiologically at various authorised locations,' proclaims Japan's official Forest Therapy Society site. When it comes to therapeutic bathing, not all forests are created equal.

It's essential that medics advising people to forest bathe take the evidence that backs it up seriously. But knowing that it was launched as a way to encourage workers to manage stress at the weekends alters its meaning and its politics as a form of quasi-enforced self-care. Nature as self-help can be a useful intervention for people who are suffering, but without changing the way business operates, it's never going to be more than a sticking plaster: a way of individualising the problem rather than transforming workplaces so no one has to seek the forest for wellbeing as a last resort. Using nature in this way also distorts the meaning of a walk in the woods. If we're using our leisure time as a way of repairing ourselves for more work, are we really calm and free?

By the time we reached the end of our Finnish forest bath, I wasn't thinking about its contradictory politics. I was trying to hide my embarrassment. The fact is, though I'd enjoyed parts of the walk, keeping the right distance from the person in front of me had made me nervous, and the planned-out route had felt predictable and dull. I'd been distracted by my partner's bored glances at his phone and by the endless assaults from mosquitoes, whose bites bring me out in angry red welts. Standing in a circle outside the visitor centre after the 'bath' was officially over, we chatted informally about our experiences, and I smiled and thanked our guide. But being here affected me less than so many other trips into the woods I've taken. How was it that I could be so numb, all of a sudden, to a place that has always affected me so profoundly?

I think what felt so strange and unappealing about the forest bath was the sense that I was on a walkway, like the travelators they use to shuttle people around airports. We use the metaphor of the 'journey' so offhandedly that it's lost all meaning, but when I walk in the forest alone, I set my own pace, leaping off the path when I want to, stopping altogether or climbing a tree when I want to be still and alone. These 'journeys' are led by my mood, and they shape my thoughts and feelings too, in an intimate, spontaneous dance. It's not exactly a solitary activity: often I walk with friends, or am led astray by the traces of the countless walkers who have gone before: the old marks made by woodlanders and foresters, the people who lived and worked in these places, pollarding and coppicing, lighting fires, building dwellings, grazing animals, clearing, felling, even quarrying, decades or centuries ago. It's in the lines of desire made by animals too: the rabbit and deer paths we may follow by accident, thinking them made for us, and realising too late that they're too steep, muddy or narrow for human feet to trace. These other presences and intelligences sway me when I walk in the forest, in ways I find it hard to interpret or decipher.

The path we walked in Finland wasn't an accessible, well-marked route – in fact it involved high, slippery slopes and snarled-root stumbles. But walking the regulation distance behind the other bathers, I felt like I'd got onto a ride and couldn't get off. This is the problem, I think, with forest bathing as a state-sanctioned, scientifically calibrated medicine. You don't need to leap from the path to really explore the forest. You don't even need to move from your position in space. But your thoughts and feelings should be your own. They should be allowed to emerge from the place, in dialogue or in concert. That's what seems to get lost when tests, government advice and clever designs have already decided how we're meant to think and feel, and how we're meant to change, on each turn of the 'Therapy Road'.

By prescribing normative feelings and emotions, I worry that we risk narrowing the range of experiences that we value, even erasing the darkness altogether. That seems to be another way of saying that it's not OK to be sad, to feel fear or loneliness.

This feels particularly wrong, because sadness, fear and darkness are inherent to the forest. The Old English roots of the word 'wood', after all, branch out from *wōd*, meaning mad and frenzied, and *woda* or *wuot*, from Old and High German, meaning violently possessed. Mad King Sweeney of Irish legend discovered this when he was cursed by a saint, traumatised in battle, then fled to the wilds of the forest to bear his pain in the form of a bird. In folktale and mythology, woods have always been the most restless of retreats, home to wild men, fairy folk, and the ritual madness of the Bacchanal: a wine-soaked festival of masks and phalluses, it celebrated the 'runner in the woods', a god ensnarled in sex and savagery. Classical drama evolved from ancient fertility rites – performances to celebrate the passing of the seasons and improve the abundance of the harvest. When Bacchic worshippers worked themselves into states of ecstasy, they weren't just loosening their inhibitions. They were affirming bonds between humanity and a nature that was anything but quaint and picturesque.

So too with the German *Wald* – the place from which so much European forest worship emanates. These Black Forests are as tied up with fantasies of back-to-nature simplicity as they are with the threat of violence and enchantment. Gustav Klimt – better known for his richly adorned, gilded paintings of lovers and goddesses – captured this sense of haunting beauty and unease in his pine- and fir-wood canvases. Slim slips of white birch hover like spectres, while black boughs of pine rise from livid red leaf-strewn floors, in a forest without footpath or boundary. In the English tradition, Shakespeare's *A Midsummer Night's Dream* shows the forest as a prism in which the human is caught like a beam of light and radically refracted. In the forest, extremes of mood and behaviour are revealed in their most vivid and intense light. Sexual inhibitions, social boundaries, even our affiliation with our own species – captured in Titania's passion for the donkey-headed Bottom – may be unleashed and abandoned.

Danger and alterity are intrinsic to our history of relations with the forest, and at the heart of what makes woods desirable and powerful places. I wonder, then, if it's possible to make forests feel *too safe* – to erase their strangeness with the wellness industry's dazzling light? This is a difficult and contradictory question. What might we lose if we sanitise the forest altogether, stripping it of danger, mystery and darkness, losing its wildness as an unpredictable environment, a place of unexpected encounter? And how do we balance the desire to embrace darkness in nature with the right to be safe?

At night, the windows of our little cottage in Savonia become frightful. Black night presses against them and the hand-stitched curtains seem flimsy and transparent. From the darkness, eyes that were invisible in the daytime seem to press and stare. Even the outhouse, ten or so metres away from the house, becomes a place of numbing, impossible danger. My torch flickers against the white tree trunks as I stumble forward into nothingness, and suddenly our little idyllic world is transformed into a scene from *The Blair Witch Project*.

The sudden lurch from joy to horror is something I've come to expect from forests. There's a place I often walk, a mile or so from my home in Bristol. The Avon river valley cuts a deep channel into the wooded hillsides there, and I walk alone in summer and winter, on rainy days, sometimes to swim late in the evening. Often it's silent. At other times the paths are crowded with families. It was on a gorgeous, sunlit, late-autumn afternoon like that when I overtook two women walking with kids and a dog on a wide forest path. Before I had gone far, I heard the older woman call out to me, 'Aren't you frightened to be in the woods by yourself?'

Her question stopped me. I turned on the spot and smiled at her. 'No, not really,' I said brightly, and quickly left the family behind. But that question rang in my head for hours, poisoning the day. I felt angry at the woman for picking me out like that, trying to put me in my place by challenging me not to feel afraid. But the longer I walked, the more I felt sorry for her. Maybe her question was honest. Maybe she wanted to walk here alone herself, but felt afraid.

Of course I know what it's like to be frightened. I was raised on a diet of crime and Gothic fiction, where a woman walking alone in a forest is the most basic recipe for disaster. Even before I started watching detective dramas – lurid Scandi noirs where women are stalked screaming through gnarled undergrowth – I'd learned the lessons of fairy tales. Little Red Riding Hood, Snow White, Hansel and Gretel, all replay stock images of the frightful forest again and again. Even in Disney's sanitised versions of fairy tales, the forest is a place where bad things happen, where a promising day turns into a dreadful night.

As a woman who loves to walk in the forest, and especially to walk alone, I have had to work hard to filter out the stories of doom and danger before taking my first steps beyond the treeline. I don't feel this way on mountains, where other walkers are visible a mile or more away, or on beaches, fields or parks (at least not in the daytime). I'm always on edge in a forest, my senses swimming with pleasure one moment, wired and frantic the next. The forests I've walked in since I was a child are so deep in my imagination that they form the landscapes of my dreams, but even they have the capacity to terrify me. A crackle of leaves, a branch snapping, and a surge of panic grips my chest. This is the fight-or-flight reaction, in which the senses are tuned, cortisol floods the blood, and muscles are primed with adrenaline. All this takes place below the surface. Consciously, I grip my keys in my pocket, calculate the miles or metres to the forest's edge. My animal senses switch on.

In the 'nature and wellbeing world' – the eclectic community of medics, carers, campaigners, researchers and alternative healers interested in the connection between health and nature – the accepted narrative is that we're primed to experience relaxation in nature, and that forests appeal as a kind of primal, prehistorical human habitat. But so often my body tells me otherwise. I've heard the same thing from friends. I remember walking out with my cousin in a forest in the late evening. She had recently become interested in photography, and we were creeping quietly down a path to a spot I knew deer could often be seen. That evening we were lucky. A stag and two does were feeding in the field. She took her photos, and then the deer scampered, barking out a warning to their friends. 'I don't know why, I didn't use to like going to the woods,' she said, suddenly. When I pressed her, she admitted that they used 'to spook her out'. Going into the forest with someone else, and with a camera, had dissipated that fear. Behind the distancing gaze of the lens, she felt for the first time less vulnerable, more in control.

Peering into a dense thicket, you can see why the forest has become a metaphor for the dangerous unruliness of the wild – the threat of violence that lurks under the bright green facade of 'nature'. Woods are the heartland of witches and their enchantments, of occult ceremonies and sightings of the devil at midnight. The sorceress Baba Yaga mixes her potions in forests, while in Norse legend the mythical Myrkviða (later revived by Tolkein as Mirkwood) is the site of heroic struggle, a dark landscape of magic and danger. Modern horror movies squeeze every drop of terror from these places, a TV trope that's seemingly inexhaustible. The evil dead rise up there, flesh-eating creatures, giant spiders and dementors stalk. In some myths of the forest, the trees themselves pose danger. In George MacDonald's *Phantastes*, a fairy romance published in 1858, the hero Anodos is stalked through fairyland by the Ash tree and the Alder, who disguises herself as a beautiful maiden and threatens to enwrap him in her web of tangled hair.

This element of eeriness is something I adore. As a teenager, I learned to love forests because of the range of emotions they inspired in me – not all of them happy or, in the most banal way, 'good'. Going to nature often meant not feeling *better better*, but feeling *bad* better. I didn't go to the forest to cheer myself up, or to find myself. I went to the forest because I needed a place to go 'mad', a place to get lost.

I don't think that means the forest somehow 'wasn't working', but something very different was going on. Feeling happy all the time can be exhausting, and oppressive, too. And why should we only take simple, sunny solace from nature? The eco-philosopher Timothy Morton pushes against this idea: 'maybe at heart I'm an old-fashioned goth, but when I hear the word "bright" I reach for my sunglasses'. Follow the logic that nature means bright green joy and health, and you'll soon end up believing that sickness and sadness, low mood and anger somehow take us *outside* of nature. This is stigmatising, and contradicts so many ancient stories about the alluring gloom of the forest, and the fact that nature has been as associated with sadness as it has with joy.

Hippocrates, the Greek physician who first connected sickness to climate, associated melancholia with the earth and with the waning pathos of autumn – the time the forest comes into its own. The history of melancholia also shows that nature has long been a backdrop to this desirable disturbance. Desirable, because as early as the Middle Ages, melancholia was becoming a fashionable disease, associated with art, poetry, and the extreme vicissitudes of genius. As the historian Clark Lawlor puts it, melancholia 'often seemed less of an illness and more of a blessing for ... anyone who desired to seem in the slightest bit sensitive or clever'. At the same time, nature became a medium, a conduit, for glorifying anguish – a place to meditate, seclude oneself, and wallow. Giovanni Benedetto Castiglione's etching of *Melancholy*, made in the 1640s, shows a typical forlorn figure reclining pensively in a gnarled and crumbling grotto, while the frontispiece of Robert Burton's *Anatomy of Melancholy* (1621) shows a wretched philosopher, his back turned to a bright and orderly garden, while ominous forests beckon all around.

'Melancholia' doesn't perfectly map onto the modern diagnosis of depression. When I think of melancholia, I think of brooding, creative sadness, pathos, longing, an emotional intensity that colours everything with a raw, anarchic beauty. Depression, as I've known it, is blankness and an evacuation of purpose. It's sleeping late, or not sleeping at all; a flat, unemotional awareness that you're not good for much, and that it doesn't matter. These aren't the states in which I make great art, when I feel 'sensitive or clever'. They're the times I stay in the house watching hours of daytime TV, or walk through the forest like a thin and emptied shell.

Sometimes nature has broken me out of these states of flat affect, but what it gives me is not always joy, but the flood of true emotion – ugly, beautiful tears, pain that has a chance of being cathartic – reminding me that I can feel things ferociously, and survive them, even find beauty and purpose in their intensity and strength.

A walk in the woods rarely makes me feel such a clash of emotions today. I'm no longer a child or an adult-in-process, able to be so absolutely transformed. But I hang on to the forest as a place to sit with darkness, to meet nature and myself in our mutual complexity. The forest can be a place to handle grief, to hold it up to the light and to let it breathe in the shade. The beckoning path of Therapy Road rubs off those edges for me, leaving me smiling in a hollow way, assuring my hosts, *I had a lovely time – we must do this again soon!*

Accepting the darkness and fearfulness of the forest may also help us restore part of our broken relationship with nature. In *Grizzly Man* (2005), his disturbing documentary capturing a man's fatal attempt to immerse himself in wild nature, Werner Herzog announces that he believes 'the common denominator of the Universe is not harmony, but chaos, hostility and murder'. I don't exactly agree with him (there's too much collaboration in nature, too much co-dependence, for his red-in-tooth-and-claw pessimism to be true). But it's fair to say that we can only idealise nature when we no longer feel like it's going to kill us every second. The same 'nature' we like to beautify also includes poisons, insects and extreme weather. Pandemics are just another reminder that nature can't be sectioned off from culture, and only visited occasionally when we need a break from our 'real' lives. 'Nature' is the cells of our bodies, the air we breathe, in beneficial nutrients as well as viruses and pathogens. When we talk about 'healing nature', we're telling just part of the story of how enmeshed we are in a living world made up of what Timothy Morton calls 'strange strangers', as well as the domesticated and familiar.

Realising that we're a part of nature – including the scary, strange and fatal bits – can be disconcerting. The literary scholar Simon Estok has called fear of nature 'ecophobia', and suggests it comes from 'an irrational and groundless hatred of the natural world', which shows up in our efforts to cut down forests and build shelters against the darkness without, and within. From the Middle Ages European communities drained bogs and marshes because they thought of them as 'places of evil and monsters'. Creating tidy parks, well-ploughed fields and pretty gardens instead of forests was seen as a less threatening way to live with the abject mess of nature, and a tasteful, more productive one.

But why should we detest dark places, or any living organism? Surely that latent hatred only makes those lives and those ecosystems easier to destroy? It's just another expression of anthropocentrism – a way of organising the world that puts humanity at the top, and everything else underneath. This way of organising the world simply hasn't worked. But accepting fear and otherness, and embracing darkness in nature may help us move beyond this demand for control, replacing ecophobia and dominance with respect for the 'strange stranger'.

Of course, fear of nature is a very different thing than fear *in* nature. Fear experienced in natural environments is unfairly distributed in society – meaning some people walk with abandonment and ease, and others are unjustly alienated from life out of doors.

It is not really the supernatural that haunts me when I walk in the forest, or that makes my palms sweat. I'd love to say I'm only frightened of spells, ghosts or dementors, but it's not true. I should be so lucky to meet a witch, or stumble on a magical ceremony in the woods. Neither do wolves or bears frighten me. I've never walked in a forest inhabited by creatures more threatening than hawks or deer. What frightens me is men – they are what I fear might be tracking me down the path. They're what my parents warned me about when, as a teenager, I pulled on my boots and told them I was going to the woods.

Fairy tales can be read as morality tales: encoded lessons about how to navigate the world, clues as to where threat lies. You don't need to be a trained psychoanalyst to see that in these stories the forest represents a place of risky encounters with men that lure girls to their deaths. And it works. These are the environments that can shake me most profoundly, making my heart race and my hands turn cold with sweat. This is in spite of the fact that I've never actually been followed in the forest, while I have been harassed in so many city streets and parks.

The stories we tell affect our ways of being in the world. Whether they are fairy tales passed down across generations, news stories about women being attacked in the wild, or repeated reminders not to go out alone, this common stock of wisdom about our vulnerabilities adds layers to the anxieties we carry around with us, affecting our wellbeing in profound ways.

In a 2015 study, Laurel B. Watson of the University of Missouri examines how being seen as a sexual object influences women's experiences of psychological distress. 'A sociocultural context that objectifies women and their bodies is related to their sense of safety and security in the world,' she concludes. This insight will be no surprise to anyone who's experienced prejudice. Anti-street harassment groups like Hollaback! and Everyday Sexism have done much to expose how direct attacks and microaggressions – a term coined by African American psychiatrist Chester Pierce – create a sense of pervasive anxiety that can become debilitating. Research suggests that persistent experiences of racism, sexism and threats of violence produce psychological effects akin to trauma. The clinical practitioner and feminist psychologist Lillian Comas-Díaz coined the term 'racial trauma' to describe the 'insidious type of distress' experienced by people of colour and other marginalised people in cultures where racism, homophobia and classism abounds. A socio-political ailment that's as slow-drip as it is defined by sudden, shocking events, racial trauma doesn't map easily onto current definitions of PTSD. But those definitions need to change, to recognise traumatic experiences that are as cumulative as they are collective.

These traumas change how people live and how we feel about the places where we are expected to find comfort – including in nature. As a woman who loves to walk alone, I refuse to be intimidated. But I still experience fear when a man gets too close on a quiet path, and grief and hot white rage when I hear of an attack. Living with these emotions and with the real threat of violence is suffocating. In a society that refuses to address misogyny and to provide justice for victims of male violence, even the simple release of nature is closed off to so many women and girls. It's only by addressing this violence structurally – from education in schools, to rethinking the entire criminal justice system – that we might hope for change. And this is something that men have to be a part of, and to take responsibility for. Avoiding getting too close on a forest path is polite and helpful, but it is going to take so much more than that.

Combined with misogyny, racism is a toxic obstacle to accessing nature for women. The photographer Ingrid Pollard captured this sense of unease in her photograph series *Pastoral Interlude* (1988). A woman from the city alone in the Lake District, she wanders, the text lying beside the image tells us, 'lonely as a Black face in a sea of white'. 'A visit to the countryside is always accompanied by a feeling of unease, dread … feeling I don't belong. Walks through leafy glades with a baseball bat by my side.'

Fears of the countryside and the prejudice associated with it are difficult to disperse, and research suggests that people of colour in the UK are less likely to exercise outdoors because of legitimate fears about safety. The writer and environmentalist Mya-Rose Craig has spent years exploring and exposing the reasons for this, and fighting for change with her organisation Black2Nature. At a race-equality conference held in Bristol in 2016 – and organised when Mya-Rose was only fourteen years old – she brought experts and community representatives together to discuss how racism at national parks, anxieties about being attacked or experiences of being targeted as criminals by the police limit people's engagement with nature. Black2Nature's work is all about challenging these perceptions and highlighting the whiteness of the conservation sector and the systemic racism that has meant environmental organisations are slow to address their own prejudices. Mya-Rose has run outdoor camps to introduce Black and Asian teens to skills like bird-ringing, and at the same time insist that nature is for them too. Other work, like celebrating visible ethnic minority role models in the outdoors, and telling her own story of birding and fighting for racial and environmental justice as a teenager, are all parts of an integrated project to turn fear and alienation into power, so everyone has an equal stake in enjoying forests and wildlife, and fighting for their protection.

One of the qualities that's so important about this work is pleasure: when focusing on pain and suffering as is so often essential, we can forget to highlight love, connection and joy too. The poet Camille T. Dungy treads this path in her anthology, *Black Nature: Four Centuries of African American Nature Poetry* (2009). Many of the poems collected explore nature and the forest as places of inherited trauma, where bad things happen. 'The traditional context of the nature poem in the Western intellectual canon, spawned by the likes of Virgil and Theocritus and solidified by the Romantics and the Transcendentalists, informs the prevailing views of the natural world as a place of positive collaboration, refuge, idyllic rural life, or wilderness,' Dungy explains. But 'the poetry of African Americans only conforms to these traditions in limited ways'. Absent is the notion of nature as a diversion, embodying an innocence and healing. Instead, writing comes from the perspective of workers with 'no leisure … / No right to waste at trees', as the poet Gerald Barrax puts it. But there are stories of survival, too – reflecting the fact that in the most difficult periods of African American history, woods and swamps served as vital places of refuge, where people found nourishment at times of desperation. These histories of dependence open up space for expressions of radical solidarity and meaning-making: of empathy expressed by oppressed people for exploited nature, and 'recognition of the connectivity with worlds beyond the human'.

So much nature poetry collected by Dungy captures the pay-off of nature: experiences of awe, wonder, brief respite from pain, which makes us feel stronger, and more open to meeting the real conditions of the present. Being in the forest isn't a distraction. War, grief, history, tenderness, all sit alongside wonder at the sweetness, the vastness of the wood. Maybe the forest is so vital not because it is a simply a place to heal, but a place to experience sadness and grief and empathy at its fullest intensity.

Deep in the forest in Finland, in the late, white evening light, I head out to pick mushrooms. I'm no confident picker, but I can spot the orange frills of the chanterelle strobing above green clumps of star moss and tangled wolf lichen. I'm kneeling down, my gloved hands severing the fruiting fungus from its web with a pocket knife, when I hear leaves crackle and footsteps coming up from behind me. I know my partner is a mile away, lounging with his headphones on in the cottage. The familiar sick thud of my heart starts up as I stand and turn around to face a man who must be six-foot two, walking towards me from the green shadows. He's wearing camo print head to foot, with a gun over his shoulder and chunky black boots on his feet. His face is half-covered in fabric, sunglasses cover his eyes. For a second every horror story I've heard about the forest rushes through my mind. I'm the murder victim in a Suomi Noir thriller. I'm being pursued by a *yurai*, a violent woodsman. This is so close to my worst nightmare that I almost cackle with dumb terror.

But then the man slips off his face covering. It's not a murderous mask, but a guard against mosquitoes. He introduces himself as Tuomas, one of the two brothers who own the cottage we're staying in. He spotted me from the road and wanted to check that everything's all right: have we found our way around? I say gracious things about the house, elated I won't meet my death today. He tells me, at embarrassing length, about his plans to improve the compost loo, and advises me to wear the bright orange hat that's hanging from a peg in the hall when I'm walking in the forest. It's almost hunting season, and it's easy for the guns to hit you.

Tuomas leaves me as the light is falling and the forest is transforming into a blue landscape of shadows. It's been good to meet him, to place this house and this experience back in time. It's tempting to think of the forest as timeless, as separate from human struggles and history. But the decaying structures in the forest tell me people have lived and died here, and that for the families that are still trying to make a living here, the forest is still very much part of our changing, frightening present. A year after our visit, I would read news reports of how the summer's excessive temperatures had dried up mosquito breeding grounds, bringing silence and stillness to the forest where I stood that day. Tuomas and his family were lucky. On the other side of the country, fires ravaged the forests of Pyhäranta, and woodlands high in the Arctic Lapland burned.

There's still time to pick more mushrooms and berries for dinner. I weave through the trees, following the line of the path that leads me home. The birds are silent now, even the mosquitoes have quietened, and I risk taking off the hat and net I've been wearing as protection to listen, slowly, to this settling, breathing world. Somewhere, a little way off, a large creature is stomping through the trees. I guess it must be a deer, or even a moose, which Tuomas told me you can hear calling at night. Before I move on, back to the warmth and flickering light of the house, I look up to the treeline, along the white strips of bark pointing at the sky. Then I let my head tilt gently downwards until my chin is pressed against my sternum, and my eyes take in the black and moss-green mass of teeming, fruiting life beneath my feet.

It is all so beautiful and strange, I nearly stumble as I lift my head and feel the blood rush through me. This is more than a sunny, healing landscape: it's a web of mineral exchange, violence, creation, destruction, desire and encounter, where microbial, fungal, plant, animal and bacterial life form strange new relations. In the mulch and web and weirdness of the forest, I've got a glimpse into how all this pulsing life connects, and how the matter of life – oxygen – is born. Being present as unseen processes take place around me is a reminder – simultaneously beautiful and anguished – that our dependence on nature is absolute. Our oneness with the otherness of the forest can be both thrilling and terrifying.

Garden
A Cure for Loneliness

During one of the longest periods of depression I've experienced, I kept a garden. I was living in a tiny room in a flat in student halls, six floors above a busy London street. Traffic backed up all day, horns blaring and engines revving. At night, rickshaws would shake and rattle their way home, slotting into garages and under tarpaulins in the yard across the road. I grew my garden in yoghurt pots and egg cartons. Soon they covered the narrow windowsill, enjoying the inch of sunlight that fell across the high-walled road as winter turned to spring. I begged my flatmates not to bin Pot Noodle pots and to save their tubs of margarine. After a week or two of watering, seeds began to sprout. Stems twisted above the dusty rows of vodka bottles lined up on kitchen counters. I'd head to lectures in the morning and come back to find each slender shoot an inch or two taller. In my room, slim green vines caught and looped round rusty metal handles, or burrowed curiously into the gaps between the panes of glass. Another week passed and leaves began to bud, folding out of nothing like fans unfurling from smooth green flesh. All I'd done was plant a pack of seeds and add soil, water and a patchy ray of sun, and the dull grey room had come to life.

I've moved many times since then, but I've always tried to keep a garden. In one rented flat, a friend and I spent a day hacking through a deep mass of brambles just to get to the other side of the long-forgotten plot. In another, I had to squeeze my torso out of the window to water the pots on what I called the 'balcony' (it was a gutter), while testy nesting gulls dived and screamed at me for disturbing their young. But in every case, the pleasure of involving myself in plant life – the jostling, unpredictable busyness of it – was worth every cut and scratch; worth even the threat of attack from angry mother birds.

Like many children, I read Frances Hodgson Burnett's *The Secret Garden* (1911) when I was growing up, and there's no doubt it shaped my idea of what a garden should look like. In the novel, a girl discovers a locked garden behind a crumbling, high brick wall in the grounds of her adoptive family's home. For Mary, and another isolated child she discovers on the way, the garden is a sun-soaked place to play, learn and grow, with beautiful old walls that shut her in, so that 'no one knew where she was'.

We're used to thinking of the garden like this – as a bubble in which we can escape the world. But only a tiny minority get to enjoy crumbling walled gardens.

The rest dig, plant and dream in spaces where the noise of traffic and shouts of neighbours penetrate, in paved rented yards, on narrow balconies or nothing more expansive than a windowsill. Across the major cities of the world, precarious communities suffer fatal housing crises. Too many people don't have the internal space to live, let alone the external space to rest, restore and flourish.

Growing plants has become a trend in recent years. Opinion pieces describe how young people are stocking their microscopic, short-term lets with pot plants, cacti and succulents, anything that can survive on a little sunshine and a small square of counter or sill. Landlords ban pets, new flats are built with limited to non-existent outdoor space, and stable housing is a fantasy from another generation. Even the hope of raising children is, for many, inhibited by low wages, the miseries of universal credit, or long shifts on zero-hour contracts, where pay can vary wildly from month to month, even week to week. There are massive, terrifying limit factors too, like the climate crisis. If recent statistics are to be believed, an environmental crisis characterised by sea-level rise, heatwaves, droughts and fire is turning a generation off starting a family and convincing new parents to limit the size of their brood.

In such unstable and unfertile times, it makes sense that people are embracing houseplants, channelling unrequited instincts to nurture and nest. The environmental philosopher Donna Haraway has called such work 'kin-making', urging would-be parents to find new alternatives to the traditional family by *making kin* in more radical ways: with each other and with other species, including plants. It's not about literally marrying your cheese plant (although in 2018 a group of Mexican environmental activists in Oaxaca did perform a series of weddings with trees to protest illegal logging). It's more a recognition that in high-consumption economies the annual carbon cost of each new child can be as much as 58.6 tonnes – a striking figure, considering that in the African nation of Burkina Faso, the estimated carbon footprint for an average person is 0.16 tonnes a year. When we joke, calling our pets or our plants our children, maybe we're responding to deeper urges to make kin of all kinds in a devastated world.

I've never wanted children, but I sought plants at points in my life when other kinds of uncertainties and relationships were lacking. Taking care of them helped me feel better about myself, and less alone. When I was a student, my three-by-five-metre room represented incredible new freedom and independence, and I was absurdly privileged to live so close to central London in subsidised accommodation. But I still found myself floundering, unequal to the task of establishing a new identity among strangers in a chaotic, synthetic environment, while navigating all the mundane duties necessary to stay fed, washed and alive. Mental health problems are known to spike among students, particularly in their first year at university. Many experience imposter syndrome and self-doubt, or lose their sense of who they are under the compounded pressure of coursework and deadlines, zero-hours jobs and an increase in student debt unimaginable to previous generations. The student mental health crisis is not helped by the disturbing 'real world' that hovers on the post-graduation horizon. The grey pod that I stocked with plants, forty feet above a smoke-choked London artery, now retails at £221 a week. It's no surprise a kind of furious nihilism runs through the inspirational polemic of youth climate activists who ask, with good reason, why prepare ourselves for a future of precarity and catastrophe?

A yearning for stability and contact through gardening seems a far cry from many of the posts you find on #plantsofinstagram. Well-curated displays of rattlesnake plants and *Monstera deliciosa* are stylishly posed in front of impressive interiors. A #plantshelfie in a million-pound London flat often comes with the hashtag 'self-care', but no acknowledgement of the privilege it takes to have so much space, and so much stability. It also sits uncomfortably against the narrative that all twenty- and thirty-somethings are turning to plants, or avocados, or avocado plants, because they're broke. Of course, just because a house looks fancy and a life perfect, doesn't mean that's the reality. It's become almost obligatory to perform wellness online, either as a way of covering up the fact that we're struggling, or projecting a different kind of self in the hope that we might transform into that person – a kind of visual 'future self' journaling, with the messy parts of life cropped away.

Even if there's truth in the accusation that houseplants are popular because they look good on social media, the fact that people are turning to gardening at a time of ecological crisis is a sign that the nature cure is alive and well, and finding new expression. One of the words that's constantly repeated in conversations about the nature cure is *connection*. It's used so often that it's lost all sense. But in a practical and hands-on way, growing plants from seed tethers us to more-than-human life. It's not that plants inhabit a different sphere from us – ecology and the climate crisis tell us that there is no separation between 'the human' and 'the natural' world. But with plants, ecological processes become our friends and familiars, tangible and reminding us of the wider world of which we are a part.

Of course, plants aren't substitutes for a fair society. Keeping a garden will not, in itself, stop climate change (though it might do a lot to save ailing insects and wildlife). But that doesn't mean that the kind of work that goes into tending a garden isn't part of a bigger story of rebuilding the relations necessary to guide us out of this crisis. This is the story I want to tell. It is a story about loneliness, but it is also a story about connection.

We must start with the idea of the healing garden as a symbolic and cultural space. Gardens have long served as spaces to find spiritual refuge, to step through a portal into another way of being in the world. Across time and across cultures, people have seen humanity's wellbeing mirrored in the abundance of nature. And they have tried to capture that symmetry in the garden.

Across Central Asia, Syria, Spain and Northern Africa, you can find green squares of lawn and flowering orange trees arranged around intersecting courses of water. These are Islamic Chahar Bagh gardens, laid according to ancient designs in honour of the four gardens of paradise written of in the Qur'an. Beds and lawns extend in a quadrilateral pattern from the central fountain, turning the garden into a sacred space, a microcosm of the living and heavenly world. Their watercourses are symbolic of fertility and abundance, but they also give a clue to their origins. From the deserts of the Middle East, Chahar Bagh tell the story of centuries of labour, bringing fertility out of harsh arid landscapes through networks of irrigation channels surrounded by methodical planting, oases of greenery rising from scorched sand. From their earliest practical functions, these gardens developed into a unique spiritual art form, acting as a map and compass of the earth and paradise. Although the climate of the Islamic world varies as widely as the historical traditions of the nations it encompasses, it is striking how aesthetically similar the Chahar Bagh design remains across time and across continents. While every garden is planted and matures in distinct ecological conditions, in the Chahar Bagh concept 'the balance between natural forces and cultural values' unravels 'in a cyclical temporal context'. Repetition represents – and also reproduces – continuity across cultures, territories and time itself. Envisaging paradise in the afterlife, the designers and users of these gardens make a statement about a religion and an attitude to God and nature that is, for believers, both healing and reassuringly eternal.

Another powerful example of gardens as spaces of psychological sustenance are those created by enslaved people in the Americas and the Caribbean. In the living quarters attached to plantations, abducted Africans and their descendants were given tiny plots of land, which they had to tend to sustain themselves. But beyond their vital agricultural uses, these plots took on special significance. As well as necessary crops, scraps of poor soil were used to grow medicinal plants and even flowers. As Dr Geri Augusto – professor of Africana Studies at Brown University – explains, you can think of gardening under slavery 'as part of resistance'. In conditions of utmost brutality, survival itself is a radical act, but for enslaved people, the garden was more than this. It was a 'small, small patch in which they could be human'.

In the modern-day Center for the Study of Slavery and Justice in Providence, Rhode Island, Dr Augusto has helped reimagine slave gardens, to 'render imaginatively a small part of what the slaves knew and wrought; and what they might have thought, as they created new landscapes against all odds'. Flowers, food and medicinal plants brought over from Africa sprout from broken pots and gourds half-buried in the soil, alongside plants that would have been growing on Indigenous American land. And set into the lawn, a *dikenga dia Kongo* – a Kongolese cosmogram in stone. Planted with herbs and flowers, the cosmogram incorporates a traditional Kongo cross, marked with a horizontal line of stones depicting Kalunga, the sea dividing the worlds of the living and the dead. Larger stones mark out moments in the journey of life – a black stone signifying birth, red for the prime of life, yellow for spiritual health, and death in white. It is unlikely enslaved people crafted such ostentatious spiritual markers in their plots, but there is evidence that gardens were used as sites of cultural expression and psychological survival.

The design of a garden and its meaning to those who use it is often shaped in this way – by inheritance. The origins of the traditional Chinese garden stretch back to the fourth century BCE, to the founding myths of its civilisation and culture. In the lakes at the centre of these gardens, you'll often spot a cluster of rocks adorned with miniature pagodas. They are symbolic mountains, and they're meant to evoke the paradisal

Mount Penglai described in *The Classic of Mountains and Seas* (third century BCE to second century CE). This compendium of myths tells of an island inhabited by immortals, dotted with palaces built of precious metals and trees laden with fruits and jewels. During the years of the Qin empire (around 221–210 BCE), the promise of this legendary mountain even inspired quests into the Bohai Sea, and though no ships came back bearing the elusive elixir of life, the legend of the isle of immortals is still celebrated in garden design. A single island or a stylised archipelago rises out of an artificial lake, while on land, wildly diverse geographical features of the empire are recreated in compressed 'scenes' by ingenious gardeners: forests, mountains, caves, lakes, streams and waterfalls, all in captivating miniature. The garden also holds spaces for contemplation, rest and retreat. From the Garden of Solitary Joy built at Luoyang in the eleventh century, to the Retreat and Reflection Garden at Tongli of 1885, classical gardens affirmed the association between solitude, creation and restoration. Stocked with *gonshi* – porous, asymmetric rocks like petrified coral, supposedly beloved of scholars – gardens were recognised as the retreats of philosophers and poets, a place to gather where inspiration was guaranteed to strike.

The Chinese metaphor of the sacred mountain appears again in the Japanese Zen garden, where it is pared down to its most minimal expression. In a dry landscape stylised rocks rise out of a rectangle of pale gravel. Natural elements are limited: the garden might have foliage and running water, or they may simply be suggested by lines raked into stones on the ground. Gardening – far from being a practical activity – may be as simple as raking, or sitting in the presence of *zazen-seki* meditation stones. The purpose in such a space is not to immerse yourself in living nature, but to treat the garden as a space of reflection, ringing with the *idea* of natural forms. Quiet reflection on these simple elements – rocks, water, and the relations between these entities in space – are organised to produce the same tranquil pleasures as more organically rich and verdant gardens.

But the Chinese gardens that inspired the Zen tradition were also places where people could congregate, where creativity and pleasure were experienced as part of a community of like-minded others. In 296 CE, the aristocrat and military officer Shi Chong brought a group of thirty friends together in his pleasure gardens to talk, drink and compose. The setting was palatial: 'limpid springs, lush groves, diverse fruit trees, bamboo, cypress and medicinal herbs' lay all around. For long days and nights, the guests wandered from garden to grotto and pavilion, or took a ride on one of Shi Chong's wagons, accompanied by an orchestra of zithers, and with food and drink to feast on. No wonder they were inspired. Settling down beside 'water mills, fishponds, caves in the ground, and all things to please the eyes and gladden the heart', the friends took turns to compose 'a poem in order to express his feelings', as Shi Chong explains in his '*Preface* to the Jingu Garden Poems' (*c.* 296 CE). The poems themselves are now almost entirely lost, but Shi Chong's preface preserved a view of the garden that shaped centuries of Chinese poetry and garden design. It should be a place that encourages the inward focus necessary for artistic creation. In the garden people will relax and unwind. Relations between acquaintances are transformed, and together they become playful, creative, open to inspiration, emotion, and floods of sheer, unabashed joy.

The relationship between the garden and wellbeing was taken for granted in ancient Chinese culture, and green and growing places set aside for overworked officials, philosophers and poets. But it's not only the wealthy and powerful who need restoration and quiet. Gardens have also been seen as essential in all kinds of institutions – from hospitals to schools, asylums to penitentiaries. In 1798, the 'Father of American Psychiatry' Benjamin Rush observed the benefits of gardening for prisoners: 'Let a garden adjoin this house, in which the culprits may occasionally work, and walk,' Rush advised. 'This spot will have a beneficial effect not only upon health, but morals, for it will lead them to a familiarity with those pure and natural objects which are calculated to renew the connection of fallen man with his creator.' It's a revealing reflection on how histories of punishment and confinement are entangled with the origins of the nature cure. In Rush's healing garden, people weren't just finding gentle, forgiving nature, but the hand of God, reaching out to reclaim the lost soul through the living world.

Rush's interest in the therapeutic value of gardens was matched across the Atlantic. One survey of English hospital gardens suggests that in 1860, out of sixty-seven general hospitals, forty-six had gardens of some kind, and only three were absolutely lacking in greenery. From the early 1700s, more and more hospitals had been founded in Britain, and the importance of fitting nature in and around bricks and mortar seemed obvious to designers and doctors too. Writing in 1760, Edinburgh medical student Edward Foster confidently claimed that a garden 'is very requisite, no one can deny, who knows, how necessary exercise is, to the cure of the most chronic diseases, or who considers how salutary a pure, fresh air must prove to people confined, for any time, in a bad one'. Architectural magazines like *The Builder* went further, claiming that 'sunlight, trees, plants, grass, and the external air, would do more for patients than all the medicine and doctors in the world'. Florence Nightingale favoured pavilion-style hospital designs, and advised that 'Whenever the weather permits it, the windows of every sick ward should be more or less open'. A look at the maps and plans of these nineteenth-century institutions, like Old Leeds General Infirmary, suggests that some architects were modelling their designs on the palaces and gardens of aristocrats, with inspiration coming from Italian palazzos and ornamental pleasure grounds. Although it was air and exercise most of all that was thought to be the virtue of the hospital garden, the beauty of these places wasn't irrelevant. Bordeaux Hospital delighted in its plantations of evergreens and flowering shrubs visible from every ward. Touring the hospital of Santa Maria Nuova in the 1780s, a sprawling medical centre in Florence, Italy, that traces its roots to the thirteenth century, one British hospital reformer was impressed by the pleasant gardens he saw there, 'contrived for promoting the health and spirits of the patients'.

It seems that a fair amount of accepted wisdom about the relations between wellbeing, beauty and nature was lost with the coming of modernity. Even in the early twentieth century, open-air sanatoria were still in fashion, giving patients direct access to the fresh air and light, which were known to help in the management and treatment of infectious disease. The tide turned in the post-war years, as more and more hospitals were built along brutalist designs. Marvels of concrete and glass, tall buildings and flat slabs of grey became the norm. Inside, treatment space became intensely rationalised, while unnecessary garden spaces were paved over, turned into smokers' corners and left to weed. That's not to suggest the coming of the National Health Service is to blame, even though the decline of the hospital garden in the UK coincides with the rise of socialised care, free to all at the point of demand. Instead, better to blame a new health paradigm focused on pharmaceutical intervention in isolation from all other kinds of treatment and care, including natural surroundings.

The philosophy about hospital gardens is, however, changing. Therapeutic horticulture is now a respected and well-evidenced approach to mental healthcare and rehabilitation, and studies of gardening interventions have multiplied since the early 2000s. Professor Anita Unruh – a researcher whose severe scoliosis inspired her interest in holistic treatments – highlighted the importance of symbolism in the garden and its power in helping people reframe difficult experiences. 'The seasonal nature of gardening recreates a cycle of growth, maturation and death,' she noted in a study focused on the experience of cancer patients in particular.

In practice, charities like Maggie's have brought about a transformation in hospitals and clinics, with gardens at their core. The organisation was the invention of Maggie Keswick Jencks, a writer, gardener and designer. After five years in remission for breast cancer, Maggie was told by her doctors that her tumour had returned. She and her husband were then escorted to a windowless corridor to reflect on the devastating news. That got her thinking. People receiving cancer diagnoses deserved more supportive places in which to recover from that first shock. The Maggie's Centre was her innovation: a calm interior where patients could rest and receive difficult news, surrounded by beautifully designed gardens. 'Above all what matters is not to lose the joy of living in the fear of dying,' Maggie believed. The first Maggie's Centre was opened in Edinburgh in 1996, and they have since been built across Europe, in Hong Kong and Tokyo, often incorporating traditional elements of garden design. Their purpose is to create a holding space for anyone who needs it. In times of crisis, this is what a garden can become – a refuge to hold emotion, a kind of bath to slip into and out of the world, until you are strong enough to emerge.

Underpinning this new medical trend are two core theories of the 'nature cure': stress reduction theory (SRT) and attention restoration theory (ART). To the layperson, the distinction between the two can seem fairly academic, but it is significant. To put it simply, SRT considers how exposure to stress affects the body and mind. When we're faced with challenging circumstances, the sympathetic nervous system kicks in, flooding the blood with adrenaline and cortisol and making our hearts race (a process that's already been discussed in connection to *shinrin-yoku*). In the early 1990s, a professor of architecture and health called Roger Ulrich became interested in how different environments might help us recover from stress. What he proposed was that natural settings seemed to help our body's soothing system – the parasympathetic nervous system – to operate, calming us down in the short term, and potentially helping ward off more serious conditions in which chronic stress is a factor. Interviews with participants who had been exposed to natural settings and empirical tests focused on capturing changes in blood hormone levels, heart rate, sweating and muscle tension all produced convincing findings. SRT was born.

As bubbles of quiet, unthreatening nature, gardens were perfect environments for SRT studies. But gardens also offer themselves as ideal settings for ART – the brainchild of Rachel and Stephen Kaplan. After receiving a grant from the US Forest Service to evaluate the impact of an outdoor programme in Michigan, the Kaplans were inspired to research nature's effect on our emotions, behaviour and cognition. What they found was that people responded very differently in natural settings to interiors and cities, and that much of this difference connected to their attention levels. To focus on an activity and achieve a goal, we need to cut out distractions and direct what the Kaplans call our 'voluntary attention'. This takes effort and leaves us vulnerable to exhaustion, irritability and stress. But, they theorised, attention can be restored by relaxing our 'involuntary attention'. The senses are given freedom to explore and engage with the environment in aimless wonder. Unlike sleep, involuntary attention restores us because consciousness is given free rein: it is an 'alternative mode of attending', requiring limited effort, allowing our attention to recover.

If we break the spell of modernity, immerse ourselves in nature and really let our minds wander, we may be lucky enough to experience what the Kaplans call 'being away'. It's that sense of timelessness, of stepping away from yourself, letting thoughts and impressions bubble over and flow free. It's connected to another ART term – 'fascination'. Fascinating objects or scenery hold our attention without quickly exhausting it. They can be 'hard', like TV, or 'soft', meaning they allow us to reflect on other things at the same time.

Some scholars have criticised ART, calling its terminology vague and its framework inadequately tested. However, it remains one of the most influential accounts of how natural settings may transform cognition and emotion, underpinning theories of why therapeutic horticulture might work. The garden isn't the only attention-restoring space, but following the Kaplans' logic, it's an ideal one. Natural settings are rich in things that 'readily hold the attention, but in an undramatic fashion', like 'clouds, sunsets, snow patterns, the motions of the leaves in the breeze' according to Stephen Kaplan. Gardens incorporate all these elements and more. Birds nest and feed, the water of an ornamental pond trickles, benches are spaced at intervals, giving people pockets of privacy, while walls or planted hedges screen surrounding distractions and noise. All these features of design combine with the ecological liveliness of the place, creating spaces of calm and quiet, where we can 'be away' together.

Togetherness is important, as although gardens are comforting places to sit in solitude, gardening is good at nurturing connections between people too. In one study, I read about a group of school-age children from the most socially marginalised groups, who visited a gardening project in North West England in 2012. The greatest improvements in their wellbeing, according to the study, were connected with social interactions. These children gained a greater sense of belonging, felt more involved and valued, and built stronger relationships with other children as a result of shared time in the garden. For the younger children, these relationships were nurtured with tea ceremonies, where facilitators asked them to explore the garden for herbs that could be brewed, then brought them together to make tea and talk over their difficulties. Older children were given more demanding group tasks, like digging a large root mass out of the centre of the plot, then posing for photos after they'd succeeded, holding it aloft like a trophy. Story corners were set aside, and children came up with their own ideas for planting different fruits and herbs. In this hard-won sliver of urban greenery, the connections that grew would define the children's experiences of the garden for the better.

That doesn't mean that therapeutic gardens are high-pressure social environments. In fact, they can nurture low-key socialising, blending a feeling of immersion and peace with a deep sense of belonging and rootedness. I read about how this works in another study, conducted at Cherry Tree Nursery in Bournemouth in 2018. The setting is a garden for adults with severe mental illness, providing sheltered work rehabilitation. Many of these volunteers express how at home they feel in the garden. 'Everybody knows there is no need to worry here,' says one volunteer. 'Cherry Tree is a haven … from the stress and strains of normal, so-called normal life. And it can be tranquil, and it can be busy. So, whatever your mood, there's something you can relate to.'

One question often raised by nature-cure sceptics is whether the social benefits of gardening and other green-care activities are more important than connections with plants, animals and the soil. If gardens are only useful as cures for loneliness, then community centres, bingo halls or art clubs might all achieve the same positive effect. While these other ways of socialising and forming communities have their own benefits, I wonder if relationships would develop in quite the same way without the 'nature' – the plants, earth, weather, creatures and water that bring people together in the garden. After reading the accounts of people working at Cherry Tree, the differences are clear. The garden is not simply a backdrop for social experiences. The 'safe haven' described by volunteers at Cherry Tree is both a real place they visit each week, and a powerfully supportive environment they can access imaginatively when life keeps them away. Even as they begin to approach the garden, the volunteers experience a marked shift in mood. As two volunteers explain:

'I feel better as I walk down the track – off the roundabout and into the trees.'

'It's as if you're going into another world. Like the past, without the cars. Although you can hear the cars, it's softened, insulated by trees ... you know it's there but in the distance.'

The distinctive layout of the garden – down the end of a winding track – helps build this sense of going into another world. And what awaits them at the end? Not a secret world apart, hidden behind a crumbling wall, but a world that is shared – with other volunteers, with plants, birds and all kinds of creatures. It's a place where 'strong friendships and bonds were likely to form', bonds that 'take many forms, not necessarily indicated by verbal interaction'. In the garden, people can be absolutely themselves, experiencing the world in their own way, but knowing they are part of something bigger. As one volunteer explains:

> I see Cherry Tree as an ant's nest …'cause there's that little world that's doing its little things, and all around there's lots of little worlds, and I'm in my little world. … I really do not have much to do with anybody else. I do not know what else goes on cos I come just one day a week, but they're all independently working [but that doesn't mean that you can't join in, and then], they've joined in that bit of the nest, and they belong in that bit of the nest … So, it's dynamic from that point of view… it's just magic

One late summer afternoon, I take a short walk down the cycle path by my house in Bristol to visit the local community garden. I've gone past the hand-painted sign signalling its whereabouts a hundred times, and from their Facebook page I know that on Thursday afternoons the gates are opened to volunteers and visitors.

It's a little tricky to reach: down a track that seems to lead to an industrial estate, but then veers off to the left to reveal a long steel barred fence and a set of gates. They're swinging open now, and in the early afternoon sun I see veg patches laid out all around. Fresh flowers are blossoming between crops: marigolds to ward off blackfly and nasturtiums to tempt caterpillars away from the tasty bulging cabbages. Trees line the garden's edges, hiding the industrial fence so well I can almost believe there's a crumbling Victorian wall behind them. Almost.

As I walk slowly down the woodchip paths between raised beds, a small ripple of attention moves over the people kneeling by them, weeding and planting. There are women of all ages, a solitary man and a teenage boy spread out about the garden. I smile and then duck my head under the laden branch of a plum tree. When I look up again I see the gardeners have turned back to their tasks. I'm now part of the garden, an occasional visitor like the flocks of starlings that land in a flurry, settle for a moment, then move on.

Conversation, when it starts, comes effortlessly. A casual question about how to keep slugs away turns into a short, relaxed tutorial on organic gardening, and before I realise it I'm sitting in a wooden shelter with a cup of tea in my hand, a small circle of gardeners gathered around me. I learn about how they began the garden, reclaiming land used as a tip by the local fabric wholesaler and drywall factory. The man tells me about how he volunteered to build the wooden shelter we're resting under after the tarpaulin they first fixed with ropes to the fences collapsed. And the boy – who has special support for his learning and says he often feels left out at school – talks about what it means to him to come to the garden with his aunty once a week. The conversation meanders after that. We talk about cuts to park funding, worries about wildlife having no home.

They ask me what I do and I tell them I'm a literature lecturer, specialising in environmentalism. It's a strange job, I admit. When they ask what I'm teaching, I tell them: currently a book by Margaret Atwood about a group of earthy protesters, the God's Gardeners, who try to recreate society after an apocalypse. I don't say it out loud, but this place – verdant green emerging from a concrete wasteland – reminds me of the herb gardens and veg plots in Atwood's novel. There's something comforting about the connection. When we try to imagine a future beyond capitalism, as Atwood does, it's easy to feel despair. But alternative relations may already be budding within the existing status quo, creating 'the possibility of life in capitalist ruins', as the anthropologist Anna Tsing puts it. From the detritus of one system, another one may begin to emerge – and it may look a little like a garden.

After all, gardens are proof that people can have positive relationships with nature, and that these relations can be built on acts of salvage and repair. The garden does not need to be wild, pure and untouched for us to love and live with it. It carries on its life, tangibly entangled with ours. And, most importantly, the garden creates possibilities for generosity that are rarely seen elsewhere, and in such abundance. When I left the community garden that day, a carrier bag of plums was foisted onto me, even though I was just a stranger who had wandered into the space for no more than an hour. There were so many plums in the bag I had to cradle it in my arms on the walk home.

Our relationships with others are often strengthened by sharing the spoils of the garden – fruits, vegetables, and also flowers and plants. We buy and pick each other bunches for special occasions. Flowers adorn the cards exchanged at our festivals; they represent cultures and nations. The Victorians invented an entire symbolic language around flowers, expressing love, dismay, sorrow and lust through roses, pansies, lilies and herbs. It is not too much to say that we understand ourselves through flowers.

But in some cultures, the amplification of affection through plants finds more powerful expression. Plants don't just symbolise relations between people – they materially transform them. Peruvian *curanderos* – healers from Mestizos, Shipibo-Konibo, Asháninka and Matsigenga ethnic groups in the East-Central Amazon – talk of 'plants that teach'. Used in purification and cleansing rituals, plants enhance sensitivity and intuition, and strengthen physical and mental resolve. These rituals are believed to enhance the health and wellbeing of the individual, and the wider community. The idea that relations with plants might teach us something about our relations with each other, and strengthen those relations, is folded into culture.

Robin Wall Kimmerer explores reciprocal relations with plants in *Braiding Sweetgrass* (2013), interlacing scientific botany (in which she is an expert) with teachings about plant life from her own Native culture: the Potawatomi nation of North America. Her urge to share Indigenous botany was sparked by despair. Working in the lab with young minds trained in modern ecosystems science, she was disappointed to hear her students reflect that nature was probably better off without humanity altogether. 'How is it possible that in twenty years of education, they cannot think of any beneficial relationships between people and the environment?' This wasn't just ignorance of how long plants have been nurtured by human intelligence and care. It revealed a fundamental misunderstanding of how mutually entangled the survival of humanity is with the biosphere: 'We make a grave error if we try to separate individual well-being from the health of the whole.'

What Kimmerer reveals instead is a world bound together in relations of mutual responsibility – from fruiting trees that contribute to their ecosystem's flourishing with startling reciprocity, to wild strawberries whose abundance is recognised as a gift. In gardening, too, connections between individual and whole are revealed and strengthened. Kimmerer discovers this during the slow process of clearing a pond in her backyard. When she begins, the pond is dense with green slime. Left to its own devices, it would thicken with run-off nutrients, eventually becoming bog and then land, the soil clumping so that trees could take root. By clearing it, she's arresting the earth's movement. This could well be seen as a selfish act – landscaping or 'improving' the pond, for the sake of aesthetics and pleasure. Working in the garden is always an exercise in discretion – deciding that a pond, and not a bog, is better. We make these choices when we pull plants that we decide to call weeds from their beds, when we lay turf rather than stones, grow fruit rather than bushes that we have deemed worthless. But gardening, in Kimmerer's understanding, is not simply a form of control. It is an act of mothering.

Through gardening, she is mother to 'frog children, nestlings, goslings, seedlings and spores'. She saves small, floundering creatures who get caught up in her nets because 'I could hardly sacrifice another mother's children', and dries algae ready for the compost heap so the life cycle can begin again. The slowness of the work allows ethical questions to percolate – like what does it mean to take care of a place or an ecosystem, to be a caretaker? Gardening, in such a light, is the ideal expression of a beneficial relationship between people and the environment. It is an act of making relations, of being a good mother – or caregiver, if mothering isn't your thing – to one's strange and various kin.

The archetype of the ecological caregiver was formed long ago, and is rooted in the Potawatomi origin story. Everything begins with Skywoman, a goddess who fell from the heavens and was saved from crashing into the sea by a flock of geese. Landing her gently on the water, the birds called on a chorus of animals to create a world from earth placed on a turtle's back – the original Turtle Island. That earth became a home to Skywoman, and a garden for the seeds she was clutching in her hand as she fell. Unlike Eve, cast out of Eden in Christianity's origin story, Skywoman falls into a world of natural plenty, not scarcity and suffering. This original obligation to nature is experienced as a pleasure, not a debt. And it shapes the way plants are understood and treated. It creates relations. Follow the descendants of Eve, and you find a very different way of understanding humanity's bonds – or conflicts – with nature. In cultures that have been shaped by Christianity, it's more common to see nature as 'man's dominion' to name and use as we see fit, even if there have always been counter-traditions within the faith pushing for more responsible stewardship.

This is one reason why the animacy of plants that Kimmerer describes is so unfamiliar to those raised in Christian cultures, or conditioned to the extractive logics of capitalism. Plants aren't an *it*, but a *whom*, in the Potawatomi language – they are entities who evoke an ethical response, a way of being that is all their own. These relationships and animate states of being are captured in words, even in grammar. *Puhpowee* describes the force that urges mushrooms to burst through damp forest mulch. *Yawe*, the verb 'to be', is used to describe all animate life – from the 'I am' of the human speaker to the *Mshimin yawe*, the apple that *is a being too*.

This is radically different from calling a plant or any other living being an 'it'. If we treat a maple tree as 'not a *who*, but an *it*, we make that maple an object', Kimmerer explains. 'We put a barrier between us, absolving ourselves of moral responsibility and opening the door to exploitation.' Instead, in Potawatomi, only objects crafted by people are referred to as 'it'. Everything living or participating in life is an animate being – plant, mineral, animal, even a hill, a pond or a bay. That is why the language is so empty of nouns. A pond isn't a noun-thing, but a verb-being. To be a being, to be a tree, to be a pond or garden, is to be alive and to be always involved in processes of co-becoming and transformation.

I wonder if it is really possible to experience gardening this way as someone from a non-Native American culture? Looking at my garden, I experiment with seeing it as not an *it* but a being – a living entity, pursuing its own interests, engaging in its own relations outside of my ken. When a spray of hedge garlic pops up in the lawn, or a mining bee digs its nest, I get an easy lesson in what it means to cohabit with living others, caught in the act of being a garden. I'm alert to the risk of appropriating and consuming Indigenous knowledge, though, and misrepresenting understandings of the world that are not my own. The reason Kimmerer must learn Potawatomi from scratch is that Indigenous languages were suppressed in the USA through the abusive boarding-school programme so many Native children were subjected to. At the behest of the state, a whole way of seeing the world and speaking about it was (almost) lost. The fact that people were resilient, and found a way to save and pass on the language like seed, doesn't mean that it is now common property.

At the same time, I'm cheered by Kimmerer's account of how her non-Indigenous students responded to these very different ways of thinking about plant life. As one of her class put it, 'it felt like an awakening' or 'more like a remembering', Kimmerer thinks. Though I will never be able to share the stories and the environmental knowledge of Potawatomi people, relating to plants as animate entities – as beings, not objects – can come more easily than we might expect. My own culture trains children out of relating to the world this way. People who talk to plants are often laughed at with relative degrees of affection, but the joke distracts us from the fact that there's something quite intuitive about this. Even if we lack the specific cosmologies that structure Indigenous world views, we can still identify with a desire to reach out to plants, and to respond to their reachings. There's meaning under the surface of all those Instagram posts about plant babies and plant pets. As one volunteer at Cherry Tree Nursery put it: 'They talk to me – I think there's more to plants than people know about ... They have feelings and if you do not treat them right they let you know.'

There are alternative traditions within European science too. Writing in the 1920s, at a moment when most scientists saw plants as little more than machines, the Scottish biologist J. Arthur Thomson looked at them in a far more tender light. Thomson was a rare kind of ecologist: a Christian and Darwinist who was convinced that organisms took an active role in their own evolution – reaching out into their worlds with a wilful vegetal intelligence, and simultaneously transforming that world. He was laughed at by the scientific profession, who were committed to a new kind of biology based on mechanisation, reducing all of living nature to a series of inbuilt behaviours. But Thomson wrote with palpable delight about the mountain flora he encountered around Aberdeenshire. This was a world of connection, relation, humour and surprise, and this was no less true of vegetable life, than animal. 'Many plants have something of the animal about them,' he reflected. 'It is a touch of nature making the world kin.'

I wonder if this sense of relation, this almost innate emotional tethering to vegetal life, is why gardens have for so long been associated with healing. There is something vulnerable, and at the same time valiant, about plants. Bulbs that have been lifted from the ground and furled in bundled-up newspaper over the winter can grow again. Dried beans pressed into the warming spring soil will, in high summer, bear fruit. Watching houseplants bounce back from a fortnight of accidental neglect can be a lesson in resilience. But tending a garden is more than just a metaphor for survival. Their creaturely qualities inspire deeper empathy. Maybe we *get* plants because we share their vulnerabilities: their fleshliness, their frequently unpredictable tendency to endure in inhospitable environments.

Look up 'plant intelligence' on YouTube and you'll find plenty of evidence of the liveliness of plants. Sped-up footage shows them exploring their worlds, throwing curious tendrils out into the void then pulling back, trying a different tack, reacting with a sensitivity that seems absolutely creaturely. Plants know when they're being injured, and some communicate that hurt to other plants using chemical signals in the entangled root mass they share. It's not just wild anthropomorphism to call plants kin, either. Many of our genes are shared with plants: enzymes collaborate to oxidise sugars in much the same way, while the cytochrome complex protein is involved in respiration in all species, plant and animal. The silent stretches of our DNA gesture to a shared inheritance. In eukaryotic organisms that emerged 2.7 billion years ago, and in the bizarre, often uncategorisable forms of life that flourished in the Ediacaran era (c. 635–542 million years ago) and the subsequent Cambrian explosion, nascent plants, algae, lichen and metazoans – the blueprint for multicelled animals – intermingled before they began their own evolutionary stories. In the dazzling scale of the universe's deep time history, it's not far-fetched to call plants family.

In fact, it made sense, even in European science, to describe plants as kin until relatively recently. Humoral medicine attributed physical and mental health to four bodily humours – blood, black bile, yellow bile and phlegm. Ailments and healing were yoked to corresponding elements of fire, water, earth and air. Humanity's health was tied to astrology and the movements of the stars, our wellbeing to the manifestations of these humours on earth: in medicinal leaves, roots and flowers scattered all across the earth by a cunning creator God. The work of the apothecary was to hunt out healing plants, to map out their relations to the body and mind, and to transform the raw medicines of God's pharmacy into healing poultices and draughts. For headaches, take flower-de-luce; to enliven the spirits, lily of the valley; and for melancholia, borage, yarrow, or spiked sea holly. Each curative herb could be matched to its corresponding ailment and element. Herbs, like people, were controlled by the planets and born under Mercury, Mars or Venus. In a world of perfect symmetry, humanity was tied by root, vine and shoot to nature. And in the garden, herbalists would collect a living library of healing plants: God's pharmacy in miniature.

On the banks of the Thames in the dense grey heart of west London, you can find such a garden. Chelsea Physic Garden, established in 1673, is a four-acre wedge of green disguised by antique brick walls. Here the Worshipful Society of Apothecaries laid beds and stocked them with healing plants to serve nearby hospitals and conduct experiments that would improve understanding of herbal medicine, turning folk knowledge and hedge witchcraft into a 'reputable' science.

Sitting on a bench in Chelsea on a recent visit, I attempted an experiment in time travel. I pressed my fingers against my ears and tried to imagine the plash of oars on the river and whispered conversation among the apothecaries tending and snipping their herbs. When

I released my hands, the sound of traffic roared again, the clattering of the lorries and Megabuses making their way out of the city. Now, as then, the routes around the garden are major thoroughfares. This is no accident. The men who laid the garden chose the plot because the warm air drifting upstream across the river and the sun-soaked, south-facing embankment were ideal for their purposes. From their river base, they could explore the tangled borderlands of London and land boats carrying medicinal plants scavenged from across the colonised world. Herbal medicines may have been respected as a gift of God's grace, but they were also an enviable commodity, and as colonial voyages spread deep into the forests and jungles of South America and the West Indies, explorers sought cash crops, precious metals and, of course, medicinal herbs.

Chelsea Physic Garden is no longer an apothecaries' store, but it is still a therapeutic space. The trust now organises gardening and botany sessions for people in recovery, and short courses for those wanting to learn more about herbal remedies used to treat low mood, insomnia and anxiety. Not all herbal treatments have been dispensed with in the move to chemicals, and many herbs are making a comeback. Leading the push is the Living Medicine group, who bring traditional knowledge into dialogue with modern science. They aim to better understand the deep affinities between plants and the human body and to improve literacy around the antiseptic, diuretic, endorphin-releasing, sedative and pain-relieving properties of plants. One day they hope to have a garden of their own in London, an intercultural living archive of herbal remedies.

Chelsea has also hosted talks on CBD, exploring medical and ritual uses of the much-maligned *Cannabis sativa*. This herb has been at the centre of the US drugs war for decades, since the American government criminalised Mexican immigrants who smoked it in the 1930s, and continue to prosecute African American communities caught with miserably small quantities of the stuff. Now it is being revalued as part of a wider movement to reject stigma associated with the use of stimulants and psychedelics in mental health treatment. Ayahuasca, peyote and psilocybin (magic mushrooms, which had a short-lived, glorious phase as a legal high in the noughties) are all enjoying the same tentative revival. These drugs have long been used for ritual purposes by Indigenous communities across South America, and respected as medicines with particular value for mental health. They even came to the attention of doctors who rejected mainstream psychiatry in the 1960s and 1970s, like the Scottish psychiatrist R. D. Laing and the American iconoclast Timothy Leary, whose experiments with hallucinogens at the Harvard Psilocybin Project are now legendary. But the ethics-scrambling approaches tried by anti-psychiatrists and the subsequent sneering attitude to 'hippy' culture adopted from the late 1970s meant that genuine advances in understanding and appreciating plant-based remedies for mental ill health were stalled. Now traditional knowledge is being taken seriously once again. Research papers exploring plants' effectiveness as treatments for depression are slowly dripping out in the medical journals, and with better understanding, hopefully, will come better options for people with hard-to-treat depression. Of course, the fact that businesses and scientific labs are now taking profit and kudos for reviving these drugs can be of little comfort to Black and Indigenous communities who bore the brunt of harsh policies and were criminalised for using traditional medicines.

Herbal medicine has often existed on the margins of mainstream science and medicine. At the same time as the apothecaries were building their walls at Chelsea, Nicholas Culpeper was working on his guide to herbal medicine, published as *The English Physician* in 1653. A herbalist, astrologer and physician, Culpeper set himself up with a practice in Spitalfields in 1640. The area really was mostly fields then – on the edge of the city walls, with access to the countryside and the forests bordering London. You can feel the presence of these places in the book. Under entries for the herbs Culpeper finds on his rambles, there is advice for how to spot them and when to pick them – under the cover of the forest, by nightfall, in time with the waxing or the waning of the moon. His tone is chatty and practical, the voice of someone you wouldn't mind meeting on a walk and going for a pint with afterwards. It's not snobby or elitist, but there's an insider quality to Culpeper's writing too, like the way he describes the alder tree as so 'well known unto country people, that I conceive it needless to tell that which is no news', or the angelica, 'which is so well known to be growing in almost every garden'.

I bought a copy of Culpeper's book, renamed as the *Complete Herbal* at some point when I was a teenager. The little pencil-scrawled '£3.50' is still visible on the inside page, telling me I must have picked it up from a charity shop. I can't remember exactly when, but flicking through its pages now evokes vividly the places that were dear to me then – a herbal ley on the fringes of a stubbly cornfield, a sliver of wildflower by the path on the route into a forest near my home. Reading Culpeper taught me to pay attention to these neglected patches, the homes of nature's waifs and strays. Finding wild chamomile among the daisies, spotting hedge mustard or Good King Henry poking out of the nettles, or stumbling on improbable seeds from scattered heads of fennel, it felt like I'd been given a secret map to these everyday places, revealing wonders beneath the once-blurry greenery. These patches of plants weren't just a background smudge any more, but full of colour, interest and meaning. There were things living and growing there quietly, and they were speaking directly to me.

What has this to do with gardening? I didn't know it then, but Culpeper was a rule-breaker. Before he wrote *The English Physician*, he'd ruffled feathers among the medical establishment for translating the Latin *Pharmacopoeia* into English in 1649. This text, controlled by the College of Physicians, contained all the herbal knowledge necessary for hedge herbalists to treat themselves and their families. By making the text accessible, he was breaking the monopoly of the royal colleges and the worshipful societies. Like the radical Protestant preachers who translated the Gospels to English a century earlier, Culpeper wanted to give ordinary people their own route to salvation. Most doctors charged rates that poor families couldn't afford. So, in the *Complete Herbal*, when Culpeper urges you to look in your local forests and fields, it's the common reader he's writing to: those who would never penetrate behind the high walls of a physic garden, and for whom access to free foraged medicine might be a matter of life and death.

Reading Culpeper retrained my vision, and now when I walk, I often spot things I would like to pick and eat or stew and dose on. St John's Wort, once thought to ward off evil spirits and which some people still use to treat anxiety; nettles, which make a tart and zesty soup; and borage, tonic for melancholia, which seems to sprout up everywhere, bold and wild. For Culpeper, all shrubs and herbs were common property. Even in today's high-density urban sprawl, a world Culpeper would hardly recognise, it's possible to imaginatively knock down the walls and see all the world as a garden.

When the coronavirus lockdown forces us indoors, the meaning of the garden is transformed once again. The world, suddenly, is constrained and contained. Life is lived in miniature. But plants are still growing, flowers bursting into attention-seeking life in time with the warming of the days, and ready for the coming of the bees. This is unchanging, indifferent to the scrolling of news and the new horrors announced each day.

Is it mere escapism to be beguiled by plants at this moment of crisis? I don't think so. Anxiety and loneliness are skyrocketing. Families and friends are being kept apart. We avoid each other in the street and shops, crossing the road or jumping out of the way when we turn the corner in the supermarket, scared of accidently coming too close. Social distancing is a form of social care, as painfully essential as it is loving and kind. But these are conditions of extraordinary isolation, making it harder for people to cope with the transformation of every routine they may depend on for health, security and sanity.

On our street, my neighbours start to share gardening equipment, slipping seeds through each other's letter boxes and offering to water plants for those shielding inside. I admire my elderly neighbour's grape hyacinths, and the next day I find she has yanked three bulbs from her soil and left them on my doorstep after a tap at the door and a quick run back to her house, which turns the whole exchange into a child's game. The contained world of the garden is becoming a refuge, abundant and immersive – at least, it is for the privileged few who have an outside space. For families and renters inside apartments with no balconies, with windows looking out onto dusty concrete streets, it is offensive to be told to find solace in a garden, as if everyone's house is surrounded by rolling lawns and potting sheds. But a friend living in a small rented flat shares pictures of the succulents he cultivates, their papery flowers unfurling against a grey backdrop of brick and sky. A blogger writes a step-by-step guide on how to set up a pollinator pot for beginners. Windowsills come to life. And from the incongruous grape vine, throwing its arms over a steel fence on the cycle path, or the mad Christmas tree plonked with pride in the verge by the footpath's edge, I can tell that the gardeners who tend the forgotten places when no one is looking have been active too.

I could take you on an all-day walking tour of these open-air gardens, hidden in plain sight along cycle paths and railway sidings, in the centres of roundabouts and around the scraggly feet of street trees. 'Guerilla gardening' flourished in the States in the 1970s, inspired by Liz Christy's Green Guerillas project to turn derelict urban space into a community garden. It now has its legacy in these reclaimed areas of urban flourishing, places where plants are tended in the early morning or at night, property of no one, offering pleasure and secret surprise for anyone who stops to take a look.

A daisy growing through concrete is one kind of resistance. Planting a flower bed in a public street is another. It rejects the notion that we must claim ownership of a place, turn it into property to take a part in its life. It is a political and an ecological act to grow a garden, a commitment to human and more-than-human communities, to the beauty of the present and the nourishment of the future. It's also a way of cleaving back ownership of space, to turn private land into a community store. When I take my daily walk, keeping a safe distance from others, I see these small tokens left like a gift by other gardeners, a way of being close in our shared separation. What a cure for loneliness it is to see snakeskin fritillaries growing, Gothic and magnificent, on the park's football pitch.

This isn't 'nature taking over'. The city is being tended, like a garden.

Park
Little Wellbeing Machines

I teach a course on literature and the environmental crisis at a university on the outskirts of Bath. There is a lot to talk about in our seminars, but at the heart of it all is the question – what is nature? How do we understand this entity – are we apart from it, or a part of the whole? What does it mean to connect with 'the world around us', and how do our ways of seeing 'nature' influence the kinds of places we destroy, value or create?

At the start of the term each year I lead the group around my university's campus, and I ask them, 'Where can you see nature?' They perch on a crumbling eighteenth-century wall, or sit cross-legged on the lawn, and make a list of all the green and blue things they can see: the grass, the hill, the trees, the lake. It's not a difficult exercise. When we come to compare notes, there's very little of this detail that's been missed. This *is* nature, they tell me. Except for the gravel paths and the wooden benches, it's all Nature with a capital 'N', as far as the eye can see.

The place where we are sitting is called Newton Park and it used to belong to an aristocratic family. It passed through many different hands over the years, and now we teach in their old stately home, and the students use the landscaped park as if it's their own. The fact that they see it all as 'nature' shows that the landscape is still working its magic, doing the job that it was designed to do. Because as natural as it seems, the whole layout is artificial. In the 1760s, the owners took shovels to the earth, turning it into a scene of beauty and pleasure. Hills were raised and streams diverted to fill the valley with a picturesque lake. Woodlands were cut down to create splendid views of the distant hills, and then a dense border of trees was planted to obscure the working terrain of farms and fields, carefully snipping the unseemly reality of poverty out of the frame.

The designer responsible for the transformation was Lancelot 'Capability' Brown, one of the most famous and fashionable of the naturalistic landscapers. Starting at Stowe in 1742, a stately home in the leafy county of Buckinghamshire, he tore up formal gardens, knocked down walls, and dug trenches called 'ha-has' to produce 'swept' landscapes, where the eye would move effortlessly across the expanse of the land. Capability Brown, along with contemporaries like William Kent and Humphry Repton, represented an altogether new attitude to what was 'beautiful' in nature. They offered Nature 2.0: inspired by the real thing, but perfected through subtle design.

It's difficult for us to notice now because it's all so craftily disguised. In his *Observations on the Theory and Practice of Landscape Gardening* (1803), Repton instructed designers to 'studiously conceal every interference of art, however expensive, by which the scenery is improved; making the whole appear the production of nature only'. Inspiration came from the Chinese garden tradition of 'artful irregularity', and from the work of French painter Claude Lorrain, who created a visual ideal of gently rolling hills and sinuous streams. The style was christened 'the picturesque', and combined grandeur with pleasantness, ruggedness with variety and beauty. This was a landscape that would intrigue but not stupefy; please but not overwhelm. As William Gilpin, one of the originators of the idea of the picturesque, advised, these landscapes should produce 'a tranquil pause of mental operation', followed by the swooning sensation of 'deliquium' – literally the melting away of the soul.

Arresting the attention without exhausting it, the picturesque was primed to become an ideal landscape for psychological restoration. As one of the leading thinkers of the 'picturesque school', Uvedale Price put it: 'the effect of the picturesque is curiosity … it neither relaxes nor violently stretches the fibres'. Repton also discusses how landscapes should move people in his *Observations*. Qualities of neatness and balance, integrated design and effortless elegance, all contributed to the total pleasure that the landscaped park could produce. With intricacy it could excite curiosity. With simplicity it could guide the eye around the whole scene 'without flutter' or confusion. The movement of living water or the swaying of trees in the breeze would create delight through animation. And with extent – the long, continuous stretch of a wooded avenue, the infinity-pool effect of the lawns, and the graceful paths that seem to wind on forever – the designer could produce feelings of joy, freedom, and infinite possibility.

The legacy of these grounds is visible all around the world. For the next two centuries every city park built on the English-landscape model was a replica of their designs. If you've ever stepped out of doors in a British city and searched for a patch of green like an oasis in a desert of office blocks and traffic-clogged roads, you've probably seen one. You may have seen hundreds. The Victorians and Edwardians had a craze for opening landscaped parks, and the trend spread to the USA and Europe in the nineteenth century, to create the distinctive sculpted terrain familiar to so many.

I call these landscaped parks 'little wellbeing machines'. Designed to soothe and beguile, restore the energies and calm the nerves, the landscaped park in the English style suggests that feelings, like nature, can be crafted and designed. Their little glimpses of surprise, intrigue and beauty still move us as easily and unobtrusively as the background music of a Hollywood movie. Their sensory features are perfectly calibrated to aid restoration, to gratify, excite, or soothe and tranquillise. And they do work – they really do. When I'm stressed, I often leave my home and take a walk around the park a few minutes from my door. I take the path that winds around the lawns, down past the lake and up through the long arcade of trees. It offers a simple, irresistible circuit, and by the end of it my headache has usually passed and my heart rate slowed. The line of trees around the perimeter has tricked me into thinking there's a forest, rather than a busy road, around its boundaries. This little wellbeing machine, concocted over two centuries ago, has worked its charms on me.

Much research has been done into the way parks affect people's wellbeing and health. The term these studies use is 'green space' – often blended to 'greenspace'. Green space means parks, but it also means lawns and playing fields, playgrounds and verges, streams and greenways, even street trees and cemeteries. It is any stretch of public land that might show up as green on a map, or where you might stumble across grass, mud, weeds and critters. For the last two decades, anyone interested in nature and wellbeing in Europe, the USA – and increasingly across the world, thanks to research funded by the World Health Organisation – has been preoccupied with how to increase and protect these green spaces in cities.

Take one experiment, conducted at Stanford University in California. Researchers sent a group of volunteers to walk around an area of green space on the university campus, while another marched up the noisy, polluted El Camino Real. When their brains were scanned back in the lab, the nature walkers showed reduced neural activity in an area associated with self-focused withdrawal and rumination (repetitive, negative thoughts, which are linked to depression). The city walkers, in contrast, remained frazzled. Or look at Seoul, where in 2005 a frantic multi-lane highway was removed, and replaced with a three-and-a-half-mile-long park running alongside the Cheonggyecheon River, now released from its tomb under the tarmac. In place of the 168,000 cars that used to race through the city, birds and fish returned. The temperature dropped, thanks to the flowing water and greenery that disturbs the urban heat island effect – the higher temperatures experienced in cities due to the high density of heat-retaining metal and concrete. Green space boosted air quality, and also created space for exercise and contemplation. In further studies, green space has been connected to reductions in perceived stress and salivary cortisol levels, positive changes to heart-rate variability and diastolic blood pressure, and improvements in self-confidence and mental restoration.

This is why city parks are used not just to beautify cities, but to create 'salutogenic' habitats – places that allow humans to be well. Have you ever played *SimCity*? Designing real-world salutogenic environments isn't really that different from what you do in the game. Armed with data about how we respond to nature, town planners and public health experts set up pocket environments to encourage certain kinds of behaviour. Mark a territory green on the map, and you see a change for the better in people's health and wellbeing. Create a park with places to run or sit, and you can expect some 'intentional engagements' – people heading there to exercise or take time out to unwind. Or be subtle, and build a green thoroughfare through a busy urban quarter. Without even knowing they're doing it, people will wander through and enjoy an 'incidental encounter' – a brush with nature, where a little of its healing properties might rub off on you.

With all the evidence mounting up, criticising parks feels unthinkable, sacrilegious. Parks have become the go-to solution for urban nature deprivation, and like anyone who has ever lived in a city, I know how passionately people feel about them, and how nightmarish it is to live in an area deprived of local green space. But parks aren't exactly perfect, for people or for nature. A good park can be a refuge for birds and squirrels, foxes and mice, but the quality and biodiversity of parks varies enormously, from leafy expanses with fresh running water, to 'a barren island circumnavigated by fuming rivers' of traffic, as novelist Rachel Cusk describes one London park. These barren islands still have value. You can tell this from the way people flock to them on hot days and lunch breaks, desperate for even the foggiest and most tired patch of green. But they can be grim sites of sufficient solace, offering 'just enough nature' for people, and a precarious refuge for wildlife.

At this stage of my search for the nature cure, I want to trace a line between the aristocratic park, the 'little wellbeing machines' built by the Victorians, and the 'just enough nature' of modern urban green space. If eighteenth-century landscapers innovated by turning nature into a picture, crafting little islands of ideal scenery out of whatever was there before, what impact did this have on our understanding of nature and the way we treat it? Knowing this history, and looking to the future, is it now time to do better?

Parks were invented in the first decades of the nineteenth century. As the Industrial Revolution took hold, mushrooming cities ate up the surrounding fields, and people from the countryside crowded into slums to take up work in factories. Cities became dangerous and dirty, with notorious sanitation and air pollution problems. Writing in 1845, Friedrich Engels described the seismic change experienced by rural migrants in their filthy and squalid new homes. Back in the countryside, many had worked as labourers or had smallholdings of their own. 'They had leisure for healthful work in garden or field,' Engels observed:

> work which, in itself, was recreation for them, and they could take part besides in the recreations and games of their neighbours, and all these games – bowling, cricket, football, etc., contributed to their physical health and vigour. They were, for the most part, strong, well-built people, in whose physique little or no difference from that of their peasant neighbours was discoverable. Their children grew up in the fresh country air, and, if they could help their parents at work, it was only occasionally; while of eight or twelve hours work for them there was no question.

As Engels goes on to describe, moving from country to city was devastating for these people. Losing financial independence and their connection to established communities, their free hours and access to fresh air and sun, they also lost places to play and socialise, to 're-create' themselves.

What could be done? In American cities, people desperate for a slice of nature started congregating in cemeteries. From the 1830s to the 1860s, these semi-rural spaces, built on the edges of towns, were treated as public pleasure grounds and tourist sites. It was their picturesque landscaping – inspired by the aristocratic park – that attracted admirers. In Mount Auburn, Boston, tombs were laid around 'winding avenues, paths, and ponds on hilly, wooded terrain with dramatic panoramic views over the entire metropolitan area'. Guidebooks attracted visitors, and paths led them round a 'programmed sequence of sensory experiences, primarily visual, intended to elicit specific emotions', as historian Blanche Linden-Ward explains. These were sites of melancholy reflection, appealing to Romantic sensibilities and the fashion for wistful introspection. Some religious visitors found them edifying, as well as restorative, like Lydia Maria Child, who in 1831 advised mothers to bring their children to the pastoral necropolis to culture a 'cheerful association with death'. But for some tourists from overseas, like the English socialite Henry Arthur Bright, the American fashion was a strange blend of the merry and the macabre: 'Cemeteries here are all the "rage",' he wrote in a letter to a friend, 'people lounge in them and use them (as their tastes are inclined) for walking, making love, weeping, sentimentalising, and everything in short.'

Many cities already had open spaces of some kind: gardens, piazzas and public promenades lined with trees. But the public park as we know it today was a product of the mid-nineteenth century: a place for sport and recreation, to keep workers out of trouble and sufficiently healthy and contented. The push to create them didn't just come from trade unionists and social reformers: lawmakers, town councils and factory owners also began to wring their hands in worry over the vigour of urban populations. In Britain, a series of acts was passed to protect access to open spaces and oblige local authorities to create new ones. These costly exercises were justified on economic, social, moral and even political grounds, inspired by the belief that parks made people 'happier, and therefore better citizens' according to historian Harriet Jordan.

Some of the most generous funders of the first parks were wealthy industrialists – the same people employing the workers whose health and happiness was, coincidentally, deteriorating in their factories. The landscaping of other parks, like Birkenhead – established in Merseyside in 1847 – were funded by selling off land around the edges to people who wanted to live in close proximity. If you've ever wondered why fancy houses often border parks, it's because the high rates generated by selling park-side plots for villas and mansions helped generate the revenue needed to transform the land.

Transform, because it was at this moment the aristocratic estate met the city park. In Britain, landscapers were given bold new urban commissions – like Joseph Paxton, a former garden boy who relocated from the grandiose Chatsworth House in the 1840s to shape public parks in Glasgow, Liverpool and Halifax. The sweep of lawn, the wooded plantations and the shallow fishing lakes would now be reproduced for the delight of the many. To cope with increased footfall, extra paths were laid to cut across the lawns, providing routes for exercise and exploration. In some city centres, existing private gardens and bridleways were folded into the public greenery, like London's Hyde Park, which joined together the seventeenth-century horse-ride of Rotten Row and the royal hunting grounds created by Henry VIII.

We often think of parks as little refuges of untouched nature left behind as the city developed around it, but often creating a park meant bulldozing whatever was there before. In England the first places to go were what remained of the commons. These were swathes of open land where, since the Middle Ages, people had claimed rights to fish, graze animals and cut turf – to draw the fundamental means to live from the land. Ordinary people didn't actually own the commons. Under the feudal system, the Crown owned everything, but lords of the manor were granted rights to their estates, and the commoners their commons.

I remember learning about the common land at school. On photocopied maps our teacher pointed out the swathes of common, woodland and meadows where villagers would collect their firewood, where sheep and pigs would chew grass or crunch acorns. Beside these stretches of common land lay the mosaicked strips of farmland – like modern-day allotments – over which the villagers held rights to grow subsistence crops. But, our teacher taught us, all this land was victim to the 'tragedy of the commons'. This idea was poached from a 1968 essay by the economist Garrett Hardin, and most of the nuance of his argument had rubbed off by the time it reached the GCSE syllabus. The lesson our teacher took from Hardin was that people simply couldn't be trusted to share. With each individual owner acting 'rationally' in their own best interest to use their land, resources were spoiled. Agricultural strips became inefficient, and the grazing land and forests of the common were stripped bare by so many people demanding their part. In the long term, total productivity began to decline, benefiting no one. It was much more sensible to put benevolent and competent land managers in charge. And so English law began to change from the seventeenth century. Shared farm and common land was enclosed and bought up by wealthy landowners, and the country gained a more plentiful source of food. What remained of the commons were turned into parks managed by local authorities, sometimes retaining the name 'commons', but offering none of the traditional land-use rights.

It wasn't until many years later, when I read the work of the economist Elinor Ostrom, that I reconsidered this telling of history. She was not the first to challenge the 'tragedy of the commons', but her debunking was decisive. Ostrom shows how in so many communities where land is held co-operatively, shared values and practices stop resources becoming depleted, as more people have a stake in their health and preservation. The seizure of the common lands, instead of being a necessary move to maximise productivity, was part of the long process of removing poor people's rights to the land and nature. Without strips to farm or commons to live off, they became roaming seasonal labourers, forced to work or rent at the landowner's rate. It was the dependents of displaced rural folk who migrated to work in factories and cities, and ended up using parks to replace the lost greens and commons of their ancestors.

Much of the common land had been enclosed and sold off by the turn of the nineteenth century – turned into farmland or the aestheticised landscapes of aristocratic estates, where the model of the little wellbeing machine was born. What was left became dangerous for the authorities – providing places for workers to congregate and organise. At Kennington Common – a muddled ground in south London used for cricket, games, public executions and grazing – around 50,000 people congregated for a mass Chartist demonstration in 1848. Chartists claimed the right to vote, whether or not people held property of their own. The Great Meeting of 1848 passed off peacefully, but these mass movements disturbed the British state, who were desperate to avoid a British counterpart to the French Revolution. In 1852, Kennington Common was enclosed and gatherings were banned. Railings went up, paths were laid and trees planted, and the area subject to new kinds of policing. From now on, working-class people could use the open space for leisure to recover from the exhaustion of work, but not to meet to fight for more.

Another striking instance of the park radically reshaping the land can be found in New York's Central Park. In the 1850s, as urban development crept up the island of Manhattan, city officials began to press for the creation of a grand area of urban greenery to give respite to the exploding population. On my first visit to New York a decade ago, we set aside an afternoon to explore Central Park. I was suffering a non-American's reaction to the scale of the city. Even London hadn't prepared me for the height of the buildings, the racket of the subway, the blocks that seemed to run on forever. But the park was reassuringly familiar. There was the sunken lake, framed by woodland, the expanse of meadow and lawn and the winding pathways through the Ramble. The heat and the epic skyline reminded me I was far from home, but if I squinted, or turned a corner at just the right angle, I could convince myself I was in an unfamiliar corner of a London park, rounding the lake at St James's.

It plays a strange trick on the mind, this blending of English and American landmarks. In the 1850s, the first American landscape architect, Frederick Law Olmsted, vowed to bring the benefits of the landscaped parks to the masses. As a child, Olmsted had travelled with his father across the Adirondacks, Connecticut Valley and the White Mountains by horseback, on 'tours in search of the picturesque'. He'd read *Walden*, published in 1854, which documented Thoreau's transformative residence in the forest outside Boston. Olmsted was impressed by the Transcendentalist idea that time spent in nature improved a person morally and spiritually. He'd also read *Solitude Considered* by the Swiss physician Johann Georg Ritter von Zimmermann. This essay – first published in 1796 – touches on that tricky territory between pleasurable aloneness and isolation. Zimmermann was a visitor to Hanover in Germany, and found his traveller's homesickness was eased by regular walks in a park 'cultivated in the English taste'. It surprised him that on 'so small a scale' the designer could 'imitate the enchanting variety and the noble simplicity of Nature'. What Zimmermann was responding to was nature's beauty, but as importantly the eye of the landscape artist who had compressed so many natural scenes – the forest, the lake, the hill, the grove – together in miniature. And the results were startling.

> I was not until then convinced that her aspect alone is sufficient, at the first view, to obliterate all the oppression of the world, to excite in our breasts the purest luxury, to fill our minds with every sentiment that can create a fondness for life.

Life was once again worth living, suffering forgotten. 'This magic art,' he reflected, 'makes a most astonishing impression on the mind; it excites in every heart, not yet insensible to the delightful charms of cultivated nature, all the pleasures which Solitude, rural repose, and a seclusion from the haunts of men, can procure.' In the park, he felt like he was in *real* nature, wandering alone in the countryside.

The idea struck Olmsted deeply. If all this was the case, surely it was a moral obligation to bring the wonders of nature to the city? In Central Park, which welcomed its first visitors in 1858, Olmsted did just that. Echoing Zimmermann, he believed scenery should work on people through 'unconscious influence'. The mind and body, the whole human organism, would relax and 'unbend' in perfectly designed surroundings. Park designs should meet deep human needs for restoration and solitude. Their scenery and planting should convey nature's bounty and mystery, producing effects as innately moving as music.

When Olmsted brought the landscaped park to a rapidly expanding New York, he was setting the standard for the kind of natural beauty that would be valued in a post-Independence, post-Civil War America. What Olmsted made, in effect, was a theme park, where visitors could wander through 'zones' as aesthetically diverse as Disney's Frontierland, Fantasyland or Main Street. Transitions between worlds were marked by subtle design features like regional plants, rugged stone or smart cobbles, and cunningly deflected vistas. To migrants drawn into the vortex of New York, the park could be both a respite and painfully affecting. In James Baldwin's *Go Tell It on the Mountain* (1953), Elizabeth, newly arrived from Maryland, realises that she 'liked the park because, however spuriously, it re-created something of the landscape she had known'. For others, born to city life, the park gave a potted tour of places and terrains they may never have had a chance to see: a curiously compressed landscape of lakes and Ladies' Meadows, castle follies and the pocket wilderness of the Ramble.

But what was there before, and what had been lost? When European colonists arrived in the sixteenth century, the isle of Mannahatta had been a vibrant ecology of wetlands and waterways, rocks and forests encompassing 'trees of every description', as the English captain Henry Hudson remarked in 1609. But this was no wilderness. The 'Isle of Many Hills' was home to the Lenni Lenape Indigenous people, and the habitat of wolves, black bears and mountain lions. Long before the lawns of Central Park were laid, these traces were destroyed as Indigenous land was divided up between merchant families, and the haunts of beavers, tree frogs and bog turtles broken and forgotten.

The design of Central Park has preserved a few traces of its geological heritage. The jutting prominence of Rat Rock is a monument to the outcrops of Manhattan schist that were once visible all across the island. But only an information board reminds visitors of the existence of Seneca Village, a community of around 250 free, property-owning Black and Irish families who started to acquire land on the site in the mid-1820s. Recent archaeological explorations have started to reveal details of Seneca Village, whose residents enjoyed a middle-class, almost rural existence on the outskirts of what was then the city centre. Supplied with a spring of fresh water and the rare privilege of voting rights, the village was cleared to make way for a long column of restorative greenery. But I wonder what other stories about nature and wellbeing we might be telling if this unique multicultural community had not been obliterated?

In spite of the often painful history of their creation, parks are still considered the most perfect form of urban nature, and the most serene landscape for natural restoration. But where did this idea come from? What is the science behind the little wellbeing machine?

That history proves equally surprising. A few miles away from my university campus in Bath lies the site of a very special therapeutic park. Built on part of the old expanse of Brislington Common, in its original form it might have been mistaken for the landscaped park and mansion of an aristocrat. But Brislington House, which opened in 1806, was a new kind of 'lunatic asylum', designed to rehabilitate its patients through subtle influences in their environment. Its manager, Edward Fox, believed that insanity was caused by a confusion of reason, rather than an inborn defect. Chains and bars were no longer moral or appropriate as treatments. Instead, social events, a timetable of chores, and a restorative landscape to relax in were all employed to coax patients back to sanity.

Although the house and gardens have long since disappeared under suburban concrete and brick, hospital historian Clare Hickman has revealed its forgotten features. Gardens were laid out in 'diversified walks and extensive plantations', to create the feeling of extent, and to give patients some privacy. In brochures, wealthy clients were tempted by engravings of elegant parkland and buildings resembling fashionable spa hotels, while announcements in the press boasted of the 'pure air' and 'pleasant situation, free from dangerous accidents' that residents would enjoy.

Throughout the 1800s, in Sussex, York, and on the outskirts of Paris, similar establishments began to pop up. What they had in common was the belief that pleasant prospects and picturesque scenery would 'agreeably affect both eye and mind', as one commentator remarked in 1841. Their landscaped parks were dotted with walks and grottos, gardens and 'snail mounts' (twisting paths up reinforced hills, from which patients could enjoy the scenery), even aviaries and rabbit runs where patients might 'awaken the social and benevolent feelings' in an early form of animal-assisted therapy.

Beliefs in nature's healing properties, its ability to soothe and improve the mind, had been stirred up by literary Romanticism, but medics were also impressed by how the 'mere extent of country' could 'afford delight' and 'convey grateful impressions' – for some residents, anyway. In private asylums, paying patients from the middle and upper classes were more likely to be sent outside to enjoy the grounds, while working-class residents were assigned farm and garden work. If moral management was all about returning people to their normal lives, why encourage farm labourers and factory workers to get a taste for neoclassical follies or swept lawns? They would never see such things again if they were returned to sanity.

Diagnosis also influenced the kind of scenery that was meant to be therapeutic. In one mid-nineteenth century asylum, melancholics were allowed to enjoy 'wide and variegated' scenery, while 'restless and maniacal patients' had to make do with a 'narrow and uniform view' – an acknowledgement that the different faces of nature might be overwhelming, instead of soothing. In Brislington, one patient even admitted he found the scenery worsened his recovery: 'I have no doubt that the noble view excited my spirits, awakened my imagination, and redoubled every blow of affliction, reminding me of my former health and force of mind, and liberty.' This detail is curiously touching. It reminds me of those days, in depression, where bright and brilliant weather can be more painful than a joy – a reminder that you're not well, and that life is carrying on in full volume and Technicolor without you.

In spite of the occasional rebel, the landscaped park's beauty is often seen as universally pleasing. This belief has even blended into theories of natural healing. Convinced that nature could help people recover from stress and restore attention, psychologists and landscape architects began searching for a perfectly calibrated landscape that would aid restoration and boost wellbeing.

One of the main players in this research was Roger Ulrich. His theory of stress reduction (SRT) has already been encountered in the therapeutic garden, but Ulrich was also interested in how natural beauty makes us feel. He coined the term aesthetic–affective theory to name this new field of study, explaining that 'aesthetic and emotional experiences are the most important benefits' of spending time in nature. Unlike some of the more prosaic physiological explanations of why we love nature – like the flash of green that's supposed to excite positive associations in our cave-man brain, or the biochemicals released by pine – Ulrich insisted that the perception of beauty itself could be therapeutic. This actually makes a lot of sense. If you've climbed a mountain, you know that the expectation of a stunning view can keep you going on a long and gruelling hike. It's also fairly well evidenced that a view of natural scenery out of a hospital window can help in the management of pain (and we have Ulrich to thank for this, as he was the first researcher to conduct experiments into the difference between gazing at a group of trees and a brown brick wall). These examples suggest that nature isn't just a simple backdrop, a blend of colour and light that we respond to with animal simplicity. It elicits emotion, invites admiration, and affects us because we appreciate its beauty.

What Ulrich wanted to understand was: what are the exact qualities of a landscape that make us feel attraction and delight? If he could pin this down, landscapers could finally perfect the designs of their little wellbeing machines, reducing the various faces of nature to an efficient model to maximise its health-boosting effect.

To answer this, psychologists collected groups of volunteers and showed them pictures. In one study, it was photographs of rural roads. In another, people's eye movements were tracked as they surveyed a series of countryside scenes. Sifting through the volunteer responses, psychologists got a better sense of the details their volunteers found attractive: everything from the focal point at the landscape's centre to the depth of the scene and the ground surface texture came under scrutiny. One study suggested that people liked the look of smooth expanses of lawn; another that volunteers liked a degree of openness, but found comfort in a screen of trees that seemed to 'enclose' a rural scene. Many of the researchers conducting this work were interested in evolutionary explanations, so you often find them trying to make sense of these preferences by looking to the lives of prehistoric humans. Maybe volunteers liked lawns because they were easier to escape across than rocks and scrub? Perhaps enclosed scenes appealed because they offered a place to forage, explore and hide from predators?

I wonder if there is a more straightforward explanation. Perhaps the volunteers liked certain views because they looked like the landscapes they'd been taught were beautiful. If the long history of nature appreciation teaches anything, it's that beauty isn't in the eye of the beholder. Just as fashions in costume, hair, make-up and interior décor change, appreciation of the landscape changes with time. This isn't to say we aren't drawn to nature for reasons that are more primal and instinctive. But when it comes to defining and celebrating beauty, and reckoning the worth of one kind of landscape over another, it's likely that the places we recognise as beautiful are the ones we've seen praised in heritage landscapes and country-house tours, and celebrated again and again in art and photography. They are the places we have learned to recognise as beautiful. What the volunteers were looking at wasn't nature, but art that represented a landscape that was itself a fashionable fabrication.

In one gloriously circular study, Ulrich and his collaborator showed 200 university students a series of landscapes. Not photographs of real places, but works of art by European and American painters depicting landscape scenes. Then, with the help of experts in picture analysis, they grouped together the main features of the preferred landscapes, trying to understand what people were responding to when they picked out a place as particularly attractive or particularly detestable.

They found that the scenes people classed as the 'most relaxing' were the ones that looked like landscaped parks. More than any other scene, their calm lakes, winding paths and gentle inclinations drew viewers in.

This is perplexing. Why should an artificial landscape that emerged in northern Europe in the eighteenth century be seen as universally appealing? Deserts, mountains, marshes and rainforests are beautiful, too, and the cultures that have lived with them have clearly not been lacking in opportunities to find peace and restoration. There's something both silly and strange about the notion that everyone should respond in the same way to an eighteenth-century European design that idealised 'nature', with its green lawn, gentle hills, and the landscape theatrics created by ha-has and discreetly planted groves.

There's more at stake here than simple landscape ideals. Since they were invented in the eighteenth century, English parks spread from country mansions to common land around the world. *Jardin à l'anglaise* and *Englischer Landschaftsgarten* were laid in France, Germany, Poland, Russia, sometimes for the benefit of ordinary people, sometimes for the enjoyment of royals (like at Versailles, where Marie Antoinette began to 'naturalise' her formal French gardens from the 1770s). And it's not only in city parks: the picturesque aesthetics of lawn and lake pop up in unexpected places all over the world, from the holiday resorts of Florida to the suburbs of Australia and the gated communities of wealthy South Africa. In many places they are remnants of colonial aesthetics, like the white-starched linen worn by Klaus Kinski's explorer in Werner

Herzog's *Fitzcarraldo*. In Britain, many of the families who shaped and sculpted the land built their wealth on slavery. The aristocratic park is not just a soothing refuge of nature perfected. They are also places of contradiction and pain, what historian Olivette Otele calls 'reluctant sites of memory'.

The cultural dominance of the landscape park also has ecological impacts. The park's idealised version of nature paid homage to the pastureland and low-lying hills of northern Europe. Those pastoral lands looked the way they did because of their distinct ecosystems – temperate climates, high rainfall, and the presence of grazing livestock. As drought and flooding become more commonplace, it's going to become impossible to maintain English-style parks in some of the most arid and tropical regions on earth. To keep the miles of smooth, green lawn around stately homes glittering, millions of gallons of water arching from sprinkler systems must be turned on at night. Scrolling through the advice to homeowners on Australian gardening sites, you can spot the tranche of articles advising on lawn care with every seasonal drought. Homeowners can switch to different grasses, but even the hardiest species still need unsustainable levels of water. Back in the days of the country mansion, lawns and parklands were always a high-input status symbol. What better way to prove your wealth than sacrifice a huge area of arable land for the creation of a 'scene', then hire a team to cut the lawn or a shepherd and his flock to maintain it? Now 'high input' means a massive water footprint, but also fossil fuels to power lawnmowers, as well as fertilisers and chemical herbicides.

Even in Britain, the park's claim to be a 'native' landscape is often tenuous. Many of the sites of aristocratic and urban parks were originally forest, wetlands or valleys holding little more than a stream. Recent summer heatwaves – where temperatures have soared over 30°C, even crept towards 40°C, day after day – have made the precarity and unsustainability of many parks more visible than ever. I never thought that I would lie on shorn, dead grass in Hyde Park in late July and listen to the crackle of brown leaves as they fell, parched, from the trees. So many city parks were designed to beautify and repackage nature, for the pleasure and health of humanity. But, as Timothy Morton puts it, the aestheticised construction of Nature often 'fails to serve ecology well'. Now it may be time to reconsider the health of parks – their capacity to sustain life, and their interconnection with ecology beyond the bright green island of tranquillity they promise.

Some scientists are taking notice. One day in late summer, out of the blue, I receive an invitation to Hanover. The event is a conference looking at the connection between wellbeing and nature. After two days of talks and evidence-sharing, the plan is to write a collective research paper, feeding in everyone's specialist knowledge to produce a document which, the organisers hope, will influence policies in the EU, the World Health Organisation and the UN.

We gather in what was once a palace, and is now a lavish conference centre surrounded by the most ornate and grandiose baroque gardens I have ever seen. In the opening session, people introduce themselves. I meet public health experts, exploring how our lived environments can be made more salutogenic. I meet child psychologists, describing the ideal places for young people to grow and play. I meet microbiologists, too, who are interested in how our gut microbiome regulates our immune system and metabolism, culturing an interior biodiversity of beneficial bacteria. What they all have in common is an interest in green space, and how these environments are connected to human health.

As I listen to the experts in Hanover talk, I'm reminded of the original purpose of parks – the little wellbeing machines designed to shape and influence our movements, mood and feelings. But as the talks progress, and images of lawns and trees flash across the screen, I realise we're a long way from the old healing aesthetic. The experts are realising that the green space of the park isn't really enough. Not all parks are created equal. The ecological quality of green space matters, too.

We are gathered here to explore that question of quality, and to ask: what is the link between biodiversity and human health? This includes mental wellbeing, but also all aspects of physical health, from disease resistance to lung capacity to gut flora. How is human health influenced by the complex, interconnected flourishing of ecosystems? Does the decline or extinction of species – from insects to mammals to fungi – affect our physical and mental health? If it does, how can the collected know-how of everyone in this room prove it?

Thinking of urban nature as 'green' or 'blue' space – the planner's word for water – doesn't always capture this difference. Look at any plan for a new housing development and you'll see glossy images of green squares of grass graced with trees like puffs of candy floss. But that doesn't guarantee that these places are valuable habitats – places where people or living creatures want to be, where birds, wild plants and insects might make their home. Many elegantly designed and popular green spaces are not particularly rich or dynamic as ecosystems – like the Seoul Cheonggyecheon park project, which has been criticised for using pumped water prone to sewage pollution, 'channelising' the river in concrete rather than letting it flow on its natural course, and creating a sterile environment of little interest to fish or birds.

That's the risk with using 'green space' as a shorthand for all urban nature: it can become just that, a blank, green, cut-out space on a map, devoid of beauty, meaning, biodiversity, life.

I've seen the failure of 'green space' thinking first-hand. On a grey June morning in 2017, I stepped off the train in Cambridge and made my way to the station exit. It had been years since I'd been there, and I was expecting to see a thousand bicycles chained together in a tangled mass. Instead I found myself ensnared in a building site, surrounded by a busy road, with people tripping over each other trying to catch a cab. My first instinct was to get away to the botanic gardens or the meadows down by the river that lead you far out into the fields and fens. But it was this mess of building work I'd come to see. Or, more precisely, the streak of green just visible behind a row of six-foot-high, metal-panelled fences.

The scrappy bit of lawn they were protecting was optimistically named Mill Park, but it looked more like a derelict parking lot. 'It's simply been too popular,' explained Sven Töpel. He's the CEO of Brookgate, the developer responsible for the park and the £750 million apartment and shopping complex that surrounds it.

Popular is an understatement. For the residents of a thousand small apartments and 350 family homes built by Brookgate, Mill Park was a shared back garden. Before it was fenced off, picnicking families jostled against students playing football and post-work drinkers sprawled on the grass. After sunset, they were succeeded by the late-night smokers, partygoers and, eventually, people sleeping rough.

It's not that people can't share space. It's just the scrap of land was so small, so badly designed and so inappropriately situated, that it was bound to fail. It's easy to blame individuals for misusing places, but the problem with letting property developers control the built environment is that they have powerful financial reasons to do the job in the cheapest way possible. Someone somewhere was able to tick a box that said the housing comes with 'green space', and feel that they had done their job. But behind the wire fences at Mill Park, the grass was patchy and brown. Skinny trees jutted out of the concrete, and I wondered if there would ever be space for their roots to stretch, if water would be able to penetrate the layers of rubble and tarmac that encased them. A confused bee bounced across the shrubbery in the raised bed by the wall I was resting on, but nothing was really living there. I tried hard to be generous, to see the best in the place by focusing my attention closely on the plants and trees that weren't wilting and shrivelling though lack of care. But being there made me feel angry and defeated.

This might seem like a first-world problem, but it's also a fact that inner-city communities – who are often the most economically vulnerable and ethnically diverse – have less access to nature and live in more dangerously polluted urban areas. Sometimes this is caused by eco-gentrification. Property values spike near city parks, pricing working people out, and meaning that you can only appreciate the mental health benefits of park access and a green view if you can afford it.

At the same time, in areas where house prices are soaring, parks and green spaces are being paved out of existence. Developers have a knack of manipulating planning regulations and ignoring protection orders on trees, calculating that it's more cost effective to cut them down and pay the fine than respect the law. The protest banners that pop up around threatened patches of urban greenery show that residents have the political will and love of local nature in spades, but they often lack financial resources and clout to reverse decisions taken in property developers' favour. When the last park is tarmacked over or the last trees standing in a built-up neighbourhood are chopped down, it's not just a little residue of natural beauty that's gone (as if that were a small thing). Air quality will worsen, carbon won't be stored, and the cooling effect of the tree or the park is gone for ever, creating problems for health that are immediate and resound down the generations. With nature reduced to a simple mark on a map or fleck of green on a planner's design, urban communities are left with just enough nature: the bare minimum to breathe, play, dream, live and unwind.

In their brief history, parks have often been a lifeline thrown to urban communities: islands of green space that persuade us to put up with high rents, small apartments, exhausting work and noisy, polluted streets. But in the last few years I've seen so many developments destroy even these tiny fragments of green, putting profit before people and nature. In working-class areas, the big, signature Victorian parks are allowed to deteriorate as local funding is cut, while leafy council estates built in the golden age of social housing are too often demolished and rebuilt with double the population and half the parkland. Sometimes this toxic combination of neoliberalism, austerity and 'just enough nature' reaches absurd proportions, like in Lambeth in 2019, where a new mixed development of private and social housing was built that gave wealthy property owners access to an attractive landscaped playing field, and council residents a strip of tarmac like a prison ground to play in instead. 'Our children's friends look down from their windows and can't come and join us,' as one resident observed. But like in Mill Park, the 'green space' box had been ticked. Just down the road in Deptford, protesters trying to save a beautiful and lively area of woodland called Old Tidemill Garden were told not to complain – there was green space locally. This turned out to be a strip of grass verge running alongside a noisy, polluted A-road, speckled with cigarette ends and dog shit.

Even access to the big city parks is at risk. Cuts to funding in the UK mean more parks have to self-fund through concerts and private events. Each year, in one of our local Bristol parks, fences go up, stages are built, and the park and playing ground is closed to locals. It's nice to have a festival on your doorstep and hear music playing in your garden on a summer evening. But it's no coincidence that the park sits in a working-class, ethnically diverse area, where cars speed past along the elevation of the M32 and wealth and health inequalities are among the worst in the city. Unlike the commons, public parks are technically private spaces, owned by councils, and vulnerable to being leveraged as a financial asset. That's why it's so attractive to sell off fragments of green space used by poorer communities, while the gated squares beside multimillion-pound properties in wealthy areas remain green idylls for residents with keys to the gate.

Why does this matter? Because if parks really can improve physical and mental health, then everyone needs access to them. For all their inherited design flaws, parks are the most accessible form of nature in most people's lives, giving people space to play, exercise, meet, relax, get away from work, and encounter tough urban critters in the city centre. A 2018–19 monitor of children's engagement with nature found that city parks are the most ethnically diverse and socially mixed green spaces in England, and considerably more diverse than the countryside or coast. The same survey also insists that quality of nature matters, that people find low-quality green space off-putting, and that 'people who spend time outside infrequently are more likely to report poor health and lower levels of life satisfaction'. There are other reasons for this correlation (poverty, inequality and existing health problems mean people don't have the time or the energy to get outdoors). Still, cutting access to parks or failing to invest in their improvement means that people – particularly children – miss out on opportunities to get to know and love nature locally, in ways that might define their entire lives.

What does it feel like to live with or without nature in the city? Beryl Gilroy's *Black Teacher* (1976) gives a glimpse into life in London for working-class and migrant communities when parks were few and far between. Gilroy moved from Guyana to the UK in 1951 to study and find work as a teacher, and would go on to become the first Black head teacher in London. But in inner-city schools and north London suburbs, Gilroy experienced naked and subtle racism from white children and their families. Confronting these bigoted attitudes, she developed innovative theories of teaching and child development. Often this involved nature. On her first day in a new school, Gilroy sings a spontaneous song about a pond as a way of befriending a nervous, prejudiced class:

> There was a pond
> A very big pond,
> That, one spring day, sighed and cried,
> Oh dear, Oh dear, Oh dear, dear, dear
> Why does nothing live in me?
> No fishes, no ducks, no butterflies.

Her lonely lyric brings the children out of hiding. They forget the racist anxieties that they had been taught, and begin to share knowledge of the newts and tadpoles they've stumbled across in the ruins of post-war London: 'I like nature things. I find 'em in the bomb site,' says one little girl with delight.

Gilroy went on to lead nature walks through those bomb sites, cemeteries and patchy urban woodland, helping her pupils gain in confidence as guides and explorers of a city in which they too had very little autonomy or power. These wanderings were far from idyllic, as Gilroy receives abuse from passers-by and even fellow teachers. But with the children, nature provides a meaningful leveller, expanding their sense of possibility and pleasure in life beyond narrowed horizons: 'They ran around stroking tree trunks, running, climbing, shouting – experiencing space and size – finding new textures and consciously listening to the sounds of nature for the first time,' Gilroy observes. Finding solidarity across social differences also helps the children to connect with other creatures – what environmental philosophers describe as a sense of multispecies ethics. Even in fragmentary patches of green, the children meet urban critters whose struggles they identify with, and whose fearlessness and charisma inspires them. This widens their sense of community beyond narrow boundaries. Animals become person-like. They become neighbours.

'Sparrers ain't birds,' as one girl puts it, 'they're Londoners.'

In Hanover the conversation runs late into the evening. I'm getting a handle on the scientific language, even though it's still strange to see something I take for granted being proven, methodically, by all this collective knowledge and experience. What binds us is that everyone is here to fight for more than 'just enough nature'. Each specialist adds another layer, telling the deep story of the connection between health, wellbeing and a biodiverse world.

Wetland plants, molluscs and reed beds upstream filter the water that flows into cities. The more complex and varied the tree cover, the more air is purified and noise pollution reduced, making cities more liveable and beautiful too. The more stimulating an environment, the more patterned and textured and flourishing, the more likely to promote experiences of awe, wonder and humility, as suggested by studies into the richness of trees in forests, fish in ponds, or 'afternoon bird abundances' (one of science's many fabulous, poetic phrases).

I admit I'm angry that we need to do this – to prove the worth of so many threatened species by demonstrating how *our* wellbeing and survival is entangled with theirs. But it's better than an economic argument – the kind that governments find so beguiling – and it is forcing scientists, town planners, and anyone who wants a fair and flourishing future to look beyond 'just enough' green space to envisage a totally different kind of city park, and a different relationship with nature.

In 2020 the first coronavirus lockdown makes people newly desperate to be in parks. Like everyone else, I walk out from my house across the now silent main road to the old-school Victorian park around the corner. Its duck pond is thick with green algae, and the kids' playground and tennis courts are locked. But the lawns are covered in groups – friends and families spaced out in circles, tarpaulins hanging from the trees to shield a kids' birthday party taking place in the rain. People are descending on the park – people I'm sure I've never seen here before. They're seeking pleasure, connection, normality, a place to drink and despair, or a place to be safe for a little while outside their homes.

And it's not just the park. Teenagers and groups of old men who'd usually be in the pub are drinking and smoking along the greenway of the cycle path. A food-distribution group starts running a weeknight BBQ under a bedraggled street tree, as a way of connecting with people who are slipping through the cracks. The cemetery's Gothic iron gates might be bolted shut, but a hole in the fence gapes open, and there are couples picnicking here, their kids playing beside new plots where the flowers on brightly named tributes have only just begun to wilt. We live in a high-density area, and this is the closest thing to a park near many people's homes.

The men who designed city parks did a good job of erasing the politics and history of the land – turning the commons into landscapes of picture-perfect leisure. They also radically altered ecology – diverting water-ways, culverting streams, chopping down forests and mowing meadows into oblivion. But as I walk, I am passing through places people used to hold in common, revealing different ways of living with the land that went before. Green spaces can still be sites of unpredictable, ungovernable disorder, sites of political activism and civil disobedience. In June a Black Lives Matter protest congregates on College Green, and later that day the statue of Edward Colston – which most Bristolians have wanted rid of for years – finally gets rolled from his pedestal into the harbour.

More than ever, parks are reminding us that they're as essential to democracy, protest and the fight for meaningful wellbeing as they were in their old lives as commons.

When we demand more nature in cities, we need to demand more than just enough green space. We need to fight for the biodiversity and ecology, to care about the quality of the water, the liveliness of habitats, and the long-term sustainability of parks. Living through the lockdowns, and seeing how people in built-up cities have suffered through lack of access to wide green space, has made many of us want to see things change urgently – like all the miles of land wasted on golf courses and private estates being reclaimed. It's also convinced me that we need to see beyond the picturesque beauty of the park, and value places that promote biodiversity and link the city to wider ecologies of water systems and animal migration routes.

In their reflections on the ecological horrors and human cost of modern capitalism Anna Tsing and Donna Haraway have both spoken of the need to create and sustain *refugia* – places of refuge – for people and other critters. These are places safe from the extractive ravages of industry, where we can make kin with each other, and with other species, as a kind of social and biological safeguard against the mutually assured destruction of climate crisis. 'I think our job,' Haraway insists, is 'to cultivate with each other in every way imaginable epochs to come that can replenish refuge.'

As the climate crisis worsens, parks are going to need to be *refugia* for humans and non-humans alike. Why should we keep reproducing a design modelled on the tastes of long-dead lords and ladies? What would it mean to have a wetland in a city park, or animals grazing, or places to pick fruit, or to turn city streets into forests where people learn about the natural processes that make the earth truly liveable? It might mean that we fight not just for green space in the city, but for ecology, where people can see 'real' nature on their doorstep, and be empowered to play a part in its future. If we can release ourselves from the notion that only the little wellbeing machine of the landscaped park can truly restore us, or that the flat aesthetic of green space is just good enough, it might open up the possibility of finding other flourishings of nature beautiful – ones that are more biologically rich and ecologically suited to the very hard times ahead.

One day soon, when it's safe to be back on campus, I'll veer away from the paths, up through the shrubs and undergrowth until I no longer see the picture of the landscape that the designers painted so long ago. I'll hopefully take my students with me, and tell them that though the park may not be pure, untouched 'nature', there are things living there, creatures who've found a refuge in the pretty curves and corners of the landscaped grounds. We'll walk through the nettles and stickyweed to the source of the tiny trickle that was dammed to fill the lake, and I'll point out the habitat of crested newts, the messy green pond where they like to wallow in the mud and where, if you're patient, you might see the flicker of their grey and gold bodies through the weed and silt.

People who care about the environment are often accused of being joyless and ascetic, but this makes me feel greedy for life. I don't want just enough nature. I want more.

Farm
Happy Work

'If you need any more eggs in the morning, just help yourself,' Terri explains, lifting the latch to the henhouse.

The occupants, five bolshy chickens and one strutting cockerel with baroque feathered legs, are hopping around our feet and kicking up straw. Peering into the darkness, I see a row of nesting spots all lined up and get a whiff of the musty, earthy interior. On the outside the henhouse is stained a cheerful red and decorated with carved wooden hearts.

It's the tail end of a long, weird summer, and my cousin and I have managed to escape the city for the weekend. She's been working from home in the first coronavirus lockdown, in a cold box room, with a window that looks out onto nothing but a brick wall, on a street that leads into the haze and choke of one of north London's busiest roads. I've been teaching online, getting through the headache-inducing churn of marking on unreliable digital portals. It's a culture shock to find ourselves in a barn conversion in the middle of the Shropshire Hills, surrounded by countryside and animals. Otto, Brandy and Oyster, the resident cows, are about ten feet away in a muddy yard on one side of the cottage we have rented. The sheep, their heads poking through the fence, are a constant, gormless presence at the garden's end.

On Terri's breathless tour, we're introduced to just about every creature individually: the cows, the sheep, the hens, and finally Griselda, the gargantuan candy-floss-pink pig who is so heavily pregnant that all she can do is lie on the floor of the barn, eyes closed, waiting for someone to kick an apple into her mouth.

'We are literally on the farm,' my cousin whispers in astonishment. 'We are *in* the farm.'

Terri leaves us to get settled in. It's almost eight months since my cousin and I have seen each other and we're dying to catch up. Before Terri closes the gate on our little private garden, she tells us how delighted she is to have us stay with them. Renting out this space is still new to them.

'Have you had many people here over the summer?' my cousin asks politely.

'We've barely had the chance to rent it out,' Terri says. 'As soon as we told our friends, they all descended on us.'

'It's a perfect spot,' I say.

'It is!' she agrees. 'They come here to restore.'

Restore – that's exactly it. That's what we're here for – to enjoy the pleasure of being unproductive, deep in the countryside and nature. There's something paradoxical about it, I admit – taking a holiday in someone else's workplace. But something about the farm says 'holiday' to us both. Like so many British children, my cousin and I were raised on a diet of Enid Blyton, where farms are friendly places you stay and stop for picnics and provisions, idyllic haunts of the Children of Cherry Tree Farm and the Famous Five. This wistful sense of the farm as a place of pleasure is still with us, and so many others. From Scandinavia to Italy, the USA to Aotearoa/New Zealand, city workers return to their parents' or grandparents' forest farms, crofts, ranches or gîtes to experience a quieter, simpler, healthier way of life. From Cumbria to the Dordogne, there are B&Bs and Airbnbs aplenty, and even dedicated 'farm stay' hotels, like Thailand's Baan Nork Farm on the edges of Khao Yai National Park, which looks a lot like a luxury resort built next to a petting zoo.

There's an inbuilt nostalgia to all this, and it's proved addictive to lifestyle bloggers, travel journalists, and anyone with something vaguely rustic to promote on social media. Under the influence of these powerful trends, moving from the city to the countryside can feel like moving not just in space, but back in time. In sunlit yards, sipping unpasteurised milk and petting friendly animals, we have the chance to slow down and dwell in the eternal nostalgia of summer.

But the ideal of the countryside as a landscape of wellbeing and leisure is much older than this. The pastoral world of sun, shepherds and simplicity was dreamed up in classical Athens and Rome, and perfected in Virgil's long poem the *Eclogues* (44–38 BCE). In the *Eclogues*, life is long and sweet, work light and simple. Virgil writes of fields and farms, cattle grazing and oxen pulling ploughs, but really these are landscapes of labour in name only. His shepherds are wrapped up in love affairs or napping 'careless in the shade ... on green leaves pillowed'. With its sun-soaked eroticism and diverting dramas, the pastoral is an ideal setting for restoration. Its legacy can be found in farm holidays and rural getaways, where living well means giving yourself up to the flesh and fruits of the land.

The pastoral ideal has also influenced the nature cure. 'Care farming' is now a global movement. Some smallholdings have a sideline as therapy centres, offering spaces for ecotherapists and counsellors to run treatment programmes. More common, though, are dedicated therapy farms, which are funded by charities and healthcare grants rather than by selling produce. You can find such sites all across the USA, UK, Australia, and much of Europe. There's a huge variation in what's on offer, but many combine talking therapies with animal care (or similar versions of animal-assisted therapy) with simple tasks like tending vegetables and farm maintenance, all as part of an established therapeutic community. As Liz Everard writes on the SANE Australia blog, 'They are safe places where people can practise being part of a community, in a space where they are not judged, but are accepted and respected. There is communal recognition that everyone belongs and everyone's contributions matter.'

I'm interested in therapeutic farms, and what they tell us about nature, work and mental health. Many of the dedicated care-farming sites I've visited play up their pastoral heritage. Charismatic animals, sunny green fields and the nostalgic architecture of clay roundhouses and wooden shepherd's huts abound. This is as true of city farms – squeezed into small and vibrant tracts of land between roads and housing estates – as it is for the quiet corners you find deep in the countryside.

The more I think about it, those pastoral therapeutic farms also look a lot like the farm where my cousin and I have come on holiday. The boundary between the 'real' and the simulation, the economic working space and the therapeutic landscape, have become blurred. This raises a question. Where am I supposed to look to really understand the farm's contribution to the nature cure: a real agricultural site, a cutesy care farm, or even a smallholding, where a little work takes place, but most of income is derived from holidaymakers? Should I look for the meaning and the pleasure of the farm and the toil of cultivation, or relax into the pastoral world of the lazy, sunny and unproductive?

I'm tempted to simply enjoy the fruits of the land, rather than get myself mixed up in the work of culturing them. I have a feeling, though, that the nature cure and the farm are connected by work, as well as leisure.

The next morning I'm woken up by the extravagant cockerel next door. The sun has risen behind the curtains and is casting its sad September light. I pick up my phone to check the time. I'm astonished to see it's almost 8.30 a.m. I thought cockerels were supposed to be dawn criers, dragging the whole farm out of bed for an exhausting day of work?

Over breakfast on the decking, we spot Terri taking out some feed for the sheep. She checks if we had a good night, and we ask what time she was up that morning. She and Steve get up at a sensible 7 a.m., leaving the animals to fend for themselves.

'That's later than I get up for work most days,' my cousin whispers, after Terri has wandered off, a bucket swinging in her hand. She works in market research, and the difference between her hours and our farming hosts seems somehow wrong.

There's nothing for us to do that day, so we loll about in the sun, drinking endless coffees and getting into the pastoral mood. A robin tries to land in the glass feeder hanging from a tree, and my cousin fiddles with her camera trying to get the perfect shot, while I read and stare out over the fields at the rows of hedges that seem to go on forever.

Terri has told us that we're welcome to pick fruit and veg from the polytunnel behind our cottage. Before lunch, when I'm looking for some light activity, I follow the path around the yard and let myself in through the unzipped plastic door. There are rows and rows of tomato plants in there, their cherry clusters bright red at the top, turning orange then yellow and green at the tip. I help myself to a bowlful, then twist a striped courgette off its trailing vine, spiking myself gently on its jungle leaves. I feel a bit of a fraud, enjoying the fruits of someone else's labour, but at the same time there's huge satisfaction in spotting the plump fruit and tugging it from the vine. Nan Shepherd writes of the pleasures of simple acts, like lighting a fire or drawing water from a well: 'you are touching life, and something within you knows it.' Picking vegetables, it also feels like I am touching life, doing something pure and 'authentic', after months of dematerialised work on screen and Zoom.

I'm embarrassed when I bump into Terri in the yard. With the best of her crop in my hands, I feel like a thief who's just been caught scrumping. It's a relief to see her obvious delight that we're making ourselves at home. I congratulate her on the fruitfulness of her kitchen garden (a guaranteed way to make friends with growers) and take the opportunity to ask her about the labour behind these serene scenes.

It is, she admits, hard work. The farm has been going for five years, much of which was spent renovating the run-down smallholding, working through blizzards and gales. They were beset with illness all the way, a scary bout of cancer and major surgeries in hospitals far away and difficult to access on country roads, with animals demanding attention at home.

'But is it *worth* it?' I ask. The answer's a firm yes. This was their dream for so long – to give it all up and get back to the land. So, ten years shy of retirement, they decided it was now or never. They put their house in the city on the market, quit their jobs, and started scouting round for an old farm and some land that the two of them could manage.

'It was time to finally do something worth doing,' Terri says.

Seeking a farm life wasn't about escaping from work into the sunny ideal of the pastoral. They wanted to be free of unfulfilling and stressful work, and instead take on work they believed would be more pleasurable, interesting, and inherently rewarding. It's not only closeness to nature and autonomy, then. The work of the farm itself is meant to be healing. Perhaps to find the real nature cure, I need to look beyond the pastoral, to another classical invention: the Georgic.

This tradition also originates with Virgil. In the *Georgics* (29 BCE), he told a very different story of the countryside: one of labour. Unlike the endless summer holiday of the pastoral, the *Georgics* are an extensive almanac of farming methods, with advice on when to plant and sow, how to keep bees and coax vines to fruition. This isn't a life of leisure, but happy work, where 'Round on the labourer spins the wheel of toil, / As on its own track rolls the circling year'. Each season brings its own demands, chores to be ticked off the long list in the farmer's head, with the threat of crop failure and poor harvests if things go wrong. But still, it's a worthy life, where the 'all too happy tillers of the soil' get their just rewards.

There can be something deeply comforting about this idea of rewarding labour. 'Grow your own' and home-baking seem to have a middle-class renaissance every few years, while stories of real working farmers continue to appeal to a modern Georgic sensibility, furnishing a hungry audience with 'authentic' tales from the land. There's the junk-viewing delights of the BBC's *Love in the Countryside* (where farmers are hooked up with folk from the city looking for a change) – and books too, like James Rebanks' *The Shepherd's Life: A Tale of the Lake District* (2015). A diary of a year running a sheep farm in Cumbria, it details the minutiae of shepherding in the high, unforgiving terrain of the Lakeland fells. The challenges of good stockmanship, the miracle of sheepdog training, and time-consuming, collective tasks like gathering free-roaming sheep or bringing in rain-drenched hay are described with meticulous detail, creating an addictive account of an expert at work.

The book was marketed as an 'English pastoral', but Rebanks' Lake District is no holiday park. This is a place where fly-strike takes down healthy animals, where chemical run-off poisons streams, where fatal sickness like the BSE epidemic hits, and where anything from winter to haymaking to snowfall can be 'a bitch'. But compared with life in city, these tasks are no great hardship. When he was a child, Rebanks' teachers encouraged poor farmers' kids to get 'good' white-collar office jobs. But when Rebanks takes up a summer job in the 'crazy manic atmosphere' of London, he feels rootless and anonymous. Only then does he realise why the tourists flock to Cumbria, 'to feel the wind in their hair and the sun on their faces'. This is English Georgic, with a drop of the nature cure, and it's no wonder it struck a chord with an urban readership hungry for stories of the good life and the happy work of the farm.

But just like the pastoral, the Georgic is often romanticised. It's easy to celebrate the charms of 'real' work from a distance, and to imagine that the farmer's life is full of joy when your own work keeps you tucked behind a desk. People have been idealising the work of farmers for centuries and playing out their fantasies, too. The academic and poet Helen Charman has written of the history of the 'pleasure dairy', and how

in nineteenth-century Britain, the large country estates of the landed gentry would often include two kinds of dairy: a working dairy, where butter, milk, cheese and cream were made by working-class women, and a 'fancy', 'polite', or 'pleasure' dairy. The latter construction followed an architectural trend from early modern France (enthusiastically adopted by Marie Antoinette) in which a fake dairy was installed, often with extremely ornate décor, so the ladies of the house could pretend to engage in what was considered to be pleasing, domestic, appropriately feminine work, without having to do any actual labour.

While the pleasure dairy was just farming-theatre for the rich, the promise of 'the good life' continues to tempt people of all classes back to the land. My grandparents were among teams of working-class Londoners who would up sticks in the early summer to pick hops in Kent. Farming was a holiday for them, and allowed them to experience a different kind of work – in the open air, surrounded by apple trees for scrumping, rivers for swimming, and nights spent sleeping on hay under the stars. I never got the chance to speak to my grandparents about it – they died when I was still young – but a fellow picker, Mozie Fenn, who was interviewed about her experiences in the 1950s, spoke of how 'it was hard work but so rewarding to experience the countryside. My main memories are of it being muddy and wet all the time. But we never minded. We all enjoyed each other's company. All mucking in together. It was special, pulling the last bine before we went home.'

Hopping disappeared in the late 1960s, as automation replaced hand-picking, and camping and package holidays made leisure breaks more affordable for poorer families. But farming as a working summer holiday still captures the imagination. I missed the call to go 'wwoofing' (WorldWide Opportunities on Organic Farms) in my twenties, but plenty of friends who wanted to get a slice of rural life applied for places on small organic farms, with volunteer destinations all across the world. Sue Coppard, who set up the first wwoofing schemes in the 1970s, explains her motivations: 'WWOOF answers the needs of so many people it had to happen; contact with nature is the psychological equivalent of Vitamin C. I feel that WWOOF chose me as its channel – a London secretary with no rural friends or family but pining for the countryside as I watched the autumn leaves blowing along the pavement.'

Reconnecting with the cycle of the seasons, developing sensuous awareness of living things, and going back to the land: these are the bread-and-butter treatments of the nature cure. But in wwoofing, they are brought to life by the experience of work. Tending mixed crops using sustainable organic methods, offers a kind of eco-Georgic gap year for people who don't have the money to go travelling. My friends who were drawn to wwoofing were certainly unimpressed with the kinds of precarious employment on offer in bars, shops and temping agencies. You don't get paid to go wwoofing, but you do get a place to stay, your meals cooked for you, and some useful training in farming skills. Typical wwoofers include people who want a career in conservation, or set up a smallholding, or find some kind of balance between seasonal work, environmental activism and volunteering – people trying to discover, in essence, how to live a low-impact, socially useful life, with work they believe matters at its heart.

This is the point – and what Terri was telling me as I cradled her late-summer harvest in my arms. Farm work offered an antidote to and an escape from other kinds of work. In her previous life she was a teacher – an occupation that's usually thought of as fulfilling. But the endless paperwork, underfunding, overwork, shifting targets, and the feeling the whole system was grossly unfair… over the years, they ground her down.

She is not alone. Work–based stress is one of the main reasons people who might otherwise be well experience mental ill health. If you work an executive job, you might be able to access a short course of CBT (cognitive behavioural therapy) through your employer's health insurance, or simply ask for a sabbatical. If you're a freelancer, or underpaid, or otherwise precarious, you're probably on your own. But no amount of 'resilience training', wellbeing workshops or lunchtime yoga can solve deep and structural problems with modern work. Exploitative conditions, unsafe workplaces, a toxic productivity culture, job insecurity and tasks that simply can't be completed in paid hours all make work – whether in an office, factory or building site – something that's almost uncannily designed to push people to their limits. On top of this, many people know their jobs have no purpose. It's the 'bullshit jobs' phenomenon described by anthropologist David Graeber. Society tells us to valorise work and to connect our innate self-worth with the jobs we do. When that work feels pointless, we can experience it as a 'profound psychological violence'. It can feel like life has no meaning.

But farming *isn't* a bullshit job. If you want to do something that's useful, that no one could do without, farming is one of the most fundamentally important activities going. Wresting the matter of life from the earth is a primary creative activity, meaning that even when the work is tiring and harsh, it holds intrinsic value. The harshness of agricultural life may even be part of its value, as James Rebanks suggests in his memoir.

There's a biological dimension to this too. Scientists interested in wellbeing point out that endorphins released in exercise have a strong connection with positive mood. This is why farm therapies are often likened to activities like walking, aerobics or swimming. Farming also provides a steady supply of repetitive, routine and (for the beginner) relatively simple chores. These kinds of activities can promote mindfulness and feelings of absorption: what the philosopher Drew Leder calls 'bodily absence'. We experience bodily absence when we are so preoccupied with our activities that consciousness of the body – paradoxically – disappears. Psychologists describe this experience as oneness, flow or 'being away', and call it therapeutic. It's at the heart of so many somatic therapies, from dance to art, crafts to sport. Combined with the attention-restoration and stress-reduction effects associated with nature, this helps explain why farming therapies are having their moment, and being seen as a pleasurable antidote to the sedentary culture of office work.

I think about this culture of work as I'm having a drink before dinner. The sun is on its way towards the horizon, and although the day has been warm, there's a cool bite in the air that reminds us autumn is coming. Tiny birds are hopping around the garden, cows dawdle in the field, crows cackle at the far end of the orchard. Lying on the table, my phone pings intermittently. Work is catching up with me, always, and catching up with my cousin too. We've booked time off work for our holidays, but she's taking a moment to look at her emails anyway.

'It stresses me out to know they're piling up in there,' she admits, and suddenly I feel a weight of dread about my own job – the feeling that I'm failing at it, that I'll never catch up – and that all this little respite is doing is setting us up to be more stressed when we return.

Nature is supposed to cure us of this feeling, to restore us so that we can return to our work refreshed. But the culture of work manages to infect everything. Our feelings of self-worth are just too bound up with work. Putting in face-time, staying after hours, outdoing our colleagues on whatever target has been set are all part of a boss-pleasing culture where the boundaries between our innermost selves and the job become blurred. Work is no longer just a means to an end, or a compromise we make so that we can focus on the pleasures of living at weekends and holidays. Work has become a calling, an ethic, a way of life.

The Protestant Ethic – that's what the German sociologist Max Weber called it. Writing at the turn of the twentieth century, Weber proposed that the spirit of capitalist work culture was actually grounded in religious sentiment, especially the renunciation of worldly pleasure and comfort, which would prove you were virtuous. From factory labourers to office clerks, people seemed to be obsessed, working harder and longer hours at the expense of happiness and health. Work was not just about making a livelihood. It was moral, spiritual, a vocation. Whether or not we agree with the details of Weber's account, it's definitely true that work is often held in a strange reverence, as 'a path to individual self-expression, self-development, and creativity', as political theorist Kathi Weeks puts it. Being 'hard-working' or a 'good worker' are still labels worn with pride, while 'shirker' or 'lazy' are about as brutal an insult as you can throw.

Current language used to describe mental illness reveals how deeply the work ethic has penetrated ideas about sickness and healing too. Most modern theories of wellbeing have work as a fundamental pivot, the foundation on which a good life is built. Take the Recovery Star, designed by the Association of Mental Health Providers and recommended as a wellbeing toolkit by the UK's Department of Health. With ten points, the star shows the steps needed to go from the mental health equivalent of zero to a fully flourishing life, including progress on areas like 'Trust and Hope', 'Relationships', 'Responsibilities' and of course, 'Work'. Like many state-sponsored programmes, its understanding of recovery is based on a model of 'busy-ness as usual', with work as an essential step to building self-respect, confidence, a sense of independence, and control over one's destiny. The *type* of work – whether the worker has a voice in how the workplace is run, whether the work is actually socially beneficial – does not figure so prominently.

Mental health services are often geared to this end – getting people fit and fighting again, so they can get back to work, putting one individual after another back on that treadmill of productivity. 'I have been taking antidepressants for twelve years now, and they work in as much as they have made me economically functional,' as London-based writer Narayani Menon reflects. Of course, unemployment is also one of the key determinants of mental illness. Being unemployed can be isolating, and where welfare support is impossibly difficult to access or altogether lacking, unemployment leads to poverty and homelessness, which comes with its own terrible health burden. The guilt of not being able to work, of not being *productive*, is something slightly different, though. People living with serious mental ill health often experience a painful concoction of guilt and existential despair, worthlessness and shame, which exacerbates their condition, and is perhaps sometimes even worse than the condition itself, if such distinctions can be made. And much of this is to do with the temporary or long-term inability to work in ways capitalist society deems valuable.

Nothing about this is universal. The idea that work is the meaning of life is peculiar to capitalist theories of wellness. Other cultures have found the good life elsewhere. In Chinese and Ayurvedic systems, activity is important, but 'care has to be taken to avoid overexertion and strain'. In the Qigong tradition of movement and exercise, which originated in ancient China, hard physical labour was best minimised or avoided altogether. In the Galenic medicine of ancient Greece and Rome, effort needed to be balanced with rest and relaxation. Indeed, the lazy pleasures of the pastoral are a perfect example of how dearly idleness was prized in classical cultures. The anthropologist James C. Scott even proposes that the shift from hunter-gatherer to agriculturalist societies in the Neolithic period was not driven, as has often been argued, by a sudden enthusiasm for prudent forethought, but by innovative new techniques for doing *less* work. What an intriguing proposition: that the origins of agriculture lie not in anxious precarity, but pleasant idleness.

In our farm retreat in Shropshire, my cousin and I are trying to recapture that lazy innocence. Switching off my phone, slamming my laptop shut, I'm enjoying the pastoral vibes. I'm channelling Paul Lafargue, the son-in-law of Karl Marx, who wrote the iconoclastic essay *The Right to Be Lazy* (1883). He blamed powerful leaders for casting a 'sacred halo over work', and the working classes for buying into this 'strange delusion', consenting to 'bend their backs', 'exhaust their nerves', and 'kill within themselves all beautiful faculties, to leave nothing alive and flourishing except the furious madness for work'. It wasn't just better pay and fairer conditions workers should fight for, Lafargue argued, but an end to the cult of productivity altogether. Instead of exhausting themselves creating absurd wealth for bosses and an excess of stuff, people could work much shorter days, perhaps only for a couple of hours, focusing on manufacturing only the essentials. The rest of the time they could devote to pleasurable leisure, being creative, improving their health, savouring the joys of nature and enjoying the right 'to make love and to frolic, to banquet joyously in honor of the jovial god of idleness'.

Over a century later, post-work organisations like the London-based think tank Autonomy campaign for a universal basic income and four-day week, and continue to push back against the work ethic. Post-work thinking isn't about no one doing anything, but about starting a serious, critical, hopeful and just conversation about the kinds of things that actually need to get done. There are deep and disturbing problems with work, and the fact is we do too much of it. Rather than being a path to perfect health, resisting the temptation to work ourselves to the bone is likely to improve wellbeing and limit environmental harm. It is, after all, overconsumption and excess production that keeps economies growing beyond all sense and ecological capacities. Released from the demand of overwork, overproduction and overconsumption, other issues might capture our attention instead.

This is what Jenny Odell proposes in *How to Do Nothing: Resisting the Attention Economy* (2019). When our value is determined by our productivity, doing nothing can be an act of political resistance. 'Rerouting and deepening one's attention to place will likely lead to awareness of one's participation in history and in a more-than-human community,' she writes. Restoring attention, doing nothing, isn't about cutting oneself off from the world, but more deeply committing oneself to it. Think of the Fridays for Future school-strike movement started by Swedish teenager Greta Thunberg in 2015, or the extraordinary acts of protest, education and resource-sharing that took place in early summer 2020, when so many furloughed or unemployed workers and young people whose studies had been paused turned their energies to supporting Black Lives Matter. When our attention isn't arrested or wasted on the inessentials, we might find ourselves able to do more, not less.

This 'rerouting of attention' is one of the things that first got me interested in the nature cure. What could be more joyful, and more political, than resisting work of all kinds, to turn our attention to the lazy beauty of nature? But what if the cult of work infects the nature cure? What if farm therapies begin to look less like the sunny pleasures of the pastoral, or the joyful toil of the Georgic, and end up looking like… well… work?

Earlier in the summer, I saw a supermarket TV ad promoting fruit-picking jobs, sponsored by the

National Farmers' Union and the Department for Environment, Food and Rural Affairs. Over black-and-white images of mud-stained flesh and verdant fields curiously devoid of modern technology, a voice croons a nostalgic, rousing message:

> Pick getting out of the house. Pick being out in the fresh air. Pick fruit. Pick veg. Pick tired limbs and aching muscles. Pick early mornings and bleary eyes. Pick a hard day's graft. Pick the sun on your back and the dirt under your nails... Pick being part of something bigger.

Its tone evoked the Blitz-spirit, 'Big Society' ethos that marked the UK's austerity years. Farming was something special, it announced: a summer job crossed with recruitment into a proud new key-worker land army. That's what it was going for, but as many people pointed out, its rhetoric was remarkably similar to the anti-work 'choose life' polemic of Irvine Welsh's *Trainspotting* (1993). If I was feeling cynical, I'd say it came across as a desperate attempt to lure unemployed UK nationals into precarious and low-paid work in order to fill a shortfall in seasonal workers caused by the chaos of Brexit and Covid-19.

There's nothing new about the connection between farming and the moral imperative to work. From the late eighteenth century a new kind of moral-management asylum came into existence in France and Britain. In Greatford Hall, run by Francis Willis – the man famous for treating King George III in the 1780s – or the York Retreat, set up by the Tuke family, the discipline of collective work was used to treat patients. These asylums looked like houses and were surrounded by farmland. Arriving at Greatford Hall in 1796, a visitor described how he was 'astonished to find almost all the surrounding ploughmen, gardeners, threshers, thatchers and other labourers attired in black coats, white waistcoats, black silk breaches and stockings ... These were the doctor's patients ...'

In many ways, places like this offered liberation that was radical in its day. They were inspired by the farming community of Geel, in Belgium, where, since the fourteenth century, farmers had welcomed the mentally afflicted into their homes. In this non-judgemental religious community, boarders could – and still can – find a place of solace and acceptance, away from orthodox psychiatric diagnosis or institutionalisation.

But in Geel, recovery was not obligatory. Many boarders spent their lives there, unharried and unsaved, free to be themselves, even if that meant being very different from the norm. And for this reason, the use of work in moral-management asylums evokes other, less benign institutions. The twentieth-century philosopher and historian Michel Foucault suggests as much in *Discipline and Punish: The Birth of the Prison* (1975/7). Telling the long, entangled history of healthcare and incarceration, he connects the work cure of the asylum with the management of workhouses, prisons and factories. The movement of people classed as 'mad' into the working asylum during the early nineteenth century was, as he argues, part of a seamless transition shared with these other disciplinary institutions. They were all geared to one goal: making the unemployed, poor, mentally unwell and unproductive fit to work.

Moral management wasn't confined to the cities of Europe. In the 1800s, in the colonised West Indies, the idea that organised farm labour was a good way of disciplining patients was imported by British doctors. Lincolnshire asylum manager Thomas Allen arrived in Kingston, Jamaica in 1863, and was tasked with improving appalling conditions in existing institutions there. Implementing tried and tested moral management approaches, he quickly established a work programme, directing patients to clear land and plant cotton and vegetables. Allen's asylum soon began to pull in a huge profit: so much that it uncannily resembled the plantations abolished a couple of decades earlier. Slave owners had made vast wealth exploiting enslaved African men, women and children. After emancipation, in asylums all across the West Indies, dark-skinned patients were seen as 'natural workers' by white asylum doctors, and set to labour in farms and workshops for the 'good of their health'.

We can't compare modern work therapies with these terrible histories. But there are lines of inheritance. In the USA numerous prisons operate gardening and agriculture programmes. Sometimes run in collaboration with external non-profit organisations, these 'farm to prison' projects have many laudable goals, including skills training, improving diet through access to fresh produce, and – of course – mental health and wellbeing. While it's certainly true that the dehumanising conditions of prison can be significantly mitigated by access to horticultural therapy and education, such projects are also part of a prison system that exploits penal labour for the profit of over 4,000 private companies (which all, naturally, pride themselves on the wonderful contributions they are making to society). The exploitation of penal servitude is made possible by the Thirteenth Amendment to the United States Constitution, which abolished slavery, but made an exception for prisoners. Many inmate agricultural workers go entirely unpaid, or must work for a few cents per hour. Looking more closely at present penitentiary populations in the USA – where African Americans charged with minor offences are disproportionately represented – you might conclude that capitalism is carceral, and that profit motives have dangerously distorted the therapeutic potential of the prison farm.

In the UK it's no coincidence that farming therapies began to attract a lot of interest during the austerity years of the 2010s. During this period deep financial cuts were made across public services as part of Conservative policy to shrink the welfare state. Mental health services were particularly badly affected, and health trusts under serious pressure to slim down their budgets. In such a context, nature-cure therapies began to look newly appealing. Some of the biggest costs to the health service are medicines, buildings and staffing, so green care's ability to move treatments out of doors, to use low-cost, voluntary providers with a good track record of limiting patients' drug dependency, was an obvious win for NHS finances. Even better, farming therapies could be sold as a treatment designed to funnel people back into work.

One study, 'The Economic Benefits of Ecominds' (2013) explains how this works. At the report's centre is the story of how a care-farming placement affected the life of a woman called Joanne. It begins by telling us a little bit about Joanne, how 'she had become unwell in her late teens and had never held a job', and now was 'overweight and unfit, rurally isolated and inactive'. Throwing in a little casual fat-phobia to emphasise the trough of unproductiveness Joanne had fallen into, the report then tells a positive story of her recovery. A short placement on a farm builds her confidence, and she goes on to gain a place as an apprentice and, eventually, paid work on a farm. The report then offers a meticulous breakdown of all the ways care farming benefited the public purse, saving the taxpayer over £12,000 a year. Cuts in medicine bills, nurses and consultants, even money recouped in benefits that the state didn't need to pay now she was able to work – they all stacked up.

The organisation behind the report was doing its best to sell a novel treatment to a suspicious government. They made a pragmatic decision and used the only language that a Conservative government would understand: money. Farm therapies could easily be spoken of in that language, offering an economically convincing work and nature cure. But the financialisation of mental health and nature has real-world repercussions. Although it is often expedient to accept reductive language to get projects funded and make good things happen, it opens the door to new kinds of harm. Joanne seems to have found a place of safety and independence through her experiences on the farm – and that's a very good thing. But why was it not enough to fund the services that might make people feel better, whatever the cost? And what would have happened if her treatment was not found to be a sound investment?

That's the problem with idealising the work of the farm and treating the countryside as a holiday camp. It becomes easy to forget that farms are part of the machinery of modern capitalism – and the point at which people, and nature, are so often exploited.

After dinner, I take a walk out across the hills behind the cottage where we're staying. I reach the peak of the hill as the sun sets. Below me the fields and hedgerows turn golden – miles and miles of arable and grazing land, rich in cows and corn, barley and sheep. So much of southern England looks this way – it's a landscape that's immediately comforting and nostalgic to me, more familiar and representative of quiet, restorative nature than mountains and oceans. It's hard to admit that it's ecologically devastated. Wildlife, soil fertility, water retention – all have been sacrificed in the work of producing profit from the land, pushing it to be hyper-productive in the short term without thinking of the long-term damage.

Scientists now mostly accept that we're living in the age of Anthropocene, when the environmental consequences of modern industry have made a lasting mark on the geology and ecology of the earth. It's a useful term, but I'm more convinced by Anna Tsing's Plantationocene, which traces the roots of our environmental crisis to the sugar and tobacco plantations of the colonised world, where modern agricultural capitalism originated. Now biodiverse regions are still trampled to make way for monoculture crops – thousands of kilometres of palm oil across Indonesia and Malaysia, fields of cattle that spread across former rain and cloud forests in Argentina and Brazil. These plantations drain the land of water and degrade the soil, turning rich earth to dead dust. Agro-capitalism is a major contributor to climate crisis, pollution and extinction, with carbon and water footprints to rival transport and industry. Half of the world's habitable land is now used for agriculture, and 77 per cent of that for livestock. Industrial mega-dairies, of the kind that cover much of the USA and northern Europe, are often celebrated as low-impact, environmentally friendly solutions, with a smaller land, water and carbon footprint than grazing fields. But the real impact of these farms is hidden, as the concentrated animal feed that powers them is harvested from 'ghost acres' in the Global South, where soy and cassava are harvested. Even the pellets that we fed to the sheep on Terri and Steve's farm are likely to share these unsavoury origins.

The entanglement of humanity and nature on the farm is part of what's supposed to make it so healing. But zoonotic viruses, which jump the species barrier from animal to human, thrive in the cramped and filthy conditions of industrial farms. Cost-saving practices – like feeding animals infected meat and rubbish – spread diseases, and the global trade in meat and animal tissue means that when sickness flares up, it spreads fast. Some of the recent forerunners of Covid-19 – including bird and swine flus – originated in mega-dairies and poultry facilities. Now experts warn that more devastating future viruses await us if we continue to encroach into wild ecosystems and exploit animals for profit.

Modern agriculture isn't harmless to mental health, either. Reading the recent therapeutic farming studies, you'd assume farmers must have the best mental health out there. But farmers are facing unbearable pressure. In Australia, research suggests their mental health is at a record low, with the suicide rate for young men – particularly in Indigenous communities – among the highest in the country. The fact that rural communities tend to be poorly served by mental health resources doesn't help. Neither does the fact that farmers are at the ragged edge of the climate crisis. Drought, fire, flood and disease create hardship and anxiety. In countries that are least responsible for the climate crisis, farmers are being forced to adapt quickly to cope with disturbing fluctuations in rainfall and temperature. Across the drought-prone saddle of Central Africa, the semi-arid Iberia region of south-eastern Spain, and the 'dry corridor' of South America, farmers are watching crops shrivel. More subsistence farmers are in danger of becoming climate refugees – forced to move by natural disasters compounded by deep-rooted injustices like poverty, corruption and an exploitative trade market. According to the International Organisation for Migration, up to 200 million people could be displaced by rising global temperatures by 2050.

The stranglehold of global corporations also makes farming a traumatic, even fatal enterprise. Over the last thirty years, agricultural giants Cargill and Monsanto have been implicated in spikes in suicides among farmers across the Global South. These corporations have a dirty track record of forcing their crops and pesticides onto smallholders, covering up research into the dangers of their chemical products. By offering loans to cash-strapped farmers and convincing them that only lab-modified, drought-resistant, super-high-yield seeds can solve the problems of food production, agro-tech giants force farmers into cycles of debt and poverty. As the Indian scientist and philosopher Vandana Shiva explains, this practice is particularly abusive because seed 'is not merely the source of future plants and food, it is the storage place of culture and history'. In many traditional farming cultures, growers share seeds freely, practising co-operation and reciprocity, and sharing ecological know-how. But when a seed is genetically modified and patented, the law makes it someone else's intellectual property. It can't be exchanged freely.

In places where one bad harvest may be the difference between subsistence and death, generosity and co-operation aren't just wholesome add-ons: they're essential. To survive the climate crisis, these are principles we must learn to fight for and practise, fast. Shiva speaks of the Indian principle of *ahimsic krishi* – 'non-violent agriculture' – a form of low-impact, low-cost organic farming based on compassion for all species. She also urges a move beyond the economics of scarcity – where the material of life is hoarded or kept scarce – to one of abundance, where food and essentials are produced sustainably and shared equitably. After all, the world already generates more than enough food to feed everyone. Famine and poverty are failures of distribution, not abundance.

It may seem wild in the midst of the climate crisis to be dwelling on abundance and plenty. One knee-jerk response to our predicament is to lament overpopulation and pray some techno-fix will come along to expand the planet's capacity. But we have to stop imagining that we can carry on business as usual while squeezing more from the planet with endless technological innovations. The writer Margaret Atwood has said we shouldn't really think of it as 'climate change': we should think of it as 'everything change'. And part of the 'everything' that needs fundamental rethinking is how the world farms. Our choices really do make the difference between a world of starvation, and one of plenty.

What might future farming look like? A little bit new and a little bit old – even ancient.

It might mean a return to precolonial land-use practices and a revival of Indigenous knowledge. Bruce Pascoe advocates for this in *Dark Emu* (2014), a book that reveals the suppressed history of Aboriginal Australian agricultural practices. Colonisers spread the myth that Aboriginal people weren't farmers, but instead of a virgin land, a *terra nullius*, what the colonisers really stumbled upon were cultivated fields so lush that they looked like the arable fields of England. These settlers told fantastical stories about their untouched Eden at the same time as they brutally suppressed Aboriginal people and their agricultural practices, dismissing the knowledge with which they'd turned these plains into fertile farmland over millennia. When they claimed the land, colonialists imported farming methods suitable for the soil and climate of northern Europe. But after a few generations of this 'superior' British cultivation, the land became dry and poor. Imported sheep trashed the soil, turning the fine humus, which Indigenous methods had carefully protected, into barren, infertile dust. The crops and grasses favoured by Aboriginal communities – like kangaroo grass, or the flour-producing cumbungi rush – were forcibly replaced with European crops that struggled and faltered. The central grain belt of the country, as tended by Aboriginal people, originally stretched from coast to coast through the heart of the arid landscape now called the Outback. By the 1970s, fertile land in Australia had shrunk to two measly coastal corridors.

'Wellbeing' means nothing without clean water and fertile soil. In Australia, real ecological wellbeing might be achieved by reclaiming the old methods and handing the land back to its Indigenous custodians. The principle of food sovereignty is vital in all this. It is 'the right to healthy and culturally appropriate food produced through ecologically sound and sustainable methods', combined with 'people's right to define their own agriculture systems.' And so too, the demand for common land, local control of resources, and placing the knowledge of farmers at the centre of political struggle.

When farm workers down tools and strike, or form collectives to push for change, they're taking part in a long tradition of rural resistance, saying no to the exhaustion of humanity and ecosystems in the hope of something better for everyone. It was in farming, after all, that modern socialism was born. In 1649 Gerrard Winstanley claimed that 'true freedom lies where a man receives his nourishment and preservation, and that is in the use of the earth'. He was one of a group of True Levellers who tore down hedges and fences erected by aristocrats and landowners, and started farming on the common land of St George's Hill in Weybridge. The Diggers – as they came to be known – were a breakaway Christian group, but they also represented an embryonic communism. In their manifesto, 'The True Levellers' Standard Advanced' (1649), they proclaimed that land should be held as a Common Treasury, not hoarded or sold. Peasants would work together to feed themselves and their community, not grow luxuries for landowners. They would share the essentials of life, and observe and respect the productive limits of the land. This was as much about pragmatism as it was about love, health and mutual care – all the key ingredients of what we now call 'wellbeing':

> That which does encourage us to go on in this work, is this; we find the streaming out of Love in our hearts towards all; to enemies as well as friends; we would have none live in Beggary, Poverty, or Sorrow, but that everyone might enjoy the benefit of his creation: we have peace in our hearts, and quiet rejoicing in our work, and filled with sweet content, though we have but a dish of roots and bread for our food.

These are early modern ideals, but they still have meaning now. For the last twenty years, the International Day of Peasants' Struggle has been a rallying call for hauntingly similar rights. Uniting local and national peasant networks all around the world, global organising and activism finally led to the *UN Declaration on the Rights of Peasants and Other People Working in Rural Areas* (UNDROP) in 2018. As Pramesh Pokharel of La Via Campesina writes, 'small food producers; peasants, landless, rural workers, herders, forest dwellers, pastoralists, fisher folks and people living in rural areas who produce more than 70 per cent of the world's food in harmony with nature do not get a dignified life'. But the rights enshrined in UNDROP provide a powerful point of reference for peasants 'in their local struggles for seeds, land, or better working conditions … while also offering them tangible prospects for decent working and living conditions, consequently making this world a safer place for peasants.' Co-operative farming is an act of love and care, realised in collective labour. It's capable of feeding the many without exhausting nature, and it might also be a part of repairing relationships between people and the land.

In the 1960s another farmer, the author Bessie Head, discovered the connection between wellbeing and agricultural work in her adopted home of Botswana. Head was born in Fort Napier Mental Institution, South Africa, in 1937. Her white, middle-class family quickly passed Head – a mixed-race child born to an institutionalised mother under the country's racist apartheid laws – to a poor Black family, leaving them to raise her. She would not learn about her origins until she turned eighteen.

'The least I can say for myself is that I forcefully created for myself, under extremely hostile conditions, my ideal life,' Head wrote in 1975. She had trained to be a teacher before working as a journalist on Black-run, anti-apartheid magazines. But after years of struggling, she escaped to Botswana in 1964. Traumatised and living as a stateless refugee, she 'took an obscure and almost unknown village in the Southern African bush, and made it hallowed ground'. The village was Serowe, located in a sleepy corner of impoverished land that had been largely overlooked by colonial powers. When Head arrived, Serowe was experiencing a devastating drought. Dehydrated cattle dropped dead in the bush. Crops faltered. And yet her writing sings with love for this place. She christened it 'the village of the rain wind', to celebrate the moment in summer when great gusts of wind blew cold, fresh rain across the bush, and the 'earth and sky heave alive and there is magic everywhere'.

Much of Head's writing focuses on the trials of co-operative farming in the years when Botswana claimed independence from British rule. Her first novel, *When Rain Clouds Gather* (1969), tells the story of Makhaya, a refugee who joins a community transitioning from precarious subsistence ploughing and cattle rearing to a future of nourishing staples and cash crops. These were trials Head experienced in person at co-operative projects in Serowe and Radisele, where she became familiar with techniques to conserve rain, restore tired soil, and grow crops that would survive and protect the community from starvation in lean years. Development, for her, meant collective struggle against want and racism. It was geared towards self-sustenance and independence for the whole community. Profits wouldn't be hoarded, but shared, in a modern co-operative model that blended ideas from socialism with precolonial forms of exchange.

There were successes and failures, triumphs and sore points. But co-operative farming moved Head's community away from dependence on imports, allowing poor people to build up 'their own economy, where no one is exploiting them and they control their own affairs'. The co-operation and anti-racism that flourished there, built on a collective dedication to the land, chimed with Head's own deeply egalitarian principles and her urgent need for healing. Farming contained the fundamental elements needed to recover from despair, liberate a people, and spark hopeful blows against the past. She wrote about farming as a love letter to Botswana, but also to send a powerful message back to Black people in South Africa, and to remind them, 'this is what we really ought to have'.

Head's story isn't one of simple recovery. The brutality of her upbringing never left her, and hallucinations, depression and attacks of paranoia and violence meant she was often alienated from her community and intermittently hospitalised. She wrote about these experiences in her final novel, *A Question of Power* (1972). Like Head, her heroine Elizabeth is a South African who finds refuge in a Botswana village, working alongside others in a development farm before her delusions become unmanageable and frightening.

Although farming wasn't enough to ward off another breakdown for Head, or for Elizabeth, when clarity is achieved it is often through immersion in the activities of the farm. Head found she could become 'self-absorbed' in meditative labour, feeling herself 'unfold' in conversation with the soil. In farming, she explained, one discovers the 'oneness of the soul with all living things, whether human or animal or vegetable'. There's a sheer sensuous delight in Head's description of farm work. There's less of the work ethic and more of dance and delight. In *A Question of Power*, the place where the same release happens for her character Elizabeth is described as a refuge of beauty and promise, emerging from the dry landscape, 'shimmering with bright green leaves', 'alive with gently seeping water'.

Moments of liberation are grasped in the humility and humanity of people Elizabeth works with, too. 'It is impossible to become a vegetable gardener without at the same time coming into contact with the wonderful strangeness of human nature,' she reflects. Together they learn the fundamentals of crop rotation, enriching the earth with cycles of legumes, then leaves, then roots. Bore holes are drilled, irrigation channels dug, and seeds the farmers sow flourish. Soon giant fresh vegetables begin to emerge from the earth, 'making the half-rotting orders of green vegetables from Johannesburg a thing of the past'.

Working together is a way of creating the conditions for life, uplifting communities as an act of decolonisation, unravelling the violence of colonialism in the mind and in the soil. In *A Question of Power*, Elizabeth finally recovers a sense of stability through her love of the land. By taking responsibility for developing new crops like the experimental Cape gooseberry, which flourishes unexpectedly in her own garden plot, new friends come into her life. She even becomes identified with the plant, and is nicknamed after it. Elizabeth too is a 'complete stranger like the Cape gooseberry', who 'settled down and became a part of the village life of Motabeng'. 'As she fell asleep, she placed one soft hand over her land. It was a gesture of belonging.'

I love how Head and her characters find belonging and refuge in a land that's new to them. When we think of farming, we often think of static communities with deep roots and ancient claims. These bonds can be matters of life and death for people and for ecosystems – as in Australia and the USA, where erasure of Indigenous land-use knowledge has created conditions for ecosystem collapse. But in my own context, the UK, these deeply held bonds can be exclusionary forces. Right-wing papers promote eco-fascist sentiments when they praise 'native' English connections to land and soil, stirring up dangerous ideologies of blood ties.

Respecting folk traditions, reviving beneficial ancient practices and listening to local knowledge must go hand in hand with resisting this resurgence of 'blood and soil' nationalism. So much of the story of humanity is of migration, of arrivals and departures. A friend, a migrant to the UK, once told me everyone should be an immigrant at least once in their life, because however well you know a place, every day you encounter something new. Too often migration is a last resort, an emergency created by insufferable conditions. But for whatever reason we move, estrangement changes us, making new ways of being possible. Belonging may offer roots, but those roots can be tethering, or strangling. Sometimes our mental health and wellbeing is dependent on our autonomy to migrate and grow.

On our last morning on the farm, I rise early and take my coffee out onto the decking. The sun is on my skin, flickering through the still-green leaves of the orchard. A tiny calf is stumbling around the yard. It can only be a couple of days old.

As I watch Terri and Steve pottering around the little haven they have farmed into existence, I know I am looking at a very privileged form of rural migration. Here are two middle-class urban people, taking their life savings and moving back – back to the land, back to traditions, back to a dream they have nourished since childhood.

Still, I'm delighted for them. They are doing good things here, making the land better for their presence. The improved habitats for wildlife they've created by laying new hedgerows, the organic methods they're using to enhance the soil, the solar panels on the barn's sloping roof: all are evidence that they're thinking about the future of this farm, making it a home for more-than-human residents as well as providing a little restoration for frazzled tourists like me.

There are signs that more people are seeking this life, making a new start in rural places that were abandoned at previous moments of modernisation. Experimental eco-communities have been growing in number, like in formerly abandoned villages in central Spain, or the Hebridean isle of Eigg, which collectively bought out its aristocratic landowners twenty years ago. After years of neglect, the island is now powered with renewable wind and water turbines and hosts a lively and creative community, with opportunities for wwoofers and those wanting a new start who are ready to make a commitment to the place. All across the country, the Scottish government now offers crofting grants to people wanting to lay down roots in isolated places – particularly the Highlands and Islands, whose populations were obliterated by the forced removal of people in the eighteenth- and nineteenth-century land clearances. Crofting is a farming system that originated among those displaced people, and is all about making the most out of poor land. It's not a lonely pursuit. A small community of other crofters is needed to make ends meet. Grazing land is shared, with most work dedicated to rearing beef and lamb. But modern crofters are also diversifying, growing vegetables and fruit or managing woodlands and investing in renewables. According to the Scottish Crofting Federation, crofters are also postal workers, teachers and weavers, and their existence is vital to the preservation of the Gaelic language and a window into so much traditional ecological knowledge and perception across the isles and mainland. The inevitable Airbnb also makes an appearance, offering another income stream in these inherently mixed economies.

I tell myself that I'm not doing a terrible thing using Airbnb to stay at Terri and Steve's. At least they live here too and aren't denying locals a home. This is an income stream that makes other innovations on the farm possible – and though it relies on modern technology and an ethically dubious platform, the practice of doing a bit of this, a bit of that, and opening your farm to guests, must be as old as the farm itself. 'Next time you want to come stay,' Terri tells me with a wink, 'just email me directly.'

Post-pandemic, it'll be interesting to see what remote working does for rural communities. In the UK, house-hunting and rental sites reported jumps in enquiries from city people looking to move to villages at the start of the lockdown. This might turn out to be just a trend among the wealthy, an acceleration of the stereotypical move office workers often make from city flats to suburbs to raise a family. But there's a potential for real change in these uncertain times, connecting more people to the land and to the messy reality of farming.

I began this journey suspicious of the pastoral fantasy of the farm, and the work-cure ethic that lies beneath so many agricultural therapies. I'm still suspicious, but I've realised that in farming itself there lies an antidote for those evils. We idealise the farm when we don't know anything about how our food is produced. And we romanticise hard work when we believe that the best things in life are created through squeezing every drop we can from people and the land.

But farming has the potential to be a kind of collective recovery. The innate creativity of farming can go far beyond abstract measures of 'productivity' to restore ecosystems and relations between people. I'm grateful to farmers for improving my wellbeing by the small matter of keeping me alive, and I'll thank them by paying a fair price for all I consume, supporting not just Fairtrade, but co-operative farming, where farmers own the land they work and can reinvest wealth in their communities, protecting the land they know better than anyone. And beyond that, what if farming were to grow even more free from a politics of scarcity and profit? What radical possibilities might farming hold for our happiness, our health, our flourishing in harmony with the more-than-human world? Time may tell. Meanwhile, there is no journey into the nature cure that's forced me so deeply to connect with the seeds and soil in which life and wellbeing grow.

Virtual Nature
Setting Up Signals

On a burning-hot day in Bristol, I wait with the other volunteers in a shiny new research building. The sky outside is iridescent blue and the concrete of the city is drenched in a light so stark and penetrating, it looks like it's been bleached. The air we're breathing is cool, sanitised by air-conditioning units, but it still feels stuffy behind the double layers of reinforced glass.

'Psychologically, people want to open a window on a sunny day, but that actually makes the building *hotter*,' another volunteer explains, as we perch on scratchy, mushroom-shaped stools, waiting for our instructions.

I'm taking part in an experiment worthy of *Black Mirror*: an immersive nature experience, designed to help me feel the soothing benefits of green space in the comfort and safety of a sealed room. I've not been told much about what's going to happen. The researchers want an honest response, so they intend to keep us in the dark about everything for as long as possible.

My search for the nature cure has often led me to scientific accounts of how nature affects our minds. Whether persuasive, naïve, or somewhere in-between, those accounts have gestured towards a startling and unsettling possibility: that the soothing qualities of nature might be isolated, extracted, and then convincingly synthesised. All those theories about how the flash of forest green, the whiff of woodland air or the sound of birdsong affect us raise the question of whether nature's aesthetic and sensory qualities may be convincingly reproduced by technologies that *out-nature* the real thing. Just as the medicinal plants that were once our only recourse have now been supplemented by potent pharmaceuticals based on the same principles, might some of the future forests where we seek solace be entirely virtual?

This is the question that perplexes me as I watch gulls soar and dive on the other side of the glass. I don't need to wait much longer. My turn comes, and a researcher dressed in black slips a blindfold over my eyes. For a moment I am lost, and then she gently takes me by the arm and leads me forward.

For the next quarter of an hour I'm immersed in a many-textured, multi-sensory environment. Birds chitter. Water seems to flow beside my ear. I'm pushed forward and leaves brush against my arm, causing me to yelp and laugh in surprise. Then I'm guided to the ground, to a floor lined with what seems at first to be living grass, and my hands are placed in cool, crumbling earth. I seem to have walked only five paces, but my senses are telling me I'm in a forest.

Only something's not right. The temperature is wrong. There was no plunge into coolness as we passed under the canopy. The air is stale and constant, and the sounds are coming from the wrong places. As I listen carefully, I realise the stream is trickling *above* my head, not beside me, as you would expect. The ground is too perfectly even. No forest floor feels so much like a football pitch, rolled out and pressed for the occasion. Why would there be a lawn in a forest, anyway? I scrunch my toes and realise it's not grass, but plastic AstroTurf. The more I notice all that isn't right about the forest, the more disorientating the experience becomes.

A hand clasps my shoulder. It's time for me to rise from the 'forest floor'. I want to whip the blindfold off and look at the elements that have made up this weird experience, but I know I'm not supposed to. In the waiting room, I sit down with the other volunteers to discuss what we've experienced. A couple of them are impressed. They talk about how realistic the scents and sounds were: the perfume that simulated the scent of grass, the field recording (which I later discover was a blend of dawn chorus and meadow sounds). It's impressive stuff: a carefully calibrated mix of science, theatre, technology, storytelling and some carefully positioned props.

'But I could tell it was all wrong,' says one of the volunteers impatiently. He's a geographer, and one of those old-school nature lovers who has spent a lifetime listening in forests. He's exasperated by the minute glitches in the birdsong, betraying a recording stitched together from diverse habitats and different times of the day.

'I didn't notice that,' admits another volunteer.

'Well I *did*. It's like that picture,' he says, and he points at the wall. We look up at the huge photograph that stretches from floor to ceiling and has been looming over us since we arrived. It shows a landscape of pine trees. The sun cuts through the dense green canopy, casting spots on the dark brown needle-carpet of the forest floor.

'We picked this room because of the feature wall,' smiles one of the researchers. 'More *healing nature!*'

A good-natured ripple of laughter runs through the room. But the geographer sighs in exasperation. 'It's a timber plantation. Planted for chopping. You realise you're looking at an ecologically useless space? The soil will be dead and dry. Hardly any bacteria or fungus. There won't be any animals. What would they eat?'

We look more closely at the regimented lines of trees, the perfect order of trunks planted close together for maximum profit and efficiency.

'You're probably not even allowed to walk there,' he says, shaking his head.

It's not the first time I've seen someone react like this to the promise of 'healing nature'. It's a defensive posture. Ominous paranoia, combined with a slight sense of superiority – what academics sometimes call the 'hermeneutics of suspicion'. I'm often guilty of the same reaction. It's not just raising questions and being critical; it's a dogged closedness to exploring new possibilities, what scholar Rita Felski describes as 'a curiously non-emotional emotion of morally inflected mistrust'. I've seen it and felt it at every stage of this journey, when considering if swimming really could 'cure' depression, or resisting the picture-perfect scenery of the city park. But virtual nature often inspires us to take our wariness to the next level, managing to annoy practically anyone with an interest in the connection between ecology and human health.

Why should virtual nature make us feel so hypercritical? Maybe it's something to do with seeing nature used as a tool, reduced to nothing more than a healing aesthetic. Nature doesn't only matter because of how it makes us feel, or how it looks in a picture. Ugly and scary nature is still ecologically essential, and prettifying places often obscures the real and messy connections between our health and that of other creatures and ecosystems. Virtual nature isn't alone in doing this. So many 'natural' healing places have been crafted with human wellbeing in mind. But at least gardens and parks are habitats for wildlife. From video games to VR (virtual reality) headsets, mental health apps to immersive nature experiences, the brave new world of virtual nature is entirely synthetic. It's not the first time I've seen nature used as a tool, but the bluntness of the instrument and its absolute separation from what it sets out to represent is stark.

What might it mean – ethically, ecologically and psychologically – to synthesise encounters with nature? How would we feel, for example, about an AI dawn chorus that could fool even the geographer? Thorny questions of 'realness' and authenticity get us deep into the territory of science fiction. If we start simulating nature, where will it end? Will we be able to trust what our senses tell us? And if what fills up those senses influences not just our thinking, but our hearts and souls, does it really matter if the whole thing is fake?

In *Simulacra and Simulations* (1981), the philosopher Jean Baudrillard explored how the postmodern world is shaped by fakery – what he called 'hyperreality'. In postmodernity, we live through simulations, weaving a reality for ourselves from cartoons and corporations, augmented realities, brands, logos, movies and fake news. Baudrillard found the perfection of the hyperreal in the deserts, cities and theme parks of the US, as he relates in his philosophical travelogue, *America* (1988). In a landscape of cowboys and skyscrapers, lush university campuses planted with vivid green lawns and trees emerging like mirages from the geological wreckage of the desert, he experienced a spectral form of civilisation, 'a paradisiacal and inward-looking illusion'. The distinction between 'the real' and 'the unreal' wasn't clear any more, or really important. Hyperreality is a third space, 'a real without origin or reality', where landscapes look like movie sets and we experience reality cinematically.

Of course, there's an ecological reality behind the simulation. As the philosopher Kate Soper famously stated, it's not culture and language that have a hole in their ozone layer, and 'the "real" thing continues to be polluted and degraded even as we refine our deconstructive insights'. Reading Baudrillard's *America* now, it's obvious he took a squeamish pleasure in the fakery of the American west, with little thought for its ecocidal reality: 'there is nothing more beautiful than artificial coolness in the midst of heat, artificial speed in the middle of a natural expanse, electric light under a blazing sun,' he muses. Even the preposterous 'synthetic, air-conditioned oasis' of Furnace Creek – a faux ranch resort and golf course slapped right in the middle of Death Valley, which in 2020 had the highest recorded temperature on earth (54.4°C) – is a place of hyperreal allure. But there are checks on his voyeur's delight. The excess and the meaninglessness, the banality and the emptiness may be exhilarating and alien, but there is a debauched sheen to the synthetic spaces he visits as well. It's best captured in a science-fiction story he retells, about a group of rich people who

> wake up one morning in their luxury villas in the mountains to find they are encircled by a transparent and insuperable obstacle, a wall of glass that has appeared in the night. From the depths of their vitrified luxury, they can still discern the outside world, the real universe from which they are cut off, which has suddenly become the ideal world. But it is too late. These rich people will die slowly in their aquarium like goldfish.

It's a potent metaphor: a new Garden of Eden planted within a geodesic dome on a ravaged planet.

When we slip on a VR headset, or wander around the fantastical landscape of a game, are we also choosing to dwell in a hyperreality of idealised, pristine nature rather than looking with clear eyes at the real thing? Why stop at virtual worlds? What about augmented and mixed reality – wearable tech that could edit your perception of the real world you're navigating? These technologies could be programmed to sponge eyesores like power stations and litter out of view, turning the scene into a picturesque masterpiece without any of the unpleasant reminders of ecological degradation or climate crisis.

Looking at the mess industrial societies have made of the living world – the forest fires and floods, the extinctions and pollution – it's hardly a surprise that sanitised, idealised virtual worlds are more soothing than reality. But if there's nothing living in these worlds, are we really 'communing' with anything but our own fantasies and projections?

The fear that virtual realities disconnect people from nature has been voiced for years – most influentially by the writer Richard Louv. In *Last Child in the Woods* (2005) he brought the plight of children growing up in America's cities and suburbs to international attention. In landscapes of urban sprawl and strip malls, the wild places were dwindling, and what scraps remained were fenced, privatised and stamped with restrictive by-laws. Parents were more worried than ever about outdoor play, and the risk their children might be injured, lost or attacked in the woods where children of Louv's post-war generation had played and camped with wild abandon. And so play moved inside and became increasingly digital.

As far as Louv was concerned, this was a problem. The 'Nintendo kids' he met were often tech-savvy and hyper-aware of global environmental crises, but few knew much about local landscapes, plants and creatures. Trees went unclimbed, dens unbuilt. All the skills kids learn from natural play – the physical laws tested, the sense of strength and accomplishment achieved – were being lost. More than that, children were losing a sense of the infinite, of their place in a living world. Immersion in nature, Louv believes, 'exposes the young directly and immediately to the very elements from which humans evolved: earth, water, air, and other living kin, large and small'. But modern kids were missing out on this, and as a result their emotional and imaginative lives were being permanently narrowed, and their mental health compromised too.

This is the bold proposition of Louv's research: that disconnection from nature harms mental health. The term he coined to describe this absence, 'nature deficit disorder', was never meant to be scientific. It certainly wouldn't count for inclusion in the influential psychiatric manual, the Diagnostic and Statistical Manual of Mental Disorders (DSM) published by the American Psychiatric Association. But Louv's findings overlap with other facts that are known about children's lives in modern cities and suburbs. Depression, anxiety, attention-deficit disorders and stress are all on the rise. Was this caused by more rigorous diagnosis, overdiagnosis, or other factors? Could nature help alleviate these problems, or lower the rates at which they occur in the first place? And were digital technologies to blame?

The answer to the last question was a resounding yes, according to Louv. Television and computer games are public enemy number one in *Last Child in the Woods*. They're accused of 'containerising' kids, 'tunnelling' and atrophying their senses, meaning they cease to experience the world directly and to learn in an embodied, independent way. According to one British study Louv cites, 'average eight-year-olds were better able to identify characters from the Japanese card trading game Pokémon than native species'. Directly or indirectly, newspaper articles, parents' forums and outdoor-education communities regularly chime with Louv's advice. TV, tech and games have been accused of everything from making children violent and aggressive to disconnecting them from reality and ruining their mental health.

But is it really fair to dismiss tech and games as 'bad' for mental health, and a toxic alternative to nature? Dr Amy Orben, an expert on teens, screen time and mental health, advises caution. She concludes that anxieties about digital and virtual worlds are just the latest in a long wave of 'Sisyphean cycle technology panics'. 'In Ancient Greece, philosophers opined about the damage writing might do to society'; in the late eighteenth century, moralists were terrified about the harm sensation novels may be inflicting on young women readers. The rise of the radio in the 1930s was met with another wave of panic: 'Here is a device, whose voice is everywhere … it comes into our very homes and captures our children before our very eyes,' fretted one contemporary reporter. While there's little evidence to suggest screen time significantly impairs children's and teens' wellbeing, parents' perception of the danger of these technologies is just as panic-stricken as the moral outrages of the past.

Orben also cautions against connecting screen time with depression. For young people, issues like bullying and family conflict are shown to have a far bigger impact on low wellbeing than gaming. Where gaming and social media is genuinely excessive, it's likely to be a symptom rather than a cause of the problem. As her colleague Andrew Przybylski, a psychologist at the Oxford Internet Institute, explains, 'It's a bit like blaming a bed for your depression. You could call it "Bed Addiction", but that doesn't mean there's anything about the pillow making you sad.'

What about the claim that games disconnect children from nature? One thing that's rarely bought up when people are having these debates is how convincing and beautiful many game worlds are. Dazzling scenery, like the mountains of *The Witcher 3*, or the dreamscapes of *Ori and the Blind Forest*, means that modern games are as immersive as high-budget fantasies like *Lord of the Rings*. Many games even explore ecological themes. The game *Never Alone*, created in consultation with Native Alaskan storytellers, folds Iñupiat culture into puzzle solving, exploring the mystery of why an unseasonal blizzard is raging.

Admittedly, the video-game industry is wasteful in terms of its environmental impact. From plastics to electronics, it's estimated that the detritus produced by Nintendo alone adds up to the weight of 5,555 Statues of Liberty. We tend to associate 'the digital' with ethereality and lightness, a realm where things can be created, destroyed, replenished or copied with a mere tap or click. But there is a material infrastructure beneath it all, and a hefty carbon footprint. Global data centres use around 30 billion watts of electricity annually, with many units running on coal or diesel. In her new media artwork, *The Gathering Cloud* (2016), J. R. Carpenter explains that 'cloud storage' 'is an airily deceptive name connoting a floating world far removed from the physical realities of data'. It's an ironically apt name, Carpenter suggests: a typical cumulus cloud weighs about as much as a hundred elephants.

Still, as one of the major cultural platforms in the world, it's a very good thing that the games industry is addressing the climate crisis in its storytelling and outreach, as the launch of the Playing for the Planet Alliance in 2019 attests. At the same time, its designers and developers are enhancing wellbeing by creating beautiful immersive worlds that bring players so much pleasure. Because games certainly bring pleasure. It feels almost taboo to admit this in the presence of nature lovers. Those pleasures are rarely taken as seriously as the aesthetic joys of other kinds of art. When I lie on my sofa reading books about nature, I'm also immersing myself in a virtual world. It's just that literature is a celebrated cultural form and games are not, at least not among the nature crowd. And unlike literature, we rarely ask whether games could create a sense of ecological wonder that could be carried over into the real world.

Someone who has considered this possibility is the psychologist and gamer Pete Etchells. In *Lost in a Good Game* (2019), Etchells reflects on how games offered him tantalising worlds to explore as a way of escaping the dull, grey reality of the town where he grew up. These pleasures continue to enthral him as a games researcher. *Firewatch*, for example, is described as one of the most beautiful he's ever played. Set in Shoshone National Forest, Wyoming, it depicts a rugged North American landscape of rocky outcrops, birch and pine, which you, as the fire lookout, must protect from devastation. 'Watching the game unfold on the screen in front of me, I can almost feel the sun beating down on my neck. I try to imagine the smells rising from the grassy carpet of the meadow beneath my feet.' Wandering the landscape feels like hiking, and as you're trying to solve the game's central mystery, the sun is rising and falling, washing the world with mesmerising golden light. Or describing *The Legend of Zelda: Ocarina of Time* – one of the games I also played obsessively as a teenager – Etchells writes that 'it felt like I was part of a huge, living, breathing world, as fragile as it was awe-inspiring'.

Could exploring the virtual ecospheres urge people to see the magic in their everyday surroundings, or even develop hunger to explore the real thing? I'm not a huge gamer, but I remember with a deeply embodied sense the pleasures of diving into the underwater caverns of the first 3D Mario game I played on Nintendo 64. It was 1996 and I'd never swum in a river or lake, could barely dive, and loved the crisp aquamarine of chlorinated swimming pools above everything else. But in this startlingly realistic world (which now looks awfully clunky) I could dive deep into crystal water, blowing bubbles behind me as I snatched coins from snapping oysters above a sandy seabed marbled with shadow and light.

How much of the memory of navigating this place do I carry in my movements, in my muscles, as I swim now? When I close my eyes and remember those sensations, it's curiously tricky to distinguish my living body from the sprite I manipulated on screen. Game psychologists describe this as a feeling of spatial presence and immersion, where choices and movements in the game feel meaningful to the player. Neurological research even suggests we experience emotions and reactions similar to those we might do in the real world. In memory, at least, those digital waterscapes are wonderfully real and familiar.

So might the pleasure of the game be a substitute for real-life encounters with nature? I'm going to side with the geographer this time, and say no. It's not just the sensations you miss out on. The sense of freedom and chance is often denied to us in the contained world of the game. The mountains or forests that make the backdrops to many games are off-limits. Take a wrong turn or try to interact with an element that isn't enchanted with game potential, and your character is left jogging on the spot and bashing their head against a virtual wall.

This does appear to be changing though. *No Man's Sky* was first released in 2016, and since then its virtual universe has been evolving and growing. Using deterministic procedural generation, its universe contains 18 quintillion planets, all with unique biomes – wild and uncharted planets with flora and fauna, water and geology that no one but you may have seen before. It really is a kind of wilderness: even the game's designers don't know what's really out there. The game uses an algorithm to create new creatures and habitats, ecological threats and strange alien life forms, which your space traveller encounters afresh with every landing. How you navigate the game is largely up to you. You might colonise planets or trade with aliens. You may catalogue plants and species, or simply explore what's out there. And it's a durable universe: if you return to one of those 18 quintillion planets, you'll meet the same curious critters as last time. On paper at least, there is more to explore in the game than in the real world.

But is it any fun? While many gamers admire the elegance and ambitions of the design, others admit that *No Man's Sky* can be boring. However good the graphics and copious the environments, 'the uninteresting harvesting and survival mechanics that underlie it all remain incredibly grindy and frequently mind-numbingly tedious', as one reviewer confesses. Yes, 'there's an undeniable rush of excitement in discovering and exploring a planet for the first time';

navigating 'a massive water planet filled with aggressive jellyfish', staring at 'bizarre life forms that were made up of levitating crystals' or exploring 'murky caves on an atmosphere-free moon'. But since the initial 2016 release, developer updates have mostly focused on adding more established forms of gameplay – multiplayer combat in starships, building bases on planets, and so on – rather than revisiting the original aspiration to inspire ecological rapture. The truth is, after so many attempts to train alien life forms or to evade weird weather events, the thrill wears off.

This isn't something I've ever thought about nature. The closer you look at living things, the more time spent in a place, the more the strangeness and interest of it deepens. 'Knowing another is endless,' Nan Shepherd writes. 'The thing to be known grows with the knowing.' That's life's deepest pleasure. In furnishing us with endless novelty and depthless difference, perhaps the creators of *No Man's Sky* have produced an imaginative dead end.

It does reveal something useful, though: that the natural landscapes of games can't necessarily offer us the same restorative experiences of 'being away' as nature. Walking, which in real forests or mountains can be absorbingly meditative, becomes tedious in the virtual world. Hours spent lying on a shore listening to waves and birdsong is time wasted in a game. There are some ways that games mimic experiences of immersion. The games critic Simon Parkin calls the loss of time we experience playing a game as 'chronoslip', and the way he describes its positive aspects sounds an awful lot like the sense of relaxation people report in nature. The difference is that we're more likely to experience it when we're actively involved in the game's problem-solving activities than lying restfully prone.

Real VR Fishing is one new game that's exploring the blurred boundaries between absorbing gameplay and nature restoration. Developed by the VR headset company Oculus, it's not the first fishing game out there, but it's one of the most impressively realistic. At the start of the short advert used to sell the game, a middle-aged guy is slumped over his desk in a dark, empty office. He's exhausted, his stress levels are high, and he's beginning to despair. He glances over to the Oculus headset lying temptingly on his desk. He slips it on, and in an instant he's in a gently rocking boat at the centre of a photorealist lake, surrounded by mountains and forest. He's fishing! As his line is pulled tight and chubby carp leap from the waters, the man is sprightly and switched on again, joyful and awake. In the real-world office, a cleaner walking past with a trolley watches his headset-clad figure winding an imaginary rod, and shakes his head.

'Breakaway' moments like this are essential for anyone whose life involves focused, tiring work, especially in built-up places. Gardens, parks, balconies and fancy offices surrounded by terraces all serve the same function. Paintings, movies, books and soundscapes, even meditations and visualisations, offer representational encounters for people who, for whatever reason, can't access nature on tap. For every person who might be able to close their eyes and imagine they are standing on the edge of a beautiful field, breathing fresh mountain air, there's another who needs a little help from games like *Real VR Fishing*.

Thanks to substantial investment from the gaming industry, virtual-reality games like this one are getting more and more sophisticated. Headsets are now sleek affairs, handheld controllers smooth and ergonomic. Room-scale sensors adjust the space of the simulation to the real-world, so you don't end up face-planting into a wall. We're not quite talking *Star Trek*'s Holodeck levels of realism, but the graphics of virtual worlds are getting clearer and more impressive than ever. The end goal is to create worlds so seamless, immersions so complete, that even the hypersensitive biological sensors with which we adjust ourselves to the world are fooled. With enough expertise and investment, the virtual may well become, psychically and physiologically, a convincing reality.

As far as games designers are concerned, these developments are valuable if they improve quality of play. But VR natures have further applications in medical treatment and in the growing wellbeing industry, which is increasingly selling its services to business.

Take HappinssVR. Designed in California and launched in 2017, it now serves major employers like IBM, Sony and Uber. As more companies make public commitments to enhance the wellbeing of their employees, swish cutting-edge 'wellness solutions' like Happinss are stepping in to offer assistance to Silicon Valley giants. First, companies are provided with a holistic worker-wellbeing survey, which aims to diagnose points of objective and subjective stress. Then the VR headsets are rolled in and special relaxation rooms installed. The Happinss experiences you can enjoy feature a soothing voice that guides the wearer through a meditation, backed up by the immersive sound of music and field recordings, as well as visual simulations like a starry sky, beach or soothing meadow. In the future, Happinss aims to incorporate biofeedback – picking up on bodily cues like heart rate, temperature or brainwaves to adjust what users see and experience – and to use haptic technology, like vibrations in wearable headsets and gloves, to give people a greater sense of touch and presence in their virtual world.

In the UK, the company behind the Dream Machine is also collecting biometric data and using it to manipulate people's experience in real time. Its VR headsets give access to nature-themed digital worlds, using an electroencephalogram (an EEG) to monitor what's going on in your brain at the same time. Neurons are the brain's circuitry, to use a clumsy technical metaphor. An EEG can tell when we're stressed or when we're distracted by keeping an eye on neural activity. Dream Machine technology, in turn, can prompt us to pay attention and refocus, with the ultimate ambition not just to get us back on track, but to fundamentally reshape the way the mind works.

The science behind this involves neural plasticity. As early as the 1890s, the American philosopher and physician William James proposed that mental habits were not hard-wired or fixed in the machinery of the mind, but were created by pathways of 'will' that are strengthened by time and repetition. Twenty-first-century neuroscience is remarkably similar in its findings. Brain science now affirms that neurons can be retrained with enough conscious effort and practice. We can truly teach ourselves to think, feel and act differently.

Western science catches up with the knowledge of Buddhism in the most common retraining method: the meditative practice translated as mindfulness. Using focused visualisations, evoking emotion and memory, exploring how they manifest in the body, and practising ways of noticing and reframing those feelings, are all part of the toolkit used to gain a gentle hold over our habits and become more consciously and unconsciously aware. Cognitive behavioural therapy (CBT) too, helps people make new behaviours and thought processes become habitual. Behind the scenes, both are building new neural pathways that may become habitual in the future.

Now the Dream Machine promises to do the work for you – or some of it, at least. Slipping on a headset, you are whisked to a remote desert island. This is your dream space, where waves lap against the shore, palms sway in the breeze, and golden sands beckon. The only problem is, a fog keeps descending. The landscape is obliterated every time your biometric data suggests you are losing focus. You have to force yourself to ignore distractions and concentrate with all your might to see the island clearly again.

If you've ever struggled with a meditation or tried and failed to follow a yoga teacher's instructions to 'empty the mind', you'll know what's going on. The purpose of these activities is to still the raging thoughts and create a blank slate on which new ways of thinking and feeling might be wrought, but it isn't easy. The stream of consciousness bubbles away constantly. What the Dream Machine does is give you an internal nudge to get you back on track. It's like a yoga teacher who knows you're not concentrating, or a meditation podcast that breaks the fourth wall and yells at you: *Pay attention!*

Never mind that accepting failure is part of the purpose of *zazen* meditation. The best account of this

I've read is in the novel *A Tale for the Time Being* (2013) by Ruth Ozeki. Her teenage heroine Nao retreats to a monastery high in the hills of Japan to visit her Buddhist nun grandmother and to recover from trauma she's experienced in the city. Nao begins to meditate, but she's fidgety: 'When I first tried to do it, I got totally distracted by all my crazy thoughts and obsessions, and then my body started to itch and it felt like there were millipedes crawling all over me.' But that's OK, her grandmother Jiko explains:

> it doesn't matter if you screw up *zazen*. Jiko says don't even think of it as screwing up. She says it's totally natural for a person's mind to think because that's what minds are supposed to do, so when your mind wanders and gets tangled up in crazy thoughts, don't freak out. It's no big deal. You just notice what's happened and drop it, like whatever, and start again from the beginning.

Zazen isn't some magical other realm, some impossible state of spiritual bliss. It's just a part of life in the monastery, a daily practice as mundane and normal as tidying up. It teaches humility, habitual dedication, and its reward comes in the experiences of *nowness* that it opens. As Nao explains, it's like banging the temple drum: 'When you beat a drum, you create *NOW*, when silence becomes a sound so enormous and alive it feels like you're breathing in the clouds and the sky, and your heart is the rain and the thunder.'

Could the Happinss programme or the Dream Machine make us feel this way? I'm not convinced. What it does instead is try to convert an ancient religious practice into a lunchtime workout, harnessing our introspective powers as a tool for workplace resilience. Experiences with potentially significant moral and spiritual dimensions become little more than a chunk of Fitbit data. It's also worth remembering that access to these technologies depends on whether you're someone whose health is worth investing in. Like the *Real VR Fishing* advert, with its expensive Oculus headset lying around the office, much of this technology is being sold for the assumed benefit of the rich executive, not the cleaner.

At the more affordable end of the spectrum are the apps. With the near ubiquity of mobile phones, it's inevitable that more of these wellness services would move online. There are so many apps out there, and a surprising number of 'nature'-themed experiences. Bite-sized forest experiences allow you to navigate images and stories about an Arctic forest for the purpose of rest and relaxation. With Wildfulness, I can immerse myself in a soothing world of hand-drawn landscapes, sounds, inspirational quotes and guided meditations perfectly timed to be squeezed into a coffee break. With Synctuition, I gain access to a 'powerful form of binaural meditation and guided inner-reflection to dissolve feelings of stress and anxiety at their source'. Like many insomniacs, I've downloaded soothing nature-sound apps that promise to help me sleep, focus and escape to the tune of whale or birdsong. To be honest, I prefer electronic drone music, the banalities of white noise, or a decent dose of melatonin or Valium. But according to the reviews, many of the users of the app swear by it, and fair play to them.

Individually, the apps are relatively harmless and often helpful. But collectively, they're part of a bigger shift to provide more self-help and mental health treatment online. According to the 2019 Topol Review, which advised the NHS on which new technologies to adopt, a massive move to technologised healthcare is on its way, from body sensors used to track emotional state, to virtual-reality treatments, even artificial intelligence and robotics within two, five or ten years' time. There is already a flourishing field called affective computing, which focuses on teaching machines to recognise, simulate and influence human emotion. Outlandish interventions like ingestible technology that can track whether you're keeping up with your meds, or sensors on the skin that record your location, screen-time, social interactions and biophysical indicators like heart rate and temperature; they're not the fantasies of a science-fiction future, but now in development and soon to be part of our world.

To be clear, there are many good reasons for digitising mental health services. Locating patient records is easier when technology is involved. AI can work with data sets to spot recurring patterns, helping diagnosis by making connections between symptoms that might have been disclosed to different specialists over many years, meaning the details get lost. Mood-monitoring apps, where you're encouraged to track your mood on a daily, even hourly basis, can be helpful for people working with CBT and compassion-focused therapy, where understanding your triggers and gaining a hold over thoughts and habits can be hugely productive. From the medical point of view, these apps can help doctors get a more realistic, fine-grained view of the person they're working with. Most diagnoses are made through subjective assessments, usually by questionnaire, which ask you to rate your mood, thoughts and behaviour over the last week or fortnight. The problem is, it's easy to forget, simplify or cast a positive or negative spin on past experience, meaning richer details get lost. Psychiatric diagnosis is already a hugely uncertain practice, and patients are often shifted between one label and course of treatment and another. By enabling 'ecological momentary assessment', capturing people's experiences *in situ* and in real time, apps can aid the process a little, giving people more insight into their experiences, and helping communicate with the professionals who act as gatekeepers to medication and services.

Everything becomes a little more complicated the deeper we go into the world of automation, tracking and intrusive data-gathering. Phones know a lot more about us than the data we choose to enter into them. Digitised mental health services are likely to make use of all kinds of information, including 'clicks, finger movements, scrolls, locks and unlocks, notifications, charges, app usage, call and SMS frequency, and calendar data', all of which can be used to draw conclusions about our mental health. On the support side, medical technologists are optimistic about automation's potential to revolutionise and streamline services. Interactive 'chatbots' like Alexa allow us to play music, search for information and buy stuff without picking up the phone. Robots and artificial intelligences, fired up with our data and equipped with natural-language-processing skills to enable more sophisticated and personalised conversations, might soon start to replace medics and therapists for at least some routine appointments.

It sounds futuristic, but the first rudimentary medical chatbot – Eliza – was created in the USA way back in the 1960s. Running her 'DOCTOR' programme, she was set up to ask direct questions, prompt you to elaborate on your thoughts, and even murmur a sympathetic response to your outpourings. The fact that Eliza was a 'she' raises some fairly interesting questions about the gendering of therapeutic encounters and the technologists' idea of who does the emotional work of listening. Eliza's existence also demonstrates that the move to digitise and automate mental healthcare has been a long time coming. More recently, the DARPA-funded virtual agent Ellie aims to be able 'to recognize and identify psychological distress from multimodal signals', including your facial cues (although Ellie takes care to remind you that she is not a substitute for a human therapist).

A huge amount of research and development money has been spent to get us from Eliza to Ellie and the AI therapists we might be consulting in the next decade. But when you look at the take-up of technologies by medical providers, cost-cutting on staff and services is at the top of the agenda. For people consulting mental health services in the UK right now, apps are often the first thing prescribed while people wait months for a specialist or a service to become available. For all their benefits, they're not so good when very serious issues are at stake. A friend described to me how frustrating their teenage child found the 'Hallmark' language and one-size-fits-all approach to mental health on the NHS app they were offered in place of more appropriate services. The app wasn't just useless – it was insulting, impersonal and made their child feel worse. Speaking for myself, I know doing almost anything on my phone is bad for my anxiety and insomnia, as the gamified approach the apps use sends me spiralling off on ludic loops and craving dopamine highs. The truth is, I'm better off when I'm using my phone less.

But for workplaces that like to promote themselves as sensitive to wellbeing, buying an app package and encouraging staff to use it is an easy option. It's cheaper than balancing workloads, hiring more staff, or paying struggling workers fairly – providing a perfect sticking plaster for a neoliberal society committed to the project of 'unbundling' responsibility for self-care, rather than creating a community dedicated to compassion and quality of life for all. For the apps' manufacturers, the access users give to the most obscure permutations of their mood easily converts into data that can be harvested and sold for profit. Apps don't even need us to diligently log our thoughts in order to convert us into 'data subjects' and monetise and commodify our inner lives. As Shoshana Zuboff explains in *The Age of Surveillance Capitalism* (2019), seemingly 'innocent' apps like our weather reports and flashlights use 'increasingly bizarre, aggressive, and illegible tactics' to collect data about our habits and moods. Much of this is for the benefit of targeted advertising – a worrying concept when you realise that shops might be quite interested in knowing we tend to splurge when we're manic or depressed.

Even more dystopian is the use of data to 'tune' or 'nudge' behaviour through subliminal cues or carefully timed prompts. Emotion AIs that analyse our feelings from our facial and vocal expressions can adapt to offer us highly targeted personal messages. This already has applications in car technologies ('You're feeling angry – pull over!'), and the use of sensors to create smart and heavily surveilled workspaces and homes is, naturally, on the horizon. It might get to the stage that you don't need to download an app to access pictures of trees and birdsong on your phone. Your virtual nature-wellbeing system will simply be able to input data from your body sensors and home-camera systems, notice that you're feeling down, and quickly convert your living-room walls to a virtual soothing forest or stormy coast, whatever is perfectly adapted to improve your mood, or nudge your behaviour in ways that are deemed healthy, or socially and economically salubrious.

Back in the analogue world of the lab, it's time for the final experiment. I'm not blindfolded this time, but led down a nondescript corridor alone. On the floor in front of me I can see a yoga mat and what looks like an unfurled flower made of large plastic petals. It's the first time I've seen the props behind the immersive experience, and it's reassuringly underwhelming to see such a humble set-up. I lie down as instructed, take the headphones I'm handed, and watch as the flower contraption is closed around me, the petals slotting into place.

It's dark inside the flower, but not black – more like the red, fleshly inside of a womb. I expect to hear some kind of animal, bodily sound, maybe a heartbeat, but instead an a cappella voice soars from the silence. It sounds like some minimalist Finnish electronica, the kind of music I listen to when I write, or play at full volume on my headphones when I'm trying to blur out the voices of people chatting on a train. It's a very different experience from the forest: much more elegant and relaxing. Instead of trying to simulate the 'real', this one takes me deep into the realm of imagination, memory, and the non-representational. It's a relief not to feel like I'm being conned.

This immersive experience, like the forest, is a prototype. The team behind the experiment are getting our feedback so that they might one day roll the final products out to hospitals and dementia wards, places where people can't easily access forests and beaches, and where moments of privacy and quiet are hard to come by. People trapped in noisy, crowded medical environments might one day be able to slip on a blindfold and be led into a healing forest, or folded into the heart of a pulsating, sonic flower.

I know how dehumanising and oppressive hospital wards can be. Environments need to be kept sterile, as hospital cleaners are under intense pressure to ward off disease and infection. But far from the places we love, we can stop feeling fully human, fully ourselves in their sanitised wards. When I am asked to write up my own experiences in the post-experiment feedback session, I try not to be as suspicious as the geographer. So much kindness, care and intelligence has gone into the team's work. But I need to be honest too.

Yes, the sounds and scent of the forest did evoke places I know and love, but with none of the freedom, depth of sensation or pleasure that I craved. The word that best captures what I was feeling is 'glascella'. After a long season in post-operative recovery and Covid-19 shielding, the philosopher Ginny Battson coined the term to describe a curious and melancholic state of being. Taking the Welsh term *glas*, which describes natural colours, and the English words 'glass' and 'gloss', she merged it with the Latin *cella*, meaning 'small chamber, inner temple. Somewhere enclosed, a form of captivity.' A glossy, glassed cell, glascella describes the feeling of being 'trapped behind glass or screen, unable to access directly the wonders of nature that can be seen and heard on the other side'.

It's an ambivalent sensation. Screens and simulations can help us maintain a 'thread of attachment' to the world outside. The vivid multicolour splendour of *Blue Planet*, or the sky seen through a photograph on an iPhone, evoke sensations and pleasures very close to those experienced when our skin is in direct contact with ocean, light and air. But there's a slip of separation too, of which the body is always conscious. Battson describes feeling 'an ache throughout my whole being' as she gazes at wonders beyond the screen, unable to taste or experience more.

It's not often spoken of, how those simulations of nature might create pain as well as pleasure. The assumption is that it's enough to see a beautiful scene to experience a small flush of joy without any pang of longing or loss for the other feelings and sensations typical of that place. Windows and screens may give us access to stunning scenery, but it can be frustrating to be able to look, but not touch, sense, or feel the heat or cool of the landscape on the other side.

I'm only speaking for myself, of course. As the post-experiment conversation reveals, many of the other participants were delighted and impressed with the immersion – more proof that, where mental health and wellbeing are concerned, individuals know what works for them best. For me, the special effects were far less important than the efforts taken to create the experience itself. If I was undergoing treatment in hospital or indoors in a care home, I can imagine how moved I would be to have guides – like the woman in black who led me around the 'forest' – giving so much of their time and attention to improve my comfort.

The feeling of someone taking care of me was so much more meaningful than the tricks and simulations. This isn't the kind of care you pay for if you treat yourself to a spa day. It's very different, too, from the VR experiences created by the companies who are selling their wares to offices. They're designed to fix us as quickly as possible, to perk us up so we can get back on track. This is something different, involving intimacy, compassion and shared love of beauty. It is a deeply moving gesture, that someone is using all their creativity and ingenuity to create an environment that might soothe me.

During the first coronavirus lockdown, the window becomes a portal to a living world that is currently closed off. Over the phone, I speak to my mother at the same time as we both skim our cursors over a distant spot on Google Earth where we were meant to be on holiday. We try to judge the time of year the photo was taken, imagine the silver speck half-obscured by foliage is our car, parked there on some past carefree visit. I finally understand why a friend I met when we were both on work placements in Germany compulsively checked an app that told him where fish shoals were moving around his home on the north-east American coast. An experienced angler, keeping track of how fish move helped him feel connected to his father and the ocean.

On social media, well-meaning people who live by mountains or beaches take snaps and share them online. 'For anyone who needs it,' they write. I'm grateful for their efforts, but not comforted. I can google images like that in heartbeat. The internet is thick with #SoothingSeascapes, Magnificent Mountains™. Even my laptop's homepage flashes a breathtaking shot of El Capitan at dawn, spiking me with low-key sublime scenery on a daily basis. Perhaps years of burning away my brain's stock of serotonin on Twitter and Instagram has made me immune to the joy I'm supposed to get from these glossy scenes. The little pang of jealousy (or let's be honest, resentment) at someone else's lovely bucolic life is magnified when many illegal miles stand between you and the cool of salt water or the thin alpine air.

But there are some pictures I crave. Like when my friend sends me updates on the ridiculous adventures of her two cats, or when my dad shares a snap of his tomato plants, grown from seeds I sent him in the post. It's not possible to order compost, but these seedlings are making the best of it in a scrap of soil scraped from a flower bed. Each image tells me a little about how their progress is being registered for him: the wonder of making something live from a few pinpricks that were tipped out of an envelope; the pleasure of starting a project at a difficult time, linking you to someone you love. The same goes for pictures sent by a friend far away on the other side of the country. I understand a little of what swimming means to her, and how important it is for her mental health to swim outside regularly. I worry for her, stuck in the city where there are no easy spots within reach. When I receive a string of images of her, hair wet and face glowing from a dip in a strange kink of river she's discovered upstream from her town, I feel joy as intense as I would have if I were with her. It's like we're swimming together, even though the lockdown is keeping us so far apart.

'Nature' when it's distilled into a series of colours, scents and physical sensations doesn't move me. I can't look at a picture of a beach, or hear a recording made in a forest, and feel the deep delight of experiencing it in person. What I am hungry for is connection. When I see pictures taken by people I love, I experience their delight vicariously. Their pleasure is mine. It's been halved, and shared, and as if by magic, it's doubled. It's soon bigger than the sum of its parts.

In early May, I'm asked to run a workshop for the Urban Tree Festival. Because of coronavirus, they've moved their programme online so they can deliver events remotely, and I'm on in the mid-morning slot.

'Quite a few of the people who've been joining us are shielding,' Mel explains when we meet on Zoom a week before the session.

'Anything you can do to help people connect with nature where they are would be brilliant,' her co-organiser Andrew chips in. Going online means people from much further afield than their regular London crowd can sign up to the free workshops, which is great for accessibility, but it raises challenges too. 'Connect with nature where they are,' I repeat to myself. But where are they?

On the morning of the session, I'm nervous. Three months of lockdown hasn't made me immune to the headaches and strange anxious nausea I experience on Zoom calls. Just as with nature, we're finding that connecting with people virtually is very different from in person.

I'm grateful when Andrew's face pops up and he tells me he'll 'let people in' in just a moment. 'All you need to do is talk,' he says cheeringly, and then suddenly it's 10 a.m. and the room fills up with little crossed-out microphone icons. It's a full house. My audience has arrived.

There's something both comforting and creepy about giving a talk online. Andrew has asked everyone to switch off their cameras to save bandwidth, so there are no faces – friendly or hostile. It's just my house, the screen, and the glimmer of the sunlit sky beyond the window. The same view, in essence, that I've stared at for the last two months.

Anxiety quickly passes, and I get on with my talk. I start by reading a few lines from Samuel Taylor Coleridge's 'This Lime-Tree Bower My Prison' (1797). The Romantics are known as hyper-energetic walkers and climbers, long-legged heroes leaping over fences or scaling bare rock. But Coleridge suffered from bouts of arthritis and depression, as well as addiction to laudanum (an infusion of opium), which would plague him in his later years. When he wrote the poem, he was in the Quantocks visiting friends. He had suffered burns at the beginning of the stay, and while Dorothy and William Wordsworth, Charles Lamb, and his host Thomas Poole were roaming in the hills, Coleridge was ensconced in Poole's cottage garden under a lime-tree arbour.

'He's not exactly self-isolating, but his injury means he can't join his friends on the walk, and thinking about the things they're seeing and experiencing makes him miserable,' I explain. 'Well, they are gone, and here must I remain / This lime-tree bower my prison!' he begins. It's a petulant little opening, an outcry against the injustice of missing out on beauties and feelings that would have been 'Most sweet to my remembrance even when age / Had dimm'd mine eyes to blindness.' That was a fixation with Coleridge and Wordsworth – the need to store up memories and experiences of nature's beauty, which they could draw from later, when they were trapped in the smoke of the city and unable to visit the places they loved.

The poem is more than a hymn to FOMO. It's a powerful exercise in refocusing attention from grand, inaccessible landscapes to the pleasures and possibilities of the here and now. Looking at what's around him helps him achieve a calm appreciation. It's not the sublime breaking of the sea on the distant horizon, but the subtle permutations of light dappling the leaves, the sun making the black branches of the elm gleam, bats wheeling in the twilight, and the 'solitary humble-bee' singing in the bean-flower. Nature isn't some wild, distant vista we must run to in order to experience it pure. 'No plot so narrow, be but Nature there.'

> No waste so vacant, but may well employ
> Each faculty of sense, and keep the heart
> Awake to Love and Beauty!

It's no coincidence that Coleridge made this discovery after spending time with Poole – a revolutionary thinker, committed to sharing wealth with the poor and dividing property fairly across society. Visited by bats and bees, sunlight and breezes blowing in from the distant moors, Coleridge finds himself extending care to his friends from afar – a kind of redistribution of pleasure, so no one goes without. Lying in his bower, he's able to imaginatively project himself onto the heath, experiencing vicariously the joy his friends feel, 'silent with swimming sense' as they gaze over the plains unreachable to him. There's an electricity in this connection, a rebuilding of a link that has been severed by distance and pain. Now he can feel pleasure imagining his friends' enjoyment:

A delight
Comes sudden on my heart, and I am glad
As I myself were there!

I enjoy the generosity of this turnaround even more now, bittersweet though it is. The people I love are far away and inaccessible, but they are safe and finding small pleasures and joy to sustain them while we commit to the painful collective project of keeping one another well.

This is what I'm trying to express. But as I talk, I'm distracted by the attendee icons that flash on and off as people leave or enter the 'room'. Coleridge could never have imagined his poem would be transmitted this way, from one little room to another, through fibre-optic cables, Wi-Fi signals and the old-fashioned copper wires that run into my house, making our internet patchy and unreliable.

The American political activist and poet Muriel Rukeyser might have seen this coming. My favourite poems of hers begins: 'I lived in the first century of world wars. / Most mornings I would be more or less insane'. News pours from the radio, the TV, and splashes across the papers. She calls her friends on the phone and finds they are 'more or less mad for similar reasons'. Slowly, she writes,

I would get to pen and paper,
Make my poems for others unseen and unborn.
In the day I would be reminded of those men and women,
Brave, setting up signals across vast distances,
Considering a nameless way of living, of almost unimagined values.

Maybe what we're doing now over our struggling internet connections is setting up signals. When we're sharing our ways of relating to nature with others – especially those shielding, people living alone and with disabilities who've been more or less abandoned by the government – we're taking care. It's not the same thing as sharing food and material resources (far from it), but mutual aid can and should include social and emotional support as well.

In my workshop, I start to talk about the photographs I've been greedily hoarding, the window boxes, gardens, pets and kitchen herb boxes. These are the things my friends have loved and tended, the places where they have walked and dreamed and worried for the past few months. I experience them not as images – flashes of green and blue – but as shared experience. A virtual nature, created by the communion of compassion and care. When we talk about 'virtual nature', we usually mean simulations, images, digital VR experiences. These are thought of as less authentic than the 'real thing', but still, they're offered to people who are, for whatever reason, confined. But there are other ways of experiencing nature from a distance that are just as valid, and maybe more powerful too. They exist in our connections with each other, and the time they take to share their world with us.

In their essay 'Sick Woman Theory' (2015) Johanna Hedva explores the kinds of activism available to people who are chronically ill. A body that must rest in bed cannot be present for a protest, and in societies without welfare support, the task of caring tends to be lumped on the vulnerable and the sick themselves. It is simply too costly and time-consuming, in capitalist economies, to prioritise the needs and wellbeing of the socially marginalised. 'Sick Woman Theory' is a push back against this individualistic way of thinking about collective and self-care. Hedva writes:

> The most anti-capitalist protest is to care for another and to care for yourself. To take on the historically feminized and therefore invisible practice of nursing, nurturing, caring. To take seriously each other's vulnerability and fragility and precarity, and to support it, honor it, empower it. To protect each other, to enact and practice community. A radical kinship, an interdependent sociality, a politics of care.

> Because, once we are all ill and confined to the bed, sharing our stories of therapies and comforts, forming support groups, bearing witness to each other's tales of trauma, prioritizing the care and love of our sick, pained, expensive, sensitive, fantastic bodies, and there is no one left to go to work, perhaps then,

finally, capitalism will screech to its much-needed, long-overdue, and motherfucking glorious halt.

Sharing our loves, honouring the places we miss, taking the time to celebrate, mourn and listen, is different from plugging into a machine that is designed to cheer us up in a twenty-minute flash of green and blue. You don't need access to a garden or a pricey VR headset to do that.

My thirty minutes are up. I need to leave everyone time to write, as this is supposed to be a poetry workshop. I give them their prompt: think about a person you miss and the place that's bringing them the greatest joy now. Meditate on what's giving them strength and helping them take care of themselves wherever they are. Now write a poem: go! I switch my mic off and wait.

A message from Andrew pings up in the corner. My Wi-Fi has been cutting out throughout the talk, he explains. There were some delays, some crispy, incomprehensible sentences. I've been throwing out signals to the universe, and some have struck, and others dispersed into nothingness. Oh well.

After twenty minutes, I ask whoever is still there to chime in with what they've written, if they want. The message board comes alive and Andrew switches all the mics on at once, releasing a chorus of breathing and birdsong, dogs barking, babies wailing, the low hum of a radio creating disturbing feedback. We soldier on, voices emerging out of the digital blur with the lines they've typed and scribbled.

This is all the virtual nature I need right now.

Lost Places
The Messy Work of Hope

I set out on this journey to discover 'the nature cure', to ask what it is, and whether it works. The 'healing nature' I was expecting to find was the late-Romantic kind: comforting and restorative, transcendent and transformative, something we can take back with us in memory to nourish and sustain us in dark and challenging times. Duly, that version of nature sprang up everywhere: in forest baths and walled gardens, the green ripple of landscaped parks and the bucolic, and Georgic pleasures of the farm. Nature as consolation, nature as a place of innocence and pleasure welcomed me, but the more I saw behind the workings, the more I realised that it's not enough any more. Perhaps it never was.

There was another kind of nature cure emerging beyond it, though. It wasn't simply charming: it was critical and held radical potential. It was about beauty and pleasure, certainly, but it was also about injustice, inequality and our frightening future: the kinds of things we often go to healing nature to forget. Being reminded of these realities didn't somehow 'ruin' the nature cure. In fact, it gave glimpses of other ways of being in the world that allow us to 'return to reality' with a clearer sense of purpose and hope. Nature has provided a site of refuge and resistance – in the co-operative farms of Botswana, in community gardens, in mountains made accessible by wanderers of all abilities. For wild swimmers and herbalists, people shielding and those living in precarious rented flats, nature provides moments of peace and strength, solidarity and connection. Parks, forests, gardens and farms can take us outside of our situations, so that we can think about them critically and creatively. These are places to recover, to feel joy, to experience love and to organise.

When the nature cure is repackaged by business or hoarded as a charm for the privileged, its radical potential is dimmed, but perhaps not totally lost. The problem is, these wellness solutions tend to treat nature as a tool, instead of thinking about how eco-recovery might work both ways. But mutual care is intrinsic to the nature cure. Why shouldn't we want to care for the forests, mountains and wetlands that we love, to understand their inner workings so that we can tend and protect them? Or when their workings are mysterious to us, leave them to their own processes of quiet regeneration and seasonal decay? Nature is life, after all, so the pleasures we take from it shouldn't be seen as separate from its flourishing and survival. It is not frivolous, or anti-human, to consider biodiversity and thriving habitats at the same time as human wellbeing, or to reflect on the many ways in which actions that are beneficial to people and to nature might be bound together – or one and the same.

How to end a journey in search of the nature cure? This question has caused me more than a little anxiety since I set out to explore the past and future of this trend. A while ago, I read a post written by a friend mocking tired tropes of nature and science writing. So many books that set out to investigate and celebrate the natural world end in exactly the same place: on an extremely depressing chapter about climate change. There's something exhausting and defeating about that kind of finale. Coming over the edge of the book's horizon like an avenging angel, climate crisis threatens to tear up everything we've enjoyed and found solace in in the story so far. It can be tempting to close the book and walk away, our dreams undisturbed.

But the climate crisis doesn't just arrive at the end of this journey. It was there at its beginning, and has been present at every moment: in weird weather, stories of crop failure and flood, and the promise of new ways of organising society and relating to nature. Ending this journey reflecting on 'lost places' does, I admit, play into the stereotype my friend observed. But I want to bring all that is depressing about this subject into focus: to ask how we live with feelings of despair, exhaustion and anxiety, and might even move beyond them. To do this, I've travelled just a few miles from my Bristol home, to the muddy shore of an estuary with one of the highest tidal ranges in the world.

The Severn is a wide, changeable streak of silver fringed with deep brown mud which, when it dries, sets as hard as clay. On the other side of the water, the low hills of south Wales stand dark grey against a light grey sky. Above me, traffic roars as it crosses the M48 bridge, white and prim as a picket fence. The channel meets the shore before me, a line that's marked by the rotting pillars of an old jetty where a cross-channel ferry docked until the late 1960s. Now, like most of the rocks and man-made forms around me, they are half-submerged in the crackling, reedy mud.

It is a landscape of strata and contrasts, where the present meets the recent and long-distant past. Aust Cliff rises 171 feet behind me, a mass of red mudstone streaked with alabaster, holding Triassic insects and marine reptiles in its crumbling walls. The cliff is a relic of a prehistoric seabed, formed some 200 million years ago. The earth's water levels were much higher then, its land masses pressed and held together in forms that are now alien and unfamiliar. The temperature was some 20°C warmer than today. With atmospheric CO_2 between five to twenty times higher, the past really was another country then, the earth another world.

Ten thousand years ago, at the end of the last ice age, the estuary was a river valley. As water rose from melting glaciers, it turned most of present-day Somerset into marshes and mudflats. Eventually the water receded, leaving fertile fields and rivers where cities would be built. Boats carrying the wealth of the transatlantic slave trade came and, later, shipping containers from across the globe, contributing to the vast movement of synthetic materials, and the mass burning of fossil fuels that has propelled us into the Anthropocene.

Faced with the brevity of human life and the intense *nowness* of the present, it can be oddly comforting to reflect on the eternal entropy of matter, the death-drive quality of all this fragile silt returning to the primordial ocean. It's like the earth relaxing into itself, a deep, eternal bath. But the difficult reality is that the estuary is a lost place in progress. Conservative predictions show its banks will be swallowed by shallow water with as little as a seven-metre rise in sea levels. With a hundred-metre rise – the expected consequence of all sea ice being lost – the channel, Bristol city, and most of Somerset will be submerged. Reclaimed by water and sediment, a miles-wide channel will provide clear passage all the way to the new coastal towns of Dorchester and Salisbury, now currently landlocked.

As I stand on the Severn's shore, I try to imagine the forces that will dissolve this land, but I find myself shrinking from the task. Maps that show coastal areas like this one missing – along with low-lying countries like Bangladesh, the Pacific Islands, and the reclaimed marshes of the Netherlands – stoke the same sense of despair. Not just despair. Horror. Emptiness. Total imaginative collapse.

Psychological harm may not be the most obvious danger of climate disruption, but that doesn't mean it isn't important. When floods and wildfires leave people hopeless and desperate, it's natural to focus on material damage and forget the trauma and emotional distress. But those wounds matter too. Following the 2005 storm that flooded much of the city of New Orleans, many survivors experienced post-traumatic stress, anxiety and depression. One study found that rates of mental illness doubled after Hurricane Katrina, with low-income,

African American single mothers particularly badly affected.

In truth, much of the pain was caused by social inequality. The trauma of a near-death encounter with rising water is devastating, but with the right psychological and social support, it should be possible to live well again. But that assumes that societies are fair and oriented towards welfare, which we know they aren't. After Katrina, the city's most vulnerable communities became ensnarled in a toxic environment of poverty, inequality and homelessness. As climate change escalates, extreme weather events will become more common, and more precarious, struggling people will be forced to face this agonising disruption. Human and ecological 'resilience' – in the form of healthcare and environmental legislation – comes at a cost few governments are yet willing to pay.

Then come the side effects: what are known as chronic impacts. Rates of aggression and violence go up when places experience unusual increases in temperature, as do suicides and hospital admissions. According to the American Psychological Association (APA), distress caused by excessive heat and climate emergencies can 'overwhelm coping ability for people who are already psychologically fragile'. Antipsychotics and certain kinds of antidepressants impair the body's ability to cope with excessive heat, meaning people who take them are at a higher risk of dehydration and toxic overload. We may all be in the same ocean, but we are definitely not in the same boat, and we are not equally equipped to weather these storms mentally, physically or financially.

There's another kind of suffering too, a psychological 'slow violence', to use the environmental humanities scholar Rob Nixon's term. It may be spurred by the horror of witnessing extinctions, experiencing (or even reflecting on) the nightmare of rising temperatures and the coming of rising waves. This suffering is called ecological grief, eco-anxiety or solastalgia. It's a little 'out there', as far as mainstream psychiatry goes, a little new. But it's coming to be better understood – and how we understand it, and respond to it, is going to be increasingly important as the climate catastrophe takes hold.

The first clues that something was very wrong were detected among communities experiencing climate disruption. After spending time with miners and farmers in the drought-prone and industry-scarred landscape of Central Australia, the environmental philosopher Glenn Albrecht coined the term 'solastalgia' to describe their emotional pain. A blend of the 'sol' of desolation, and 'algia' (from the Greek, meaning suffering), it can be translated as homesickness for a place that has disappeared, and the loss of identity that comes with it. As the ecological relationships that ground communities are destroyed, people are left, like the place itself, empty. 'If a person seeks solace or solitude in a much-loved place that is being desolated, then they will suffer distress,' Albrecht explains. Solastalgia is that 'ongoing loss of solace and sense of desolation connected to the present state of one's home and territory'.

Albrecht never thought of solastalgia as a biomedical diagnosis, although he did wonder if it might be a trigger for anxiety and depression. Nonetheless, psychologists have picked up the term and taken it seriously. One article published by *The Lancet* claims more research is needed into solastalgia, as the 'growing reality of climate change is likely to have major mental health consequences, especially for vulnerable groups'.

There are many new terms for climate despair, each offering its own understanding of how it may affect us. Climate and health researchers Ashlee Cunsolo and Neville Ellis introduced the term 'ecological grief' to define how 'climate change can disrupt a coherent sense of self via its physical impacts upon landscapes, seasonal weather patterns and ecosystems'. Feeling our 'inability to prevent the degradation or loss of land', we experience an 'anticipatory grief for ecological changes' that have not yet happened, and anxiety about 'future losses and mourning for an anticipated future that will likely cease to be'. The APA has added solastalgia to its medical lexicon, as well as eco-anxiety (which they define as 'a chronic fear of environmental doom'). They also worry about the climate Cassandras, 'gripped by thoughts of future harm, suffering from pre-traumatic stress response (a before-the-fact version of classic PTSD) because they know the world has not heard the warnings forcefully enough'. Although these new words haven't graduated to the DSM, they're seeping into medical language, informing the decisions doctors make, and leading sufferers to define themselves as eco-anxious.

I've experienced this as an environmental educator. I teach climate-crisis literature at university, and know how hard it is to balance hope with hard truths, giving students tools to critically reflect on the problems without sugar-coating the facts. In the last few years we've seen students self-diagnose as eco-anxious for the first time. It's not simply depression or anxiety they disclose. This is a new way of being in the world, a new way of registering its harms cognitively and emotionally. It has changed the way I think about my responsibility as an educator. I already issue content warnings for books that represent difficult experiences, like eating disorders or suicide. This isn't to close discussion down, but to help those who need to prepare emotionally to talk about certain themes. Now the possible range of disturbing material has expanded. We used to need to shock our students into awareness about climate catastrophe. Even ten years ago, I had to teach classes proving that climate change was really happening, not in thirty or fifty years, but *now*. I don't need to do that any more. Instead, we must learn to care for each other, and grieve.

I've even wondered about whether I should diagnose myself with ecological anxiety. It might help to put a stamp on my feelings, to remind myself that they're real and intense enough to deserve care and concern. Like any psychiatric diagnosis, these terms can give a sense of validation and help us connect with others who are suffering in a similar way. At the same time, I worry about the tendency to medicalise so many messy parts of human experience. Are climate grief and solastalgia just the latest example of the move to create what critical therapists call 'a disorder for everyone'? The fact that medical bodies are taking climate-related anxieties seriously reflects the reality that these disturbances create intolerable situations for those living at the frontline – particularly poor and Indigenous communities. But what does it mean to say that those raging and grieving are somehow disordered or sick? Yes, by validating ecological anguish in the most powerful psychological lexicon we have, we place the mind back into the environment in radical and necessary ways. But we also risk turning legitimate anger and pain into a new kind of hysteria – framing our natural response as somehow excessive and delusional.

I wonder if what we are experiencing is actually environmental gaslighting. Two, three decades ago, when climate scientists predicted the weird weather we're seeing now, politicians and industry told us it was the stuff of science fiction. Now those predictions are coming true, or exceeding the worst expectations. Arctic forests are on fire. The permafrost is melting. Icebergs are dissolving like sugar.

But political apathy and the powerful sway of business interests still mean that nothing – or nowhere near enough – is being done. When we protest, we are called mad, cranks, lefty loons. If we want to be treated as reasonable people, we are told, we must believe unreasonable things – like the idea that technological innovations alone can solve the climate crisis, and things can carry on as usual. Like the gaslighting behaviours characteristic of abusive relationships, these contradictions distort one's sense of reality. A chorus of climate Cassandras, we've been watching the lamps flicker for a long time and known that something was wrong.

These experiences might drive us mad, but they don't make us delusional. The problems are *out there*, not in here, and trying to adjust ourselves to them can feel painful and absurd. The cultural scholar Timothy Clark recognises this when he diagnoses society and thought itself as suffering from 'Anthropocene disorder'. It is an incoherence caused by the demand that we grasp the enormity of the problems the world is facing, and try to resolve them through individual actions in daily life. What this demand produces is a 'gut reaction of repugnance', and emotional confusion as we try to tally up 'the implication of trivial actions in scale effects'. Turning on a kettle, leaving a phone charger on standby, we are mundanely implicated in the fatal machinery of global capitalism, responsible for the death of all life on earth.

Repugnance, suffering and anxiety are the sane outcomes of a broken system. For the last few decades, individuals have been told they are to blame for the climate crisis, and tasked with the responsibility of fixing it with tweaks to consumption and lifestyle. These little changes are often satisfying and helpful for solving specific problems, especially if adopted on a large scale. But at the same time, obsessing about the details lets big polluters and the governments that back them off the hook. Twelve of the twenty companies responsible for most of the world's CO_2 emissions are state-owned. Most sea plastic comes from the fishing industry, not consumer waste. As useful as our collective efforts are, only a global response can save the biosphere. When we realise this, our sense of agency and hope can easily collapse.

How do we cope? How do we survive and fight back? Reframing our grief as normal and healthy is a good place to start. In her essay 'On Grief', Rebecca Tamás cautions against environmental despair. Drawing from Freud's distinction between the pain of mourning and the self-critical defeat of melancholia, she argues that mourning is a necessary part of life, and a reminder of why what we love is worth fighting for. To accept and nurture grief is to expand and express the depth of our love, to turn it into action. As Tamás explains, 'to grieve for the ecosystems, beings and people destroyed by climate change, is to give them the dignity, respect and love which they deserve. It is right that extinctions are met with mourning, that space is made in our emotions for the enormity of the loss.' Grief should not be a closing down to the world, but an opening up.

What does it mean, in practice, to grieve for the world? We have rituals to cope with human death – funerals and celebrations of life, songs and ceremonies, which mark the passage from one state of being to the next. Looking out across the Severn estuary, I wonder what kind of funeral I would hold for this tidal landscape. What, or who, would be honoured: the mud, the water, the cliffs that have known dissolution and submersion, which are now waiting to recede again beneath the encroaching waves?

In their short experimental encyclopaedia *Anticipatory History*, Caitlin DeSilvey, Simon Naylor and Colin Sackett offer a new vocabulary of words and concepts to help us navigate the uncertainty and anxiety of a changing world. One of these is 'palliative curation'. Adapted from practices of end-of-life care, palliative curation involves an ethical and compassionate attitude to landmarks and landscapes that will be tangibly altered by climate crisis. When land is being lost, or ecosystems in collapse, 'the tendency is to look away, and pretend that all is well, until the expiration date applies'. Palliative curation invites us to bear witness to the gradual loss, and to be curious about the future left behind after that cliff or species has vanished. More than that, it asks us to be active in mourning and commemorating its loss.

'The gradual stages of unmaking could be accompanied by cultural events, rituals of leave-taking that help us bridge the gap between "there" and "gone".'

Maybe these ceremonies can act as a warning, an attempt to stop change in its tracks. A few years ago, I went to a tidal festival on the banks of the Avon. We were there to celebrate the extraordinary range and fluidity of this watery ecosystem. The Severn estuary itself can shift up to fifty feet in a matter of hours. At certain times each year, the tidal force pushing in from the five-mile-wide mouth of the river gets funnelled upstream, building in energy until it is pushed back down to sea in the form of one long wave called the Severn bore. Following a nine-year cycle that corresponds to the tug of the moon, the bore at its highest attracts surfers and anyone fascinated by its cosmic occurrence. I've not seen the biggest, 'five star' bore, but that night I stood on the banks of the Avon close to where it flows into the channel and watched the water lap over the tarmac of the road under a blue full moon. I have never felt closer to the dark mystery of water, or as caught up in its flow.

Of course, the festival wasn't a farewell, but part of a campaign to spark love for the tides. Living by a river prone to flooding isn't easy, and some locals would rather the water was kept under control than allowed to rise and rise. Plans for a tidal barrage, which will help do this, are ever on the horizon, a feat of engineering designed to harness the renewable energy of the waves and protect coastal areas from storm surges and sea-level rise. It should be an easy win for the green crowd, but the price will be the end of these tidal reaches and the unique ecosystems they support. There's the loss of the cultural meaning of the tides too – the songs and stories, the fishing and boat communities that have worked with their challenging constraints. Although the festival was celebratory, not palliative, dwelling on the future unmaking of this land was inevitable, and the tidal marshes looked a lot like land already in the process of disintegration.

That's the problem: what if the ritual is too much to bear, the leave-taking too hard to process? The poet CAConrad reflects on this in an interview about a series of poems they have undertaken, each beginning with a performance or personal act of endurance, after which they produce a poem. As Conrad explains, 'RESURRECT EXTINCT VIBRATION' starts with 'a ritual where I lie on the ground and listen to various recordings of recently extinct birds, mammals and reptiles'. The purpose is to 'return these sounds to my body; it's a returning, a restoration of vibratory frequencies'. The ritual seeks to restore lost equilibrium, to reconnect the body with the earth and its lost creatures through the intimacy of sound. It reminds me of a term used in conservation, 'shifting baselines'. As each generation grows up in a quieter, less biodiverse world, their expectations of what is normal change. They do not miss the wildlife that is gone or the ecosystems that have collapsed. Their baselines have shifted.

Conrad challenges this through their ritual. Our bodies are part of the web of life, attuned to its frequencies and the lives of which we are a part. Although these creatures are gone, their vibrations are still with us and *in* us. In some ways, they *are* us too. In speaking of the web of life, Conrad gestures to the science of ecosystems. Ecology tells us all life is interconnected, and the loss of a species ricochets out across the globe, creating a domino effect that may be subtle, catastrophic, brief or long-lasting. Speaking of the web, Conrad also evokes the Vedic metaphor of Indra's net. In the Hua–Yen school of Buddhism, the net is used to describe the interpenetration of all life, and the principle that 'what affects one item in the cosmos affects every other'. This might make us sound like little atoms, connected to each other, but ultimately alone. That's not the point. We are bound together, as if part of one 'living body in which each cell derives its life from all the other cells, and in return gives life to those many others'.

Listening to the voices of the dead is not just a ritual commemoration, but a way of pulling at the strings left dormant in the body, the little links in the mesh gone quiet after a species has been lost. Those creatures are not in the world, but in some way they are *in us* – certainly in the bodies of those who were alive on the earth at the same moment. By vibrating in frequency, the ritual tries to reignite those links and reanimate the dead. But this isn't exactly comforting. There's a zombie quality to the act of inviting these animals to return, because as Conrad puts it, 'they are NOT returning, which makes this one of the most cruel rituals I have ever done to myself'.

If we are all part of the net, enmeshed in the whole, part of one living body, then what we are grieving for is not just a landscape, not just a species, but a part of ourselves. Or more than that. In realising our entanglement, our sense of who we are and what it means to be *ourselves* changes. As Judith Butler puts it in *Precarious Life: The Power of Mourning and Violence* (2006), 'When we lose some of these ties by which we are constituted, we do not know who we are or what to do. On one level, I think I have lost "you" only to discover that "I" have gone missing as well.'

The more we dwell on loss – whether of a particular place, species, or nature itself – the less protected, the less detached the 'I' seems to be. This contradicts the basic principles of individualism. Wellbeing is all too often supposed to be a solitary affair, a personal responsibility. Whatever happens to nature doesn't concern us, because one way or another humanity will (probably) survive. The story of ecological grief and solastalgia tells us otherwise. Our ties to other lives constitute what we are; they compose us. Our baselines may shift, and a child born now may never feel deeply the loss of the extinct creatures and endlings (the last survivors of species on the brink of collapse). But we could never process our grief at the loss of the relations that bind us. Unlike the process of healthy mourning that Freud describes, we cannot slowly recover by releasing our attachment to what we have lost. We find that in the process, we have gone missing too.

In the low-lying island nation of Kiribati in the Pacific, people are preparing for the impacts of accelerated climate change. Around 100,000 people are set to be displaced across the archipelago, which at its highest point is no more than two metres above sea level. Already, salt water is penetrating the fresh-water wells, and growing crops is getting harder. As former president Anote Tong explains, the country will soon be underwater. There is no time to speculate about imagined futures. 'Either we build the islands up ... or we build floating islands, or we are not here ... we migrate.' Sea walls are being erected, houses relocated inland. A tract of land has been purchased in Fiji as insurance for the worst-case scenario. The gap between 'there' and 'gone' is thin in this threatened place.

But adjusting to the loss of land is a very different challenge in this island community. Advice to take practical steps, like make a managed retreat, does not take account of the relationships the people of Kiribati have with the land. Climate change is not feared simply because it will damage property; land here is sacred and passed down within families. 'Our ancestral lands are not bought by us, we inherit it.' These are the words of Pelenise Alofa, a Kiribati citizen and researcher at the University of the South Pacific, who was interviewed by the filmmaker Sara Penrhyn Jones in 2015. The same story is repeated by other cultural custodians and activists across Kiribati. Teweiariki Teaero, a scholar and artist, explains that in Kiribati, land 'is connected with your ancestry and your history as a particular clan'. Even the words for land and people are the same: 'You can't have one without the other.' Land underpins language and faith, and is held as a responsibility by families, binding them to the past and ensuring they are always living partly in the future, thinking about the lives of coming generations.

Living in ancestral time is alien in much of the West, though more familiar in many Indigenous cultures. Kyle P. Whyte, an environmental justice scholar and member of the North American Citizen Potawatomi Nation, has pointed out that different temporal imaginaries exist across many Native cultures. In the Anishinaabe tradition, the 'expression *aanikoobijigan* (*yankobjegen*)' means ancestor and descendent at the same time. Time is intergenerational, and it 'makes sense to consider ourselves as living alongside future and past relatives simultaneously as we walk through life'. While non-Indigenous societies are more likely to draw time as a straight line connecting past, present and future, Whyte offers a spiral as a way of describing a common form of Indigenous experience. Living in spiralling time, people ask 'questions about how ancestral and future generations would interpret the situations that we find ourselves in today'. To non-Indigenous people, this can sound a little like science fiction or time travel. But time travel is just a way of relating to the past and the future at once, and this is something we all do every day simply by participating in life on earth.

Because the people of Kiribati also live in ancestral time, 'being relocated is the biggest disaster', according to Pelenise Alofa. Relations with ancestors are not memories, but a constant presence as people navigate land and water to fish and farm. 'The line between the dead and the living in Kiribati culture is very fine,' says Teaero. 'We move easily between the two. Dead people for us – dead ancestors – are as important as the living.' In some parts of the islands, areas are given over entirely to the dead. To travel there involves rituals and polite forms of approach, ways of acknowledging relations and strengthening them, again and again.

What kinds of rituals could be invented to say goodbye to Kiribati, when it is home to the dead, who are as present as the living? It's a paradoxical question, fusing love, land and life in ways that take me – and those not living in ancestral time – further than we have thought or felt before. This is grief on a different scale, a loss of a sense of self unimaginable. 'I wouldn't know how to tell my children where I come from, especially my grandchildren, if Kiribati is not here,' says Pelenise Alofa. But at the same time, she is concerned about the practicalities. 'How can you leave a land that all your families are buried in? ... Maybe we have to dig everything, all our families up and put them together, and we go with them. Maybe that's one way.'

It's obvious that living this way – as the canary in the climate coalmine – is depressing. Ecological grief, solastalgia, climate despair: they could have been invented to describe life in the sightlines of sea-level rise in Kiribati. Claire Anterea Tangaroa of Kiribati Climate Action Network admits this: 'It is sad for me to keep saying about it, that my people will have nowhere to go.' At the same time, this premeditated mourning traps the islands in negativity. Framing Kiribati as doomed to inevitable submersion is giving in, and practically manifesting the real event.

Organisations like 350 Pacific refuse to do this. A youth-led grassroots network working across the Pacific Islands, it spreads awareness about sea-level rise, lobbies international powers like the UN, and connects with similar groups worldwide. And there's no shortage of such alliances. The Climate Action Network, of which the Kiribati group is a part, is a global network of 1,300 NGOs in 130 countries fighting the climate emergency. The goals for this network and others (like the Indigenous Environmental Network, founded in the 1990s) are to end the era of 'extreme energy', moving beyond fossil fuels, nuclear power, waste and biomass incineration, landfill gas, mega-hydro and agrofuels. Indigenous sovereignty over land and decision-making is a key part of that, as is taking on the banking sector – which is financing the fossil-fuel industry – ending extreme poverty and demanding just and sustainable recovery post-Covid-19 and in an ecologically altered world.

As I grew up in the 1980s and 1990s, the climate crisis shaped my sense of reality. It was part of my education, showing up in movies and lessons, a scary vision of the future on the far edges of the horizon. In spite of all this education and awareness-raising, very little seemed to be being done about it. When I was a child I watched older generations speculate about whether it might be a hoax, or a natural warming phase, or simply overstated. In my twenties, I participated in marches and climate camps. These actions were on the fringes though: mainstream news and public discourse were indifferent and dismissive. The climate crisis was treated as a political or philosophical question. Pundits and intellectuals questioned whether climate change was simply too complicated for governments to handle, or the human mind to grasp. Perhaps we just aren't wired to think in such grandiose scales? Faced with global ecological meltdown, the imagination collapses, thought shuts down.

Picturing the waters creeping up Aust Cliff, the Severn bridges submerged, I understand the challenge. The extreme imagery of the flood evokes apocalypse narratives as old as the Bible and the epic of Gilgamesh, as well as Hollywood blockbusters like *Waterworld* (1995) or *The Day After Tomorrow* (2004). But why should we need fantastical stories to predict the end of the world? The reality is, Indigenous people have already lived through an apocalypse. Colonisation, genocide, forced movement and ecological devastation mean the world is already post-apocalyptic. As Kyle P. Whyte puts it, Indigenous people are already living 'in what their ancestors would have seen as fantasy times. Some of their ancestors at particular times in history, were they told of today's conditions of Indigenous peoples, would have believed they were hearing fantastic tales.' If we still don't know how to understand disaster, live with the grief, and begin to create change, we should listen to the people of Kiribati. We should learn from Indigenous people, who have been living in the end times for centuries.

It will be painfully ironic if non-Indigenous people give up to climate despair the moment we see a glimpse of an apocalyptic future that will affect us in the so-called 'first world'. The fact that the ecological destruction and suffering inflicted on Indigenous people and formerly colonised countries is now returning, in the form of the climate crisis, to create pain for those who profited from it might look a lot like karma playing out. It isn't that, though – if it were, the people who pollute the least would not be suffering first and worst. What we are seeing is the result of exploitation of the world and its people reaching an obvious, painful conclusion. Treating nature and people as commodities, acting as if we live alone on this earth, and pretending the future isn't coming: these are not ways to create human or ecological wellbeing. We cannot survive and flourish without dismantling these values.

The grey water and the mud of the Severn estuary shimmer for miles ahead of me, and behind me the Triassic rocks show what the land might look like as a seabed without me even having to imagine it. When geologists first discovered the age of the earth and realised that natural processes acting over millennia had created the land they took to be ready-made by God, the experience changed them fundamentally. The age of the living earth was mind-boggling, dizzying, disorderly. 'The mind seemed to grow giddy by looking so far into the abyss of time,' as Scottish scientist John Playfair wrote in 1788 after gazing too long at the rocks. But now we live with geological time without trouble or existential collapse. Minds are constantly expanding.

Trying to actually create psychological, political or behavioural change can be miserable work. Anyone who has been involved in a movement as a campaigner or activist will know what it is like to come up against obstacles, for your ideas to go nowhere, for the police to rush in and tear up the banners and tents. Activist burnout is real and mental illness among protesters rife. 'How do people cope and retain hope under the weight of these contexts? How do individuals come to struggle; to the attempt to effect change by exerting agency?' These questions are posed by anthropologist and activist Sian Sullivan. Reflecting on her own experience and observation of anti-capitalist communities, Sullivan describes how activists become desensitised to the heartbreak of failed campaigns, or turn the anger and the pain inward. Self-harm and depression become commonplace as responses to 'the pain, fear and anger felt at the multiplicitous violence of modern society, and a yearning for release from these contexts'.

And still we turn up again and again. I beat myself up for not doing more, but I know that when I've made my way to the streets for a protest, committed to union work or gone door-knocking, I feel the most urgent outpourings of hope, optimism and love. This is as true when I believe everything is going our way as when I know the campaign to be doomed. That's not to say that organising isn't painful. The original meaning of self-care, as defined by Audre Lorde, was the time-out needed to recover strength to persist, survive and fight. Self-care is basic self-compassion, and in an economy that thrives on overwork, burnout and despair, it is radical. At the same time, as the American writer and feminist Starhawk insists, organising and taking action feels really good because we're 'taking action – particularly environmental action – to stop the destruction of the Earth, we're doing an act of healing and we are free. There are few times when we are free in this culture and this is one of them.' The freedom feels a lot like 'being away' to me, just like theories of the nature cure tell us we can be in natural places. It is a way of leaving one kind of reality – a broken and suffering one – and entering another. We get there by taking steps to imagine and create a different world.

Sometimes, calls to be 'hopeful' can sound terribly naïve. Being hopeful can feel a lot like kicking a problem into the long grass, assuming someone else will come along and sort it out later. But hope is something we do. Hope is action, and hope is messy. If there is any hope to be found in the multiple struggles, social and ecological, that constitute our reality now, it is this: because the frontlines of the struggle are everywhere, there are opportunities for empowerment, for freedom and action everywhere too.

History used to be told through the stories of great men and their powerful deeds, but now we know better.

Ordinary people make history, and big events take time, often years, to organise. In collective acts, small but persistent gestures, tides turn and the world is remade.

The same thing may be true of climate action. Timothy Clark describes Anthropocene disorder as a problem with scale-framing. We feel despair when we believe our little actions to be meaningless. But if you contextualise your actions and reframe the scale in which you're trying to act, small gestures suddenly seem less absurd. You develop a clearer sense of how they relate to mid-scale, even macro-level changes, and how they connect to someone else's campaign or protest. Recognise that you are not a lonely hero tasked with saving the world, but can 'organise together in adversity', and you will feel less alone.

It's probably a bit strange, but standing on the banks of the Severn at dusk brings this home to me. Gulls wheel and cry. Fog is rolling down the estuary and the tide is drawing in. Semi-petrified mud thins again. Air that was trapped in the sludge pops and mudworms writhe. Matter is moving, and the earth is not in a cycle of loss, but a constant process of becoming.

It is matter in motion that made this landscape. The cliffs may have been pushed up by volcanic intensity, but they were worn down and layered up by the tides and by movements of life – aquatic, vegetal and mineral. In geology and ecology, no action is wasted. Everything connects. Standing here and watching matter change state, I see how vast energies like tides, and people, and the creeping of mud-snails and sea lampreys have made the world.

Bibliography

Introduction

'These questions matter, because…' '68% of the world
 population projected to live in urban areas by 2050, says
 UN', United Nations (16 May 2018), https://www.un.org/
 development/desa/en/news/population/2018-revision-of-
 world-urbanization-prospects.html
'Nature holds the key…' E. O. Wilson, *Biophilia*, Cambridge,
 MA: Harvard University Press, 1984, p. 79
'The "hedonic" concerns…' Mohsen Joshanloo, 'Optimal
 human functioning around the world: A new index of
 eudaimonic well-being in 166 nations', *British Journal of
 Psychology* 109 (2018), pp. 637–55; pp. 637–8
'The American psychologist Abraham Maslow's "hierarchy
 of needs"…' Abraham Maslow, 'A Theory of Human
 Motivation', *Psychological Review* 50:4 (1943), pp. 370–96
'But to experience "transcendence"…' Abraham Maslow,
 The Farther Reaches of Human Nature, New York: The Viking
 Press, 1971, p. 269
'It was vital to do this…' Howard Clinebell, *Ecotherapy: Healing
 Ourselves, Healing the Earth*, Oxford: Routledge, 1996, p. 2
'Depression is one of the leading causes…' see 'Mental
 Health' at World Health Organisation, https://www.who.
 int/health-topics/mental-health#tab=tab_1

'In 2019, a report by Natural England…' 'Monitor of Engagement with the Natural Environment', Natural England, 2019, https://assets.publishing.service.gov.uk/government/uploads/system/uploads/attachment_data/file/828552/Monitor_Engagement_Natural_Environment_2018_2019_v2.pdf

'A comparable report…' 'Monitor of Engagement with the Natural Environment Children and Young People Report', Natural England, 2019, https://assets.publishing.service.gov.uk/government/uploads/system/uploads/attachment_data/file/828838/Monitor_of_Engagement_with_the_Natural_Environment__MENE__Childrens_Report_2018-2019_rev.pdf

'But nature may be somewhere…' Audre Lorde, *A Burst of Light*, Long Island: Ixia Press, 2017 (1988), p. 130

'The geographer Wilbert Gesler…' Wilbert Gesler, *Healing Places*, Washington, D.C.: Rowman and Littlefield, 2003

Water

'Once in the water…' Roger Deakin, *Waterlog: A Swimmer's Journey through Britain*, London: Vintage, 2000 (1999), p. 3

'Our minds are no longer as turbulent…' Tessa Wardley, *The Mindful Art of Wild Swimming: Reflections for Zen Seekers*, Brighton: Leaping Hare Press, 2017, p. 42

'The actual, physical water of Lourdes…' Bernard François, Esther M. Sternberg and Elizabeth Fee, 'The Lourdes Medical Cures Revisited', *Journal of the History of Medicine and Allied Sciences* 69:1 (January 2014), pp. 135–62

'Mikveh is a place…' Marjorie Ingall, 'Transgender Jews Find a Place in the Mikveh', *Tablet Magazine* (17 November 2017), https://www.tabletmag.com/sections/belief/articles/transgender-jews-in-the-mikveh

'We are people of the inlet…' Will George quoted in 'Coast Salish Territories: Indigenous Land Defenders Denounce

Canada's Criminalization at Burnaby Mountain', It's Going Down (4 April 2018), https://itsgoingdown. org/coast-salish-territories-indigenous-land-defenders-denounce-criminalization-at-burnaby-mountain/

'Environmental sociologist…' Sonya Sachdeva, 'The Influence of Sacred Beliefs in Environmental Risk Perception and Attitudes', *Environment and Behaviour* 49:5 (2017)

'Across Central, Western and Southern Africa…' Henry John Drewal et al., 'Mami Wata: Arts for Water Spirits in Africa and its Diasporas', *African Arts* 41:2 (2008), p. 60

'Rhiannon Lucy Cosslett – a writer who is…' Rhiannon Lucy Cosslett, '"Wild Swimming"? We used to just call it swimming,' Guardian (29 January 2020), https://www.theguardian.com/commentisfree/2020/jan/29/swimming-wild-trend-social-media-cliche

'At home, mother, law…' Simone de Beauvoir, *The Second Sex*, London: Vintage, 1997 (1949), p. 386

'She was becoming herself…' Kate Chopin, *The Awakening*, Putnam: New York, 1964 (1899), pp. 147–8

'One of the psychologists who has most thoughtfully…' Donald Winnicott, *The Maturational Process and the Facilitating Environment*, Abingdon: Routledge, 2018 (1965)

'In fiction and in memoir…' Tsitsi Dangarembga, *Nervous Conditions*, Oxford: Ayebia Clarke, 1988, p. 4

'In water, like in books…' Lidia Yuknavitch, *The Chronology of Water*, Edinburgh: Canongate, 2019 (2011), p. 132

'Not that the river is like the body…' Elizabeth-Jane Burnett, 'Preface', *Swims*, London: Penned in the Margins, 2017, p. 15

'In the 1960s an outlandish hypothesis…' Alister Hardy, 'Was Man More Aquatic in the Past?' *New Scientist* 7:174 (17 March 1960), pp. 642–45

'According to one poll…' Natasha Hinde, 'Can Swimming Help Fight Depression And Anxiety? 1.4 Million People Think So', *Huffington Post* (8 October 2018), https://www.huffingtonpost.co.uk/

entry/how-swimming-can-help-mental-health_
uk_5bbb1cade4b0876eda9f879b

'Swimming as a treatment for depression...' Christoffer van
Tulleken, Michael Tipton, Heather Massey et al., 'Open
water swimming as a treatment for major depressive
disorder', BMJ Case Reports (2018), https://pubmed.ncbi.
nlm.nih.gov/30131418/

'In 2000 in Finland...' B. Dugué and E. Leppänen,
'Adaptation related to cytokines in man: effects of regular
swimming in ice-cold water', Clinical Physiology 20 (2000),
pp. 114–21

Mountains

'Life, it frequently seems in the mountains...' Robert
Macfarlane, Mountains of the Mind: A History of Fascination,
London: Granta, 2003, p. 71

'Dennis was drawn to them...' John Dennis in
Andrew Ashfield and Peter de Bolla, eds., The
Sublime: A Reader in British Eighteenth-Century Aesthetic
Theory, Cambridge: Cambridge University Press,
1996, p. 59

'Standing on the edge of a precipice...' Edmund Burke,
A Philosophical Enquiry Into the Sublime and the Beautiful,
London: Penguin, 2004 (1757), p. 101

'The artist James Barry...' James Barry, 'Letter to Edmund
Burke', in James Boulton and T. O. McLoughlin, eds.,
News from Abroad: Letters Written by British Travellers on
the Grand Tour 1728–71, Liverpool: Liverpool University
Press, 2012 (1765–71), p. 183

'Writing in 1836 of the Mer de Glace...' Mariana Starke,
Travels in Europe and in the Island of Sicily, Paris: Galignani,
1836, p. 54

'Gazing on the...' Percy Bysshe Shelley, 'Mont Blanc: Lines
Written in the Vale of Chamouni', 1816

'In Byron's ...' Lord Byron, *Childe Harold's Pilgrimage*, 1812–18

'This man has overcome nature...' Gillian Carter, '"Domestic Geography" and the Politics of Scottish Landscape in Nan Shepherd's The Living Mountain', *Gender, Place and Culture: A Journal of Feminist Geography*, 8:1 (2001), pp. 25–36

'There's a pungently masculine...' Sarah Jaquette Ray, *The Ecological Other: Environmental Exclusion in American Culture*, Tucson: University of Arizona Press, 2013, p. 41

'Man is alone...' *Scottish Ski Club* Magazine 1–2, Edinburgh: T. S. Muir, 1909–15, p. 207

'As he wrote in 1939...' R. L. G. Irving, *The Mountain Way: An Anthology in Prose and Verse*, London: J. M. Dent and Sons, 1939, p. xx

'I work to expand my comfort zone...' Alex Honnold, 'Free Solo 360', *National Geographic* (September 2018) on YouTube, https://www.youtube.com/watch?v=FRGF77fB AeM&list=PL5Tx3hMIoDV6wj8fDwKBEx5pUpDcIt68v

'It's a way of reshaping the emotional charge...' Marie Monfils quoted in J. B. MacKinnon, 'The Strange Brain of the World's Greatest Solo Climber', *Nautilus* (11 August 2016), https://nautil.us/issue/39/sport/ the-strange-brain-of-the-worlds-greatest-solo-climber

'They want the startling view...' Nan Shepherd, *The Living Mountain*, Edinburgh: Canongate, 2011 (1977), p. 16

'As Robert Macfarlane puts it...' Robert Macfarlane, 'Introduction' to *The Living Mountain*, Edinburgh: Canongate, 2011, p. xvii

'Anna Fleming, an author and climber...' Anna Fleming, 'Let's go bouldering', *The Granite Sea* (6 May 2019), https://thegranitesea.wordpress.com/2019/05/06/ lets-go-bouldering/

'I have had fewer extreme episodes...' quoted in Joanna Rowbottom, 'How to harness positive mental wellbeing by rock climbing', British Mountaineering Council

(2 February 2017), https://www.thebmc.co.uk/
Positive-mental-wellbeing-through-rock-climbing

'The terrible event…' Gregg Mitman, *Breathing Space: How Allergies Shape Our Lives and Landscapes*, New Haven & London: Yale University Press, 2007, p. 17

'Thoreau admitted that he felt…' Henry David Thoreau, *Letter to Harrison Blake*, 7 December 1856

'Emerson slotted human health…' Ralph Waldo Emerson, *Nature and Other Addresses*, New York: John B. Alden, 1886, p. 13; pp. 8–9

'On "Ktaadn", as he called it…' Henry David Thoreau, 'Ktaadn and the Maine Woods', *The Union Magazine*, 1848

'Mountains became the quintessential…' William Cronon, 'The Trouble with Wilderness' in *Uncommon Ground: Rethinking the Human Place in Nature*, New York: Norton, 1996, pp. 69–90; p. 69

'A lifelong lover of nature…' John Muir, 'The Creation of Yosemite National Park: Letters of John Muir to Robert Underwood Johnson', *Sierra Club Bulletin* 29:5 (1944), pp. 49–60

'From then on, the Sierra…' John Muir, *The Writings of John Muir: My First Summer in the Sierra*, Boston and New York: Houghton Mifflin, 1917 (1911), p. 131; p. 54; p. 55

'Native people are reduced to…' Shepard Krech, *The Ecological Indian: Myth and History*, New York: Norton, 2000

'Thousands of tired…' John Muir, 'The Wild Parks and Forest Reservations of the West', *Nature Writings*, New York: Library of America, 1997 (1901), pp. 721–2

'Roosevelt returned…' Theodore Roosevelt, *Outdoor Pastimes of an American Hunter*, Mechanicsburg: Stackpole Books, 1990 (1905), p. 317

'In his attempt to save the mountains…' John Muir, 'Hetch Hetchy Valley', *Nature Writings*, (1908) p. 814

'He made derogatory comments about Black people…' Associated Press, 'Sierra Club apologizes for racist views of "father of national parks" John Muir', Guardian (23 July

2020), https://www.theguardian.com/environment/2020/
jul/23/john-muir-sierra-club-apologizes-for-racist-views

'A "nonessentialized black environmental identity"…'
Carolyn Finney, *Black Faces, White Spaces: Reimagining
the Relationship of African Americans to the Great Outdoors*,
Chapel Hill: University of North Carolina Press, 2014, p. 3

'You shouldn't climb…' Tony Tjamiwa quoted in Libby
Stewart, 'Closure of Uluru Climb', National Museum of
Australia (26 October 2019), https://www.nma.gov.au/
explore/blog/closing-the-climb

'The tourist comes here with the camera…' Tony
Tjamiwa quoted in Kennedy Warne, 'Why Australia is
banning climbers from this iconic natural landmark',
National Geographic (April/May 2018), https://
www.nationalgeographic.co.uk/adventure/2019/09/
why-australia-banning-climbers-iconic-natural-landmark

'As the organisers of Kendal Mountain Festival's…' at 'Open
Mountains: Space and Isolation', Kendal Mountain Festival,
https://tour.kendalmountainfestival.com/literature-art/
open-mountain-space-and-isolation

'The "exhilarating eight-hour journey"…' Alice Tarbuck,
'Walking' in *On Bodies: An Anthology*, London: Three of
Cups Press, 2018, pp. 17–24

Forest

'The Firesticks Alliance…' Firesticks Alliance Indigenous
Corporation, 'What is Cultural Burning?' Firesticks,
https://www.firesticks.org.au/about/cultural-burning/

'The young William Wordsworth…' William Wordsworth,
'Nutting', *Lyrical Ballads*, 1800

'Thoreau took his "tonic of wildness"…' Thoreau, *Walden*,
Oxford: Oxford University Press, 1997 (1854), p. 282

'John Muir thought…' John Muir, *The Wilderness World of John
Muir*, Boston: Houghton Mifflin, 2001 (1954), p. 312

'Under the influence of the Transcendentalists...' Ben Harris, 'Therapeutic Work and Mental Illness in America', in Waltraud Ernst, ed., *Work, Psychiatry and Society, 1751–2015*, Manchester: Manchester University Press, 2016, pp. 56–76

'Juliet is sceptical of the treatment...' D. H. Lawrence, 'The Sun' in *The Woman Who Rode Away*, London: Penguin, 1973 (1928), pp. 27–44

'In recent studies, forest baths...' see J. Lee et al., 'Effect of Forest Bathing on Physiological and Psychological Responses in Young Japanese Male Subjects', *Public Health* 125:2 (January 2011), pp. 93–100; Bum Jin Park et al., 'The physiological effects of *Shinrin-yoku*: evidence from field experiments in 24 forests across Japan', *Environmental Health and Preventive Medicine* 15:1 (2010), pp. 18–26

'In a 2008 study...' Qing Li et al., 'Visiting a forest, but not a city, increases human natural killer activity and expression of anti-cancer proteins', *International Journal of Immunopathology and Pharmacology* 21:1 (2008), pp. 117–27

'Similar changes also took place...' Qing Li et al., 'A forest bathing trip increases human natural killer activity and expression of anti-cancer proteins in female subjects', *Journal of Biological Regulators and Homeostatic Agents* 22:1 (2008), pp. 45–55

'Offices were criticised...' Koji Morioka, 'Work till You Drop', *New Labor Forum* 13:1 (2004), pp. 80–85

'Now, there are sixty-two recognised forest bathing...' '62 Forests Across Japan', *Forest Therapy Society*, https://www.fo-society.jp/quarter/cn49/62forest_across_japan.html

'The eco-philosopher Timothy Morton...' Timothy Morton, *The Ecological Thought*, Cambridge, MA: Harvard University Press, 2010, p. 16

'As the historian Clark Lawlor puts it...' Clark Lawlor, 'Fashionable Melancholy' in *Melancholy Experience in Literature of the Long Eighteenth Century*, London: Palgrave Macmillan, 2011, pp. 25–53, p. 25

'In Grizzly Man (2005)...' Werner Herzog, Grizzly Man, 2005

'The literary scholar Simon Estok...' Simon Estok,
    'Theorizing in a Space of Ambivalent Openness:
    Ecocriticism and Ecophobia', *ISLE: Interdisciplinary Studies
    in Literature and Environment* 16:2 (Spring 2009), pp. 203–25

'Since the Middle Ages...' Rod Giblett, 'Theology of
    wetlands: Tolkien and *Beowulf* on marshes and their
    monsters', *Green Letters* 19:2 (2015), pp. 132–43

'A sociocultural context...' Laurel B. Watson, 'Understanding
    the Relationships Among White and African American
    Women's Sexual Objectification Experiences, Physical
    Safety Anxiety, and Psychological Distress', *Sex Roles*
    72:3–4 (February 2015), pp. 91–104

'A woman from the city...' Ingrid Pollard, 'Pastoral Interlude',
    in *Postcards Home*, London: Autograph, 2004, pp. 18–29

'The traditional context of the nature poem...' Camille
    T. Dungy, 'Introduction' in *Black Nature: Four Centuries of
    African American Nature Poetry*, Athens, GA: University of
    Georgia Press, 2009, p. xxi; p. xxiv

'Instead, writing comes from the perspective...' Gerald
    Barrax in *Black Nature*, p. 40

Garden

'For Mary, and another isolated child...' Frances Hodgson
    Burnett, *The Secret Garden*, Oxford: Oxford University
    Press, 2011 (1911), p.66

'The environmental philosopher...' Donna Haraway,
    'Anthropocene, Capitalocene, Plantationocene,
    Chthulucene: Making Kin', *Environmental Humanities*
    6:1 (May 2015), pp. 159–65

'It's more a recognition that...' Seth Wynes and Kimberly
    Nicholas, 'The climate mitigation gap: education and
    government recommendations miss the most effective
    individual actions', *Environmental Research Letters* 12:7
    (July 2017) pp. 1–9

'While every garden is planted...' D. Fairchild Ruggles, *Islamic Gardens and Landscapes*, Oxford: Oxford University Press, 2008, p. 6

'As Dr Geri Augusto...' Geri Augusto, 'The Importance of Okra to Enslaved People', National Museums Liverpool (10 August 2018), https://www.youtube.com/watch?v=KlGylKHTI4Q

'In the modern-day Center for the Study of Slavery...' Geri Augusto, 'The Center for the Study of Slavery and Justice, Brown University', *Africology: The Journal of Pan African Studies* 11:2 (January 2018), http://jpanafrican.org/docs/vol11no2/11.2-24-CenterfortheStudy.pdf

'Limpid springs...' Xiaoshan Yang, *Metamorphosis of the Private Sphere: Gardens and Objects in Tang-Song Poetry*, Cambridge, MA: Harvard University Press, 2003, p. 11

'Settling down beside...' Shi Chong, 'Preface to the Jingu Garden Poems' (*c.* 296 CE), *Early Medieval China: A Sourcebook*, New York: Columbia University Press, 2014, pp. 533–4

'Let a garden adjoin this house...' Benjamin Rush, *Essays Literary, Moral, and Philosophical*, Philadelphia: Thomas and William Bradford, 1798, p. 150

'One survey of English hospital gardens...' and other quotes, Clare Hickman, *Therapeutic Landscapes: A History of English Hospital Gardens Since 1800*, Manchester: Manchester University Press, 2013, pp. 115–28

'Florence Nightingale favoured...' Florence Nightingale, *Notes on Hospitals*, London: Longman Green, 1863 (1859), p. 77

'The seasonal nature of gardening...' Anita Unruh, 'The meaning of gardens and gardening in daily life: a comparison between gardeners with serious health problems and healthy participants', *Acta Horticulturae* 639 (2004), pp. 67–73

'Underpinning this new medical trend...' see Roger Ulrich et al., 'Stress Recovery During Exposure to Natural and Urban Environments', *Journal of Environmental Psychology* 11 (1991), pp. 201–30

'Above all what matters...' Maggie Keswick Jencks, 'Our Story', Maggie's, https://www.maggies.org/about-us/how-maggies-works/our-story/

'Unlike sleep...'; 'Natural settings are rich...' Stephen Kaplan, 'The Restorative Benefits of Nature: Toward an Integrative Framework', *Journal of Environmental Psychology* 15:3 (1995), pp. 169–182; p.172; p. 174

'Some scholars have criticised ART...' see Yannick Joye and Siegfried Dewitte, 'Nature's broken path to restoration: A critical look at Attention Restoration Theory', *Journal of Environmental Psychology* 59 (2018), pp.1–8

'In one study...' Anna Chiumento et al., 'A haven of greenspace: learning from a pilot pre-post evaluation of a school-based social and therapeutic horticulture intervention with children', *BMC Public Health* 18:836 (2018), p. 8

'Everybody knows...' and other quotes, Paul Stevens, 'A Hypnosis Framing of Therapeutic Horticulture for Mental Health Rehabilitation', *The Humanistic Psychologist* 46:3 (June 2018), pp. 258–73

'But alternative relations...' Anna Tsing, *The Mushroom at the End of the World: On the Possibility of Life in Capitalist Ruins*, Princeton: Princeton University Press, 2015

'Peruvian curanderos...' X. Jauregui et al., '"Plantas con madre": Plants that teach and guide in the shamanic initiation process in the East-Central Peruvian Amazon', *Journal of Ethnopharmacology* 134:3 (2011), pp. 739–52

'How is it possible...'; 'We make a grave error...'; 'We put a barrier between us...' and 'it felt like ... a remembering...' Robin Wall Kimmerer, *Braiding Sweetgrass*, Minneapolis: Milkweed, 2013, p. 6; p. 16; p. 57

'They talk to me...' Stevens, 'A Hypnosis Framing', p. 265

'In eukaryotic organisms that...' A. H. Knoll, et al. 'Eukaryotic organisms in Proterozoic oceans', *Philosophical Transactions of the Royal Society of London* 361:1470 (2006), pp. 1023–38; Traci Watson, 'These bizarre ancient species are rewriting animal evolution', *Nature* 586 (28 October 2020), pp. 662–5, https://www.nature.com/articles/d41586-020-02985-z

'Many plants have something of the animal…' J. Arthur Thomson, *Mountain and Moorland*, London: Macmillan, 1921, p. 19

'Research papers exploring plants' effectiveness…' Andy Coghlan, 'Psychedelic drug ayahuasca improves hard-to-treat depression', *New Scientist* (14 April 2017), https://www.newscientist.com/article/2127802-psychedelic-drug-ayahuasca-improves-hard-to-treat-depression/

'It's not snobby or elitist…' Nicholas Culpeper, *Complete Herbal*, Ware: Omega, 1985 (1653), p. 18–19

Park

'It's difficult for us to notice now…' Humphry Repton, *Observations on the Theory and Practice of Landscape Gardening*, London: T. Bensley, 1805 (1803), p. 84

'Inspiration came from the Chinese garden…' John Fleming, Hugh Honour and Nikolaus Pevsner, *The Penguin Dictionary of Architecture*, London: Penguin, 1980 (1966), p. 296

'As William Gilpin…' William Gilpin, *Observations, Relative Chiefly to Picturesque Beauty*, London: Balmire, 1786, p. 125

'As one of the leading thinkers…' Uvedale Price in Suzy Halimi, 'The Picturesque', *A Handbook to English Romanticism*, London: Palgrave Macmillan, 1992, pp. 213–15

'Take one experiment…' Greg Bratman et al., 'The benefits of nature experience: Improved affect and cognition', *Landscape and Urban Planning* 138 (June 2015), pp. 41–50

'Or look at Seoul…' Moohan Kim, 'A Healing Environment Study focused on Attention Restoration Theory for Healthy Environmental Planning and Design: A Case Study of Cheonggyecheon', *Journal of the Korean Institute of Landscape Architecture* 45:1 (2017), pp. 94–104

'Create a park…' see M. P. White, I. Alcock, J. Grellier et al., 'Spending at least 120 minutes a week in nature is associated with good health and wellbeing', *Scientific Reports* 9:7730 (2019)

'A good park can be…' Rachel Cusk, *The Temporary*, London: Picador, 1996 (1995), p. 4

'They had leisure for healthful work…' Friedrich Engels, *The Condition of the Working Class in England*, Oxford: Oxford University Press, 1993 (1845), p. 16

'In Mount Auburn…' Blanche Linden-Ward, 'Strange but Genteel Pleasure Grounds: Tourist and Leisure Uses of Nineteenth-Century Rural Cemeteries', in Richard E. Meyer, ed., *Cemeteries and Gravemarkers: Voices of American Culture*, Logan, Utah: Utah State University Press, 1992, pp. 293–328; p. 293

'Some religious visitors…' quoted in Linden-Ward, p. 298

'Cemeteries here…' quoted in Linden-Ward, p. 305

'These costly exercises…' Harriet Jordan, 'Public Parks, 1885–1914', *Garden History* 22:1 (1994), pp. 85–113; p. 86

'This idea was poached…' Garrett Hardin, 'The Tragedy of the Commons', *Science* 162 (1968), pp. 1243–8

'She was not the first…' Elinor Ostrom, *Governing the Commons: The Evolution of Institutions for Collective Action*, Cambridge: Cambridge University Press, 2015, (1990)

'As a child, Olmsted had travelled…' Frederick Law Olmsted to Mariana Griswold Van Rensselaer (June 1893), Frederick Law Olmsted Papers, Library of Congress, USA.

'I was not until then convinced…' and other quotes, Johann Georg Ritter von Zimmermann, *Solitude Considered – With Respect to Its Influence Upon the Mind and the Heart*, London: C. Dilly, 1799 (1788), pp. 243–4

'The mind and body, the whole human…' Charles Beveridge, 'Olmsted: His Essential Theory', National Association for Olmsted Parks, https://www.olmsted.org/the-olmsted-legacy/olmsted-theory-and-design-principles/olmsted-his-essential-theory

'In James Baldwin's *Go Tell It on the Mountain* …' James
   Baldwin, *Go Tell It on the Mountain*, London: Penguin, 2001
   (1953), p. 193

'When colonial settlers arrived…' Henry Hudson quoted
   in Amy Johnson, 'The Saw-kill and the making of
   Dutch Manhattan', Gotham Centre for New York
   City History, https://www.gothamcenter.org/blog/
   the-saw-kill-and-the-making-of-dutch-manhattan

'The "Isle of Many Hills"…' in 'Recreating
   Mannahatta', Welikia, https://welikia.org/science/
   recreating-mannahatta/

'Recent archaeological explorations…' Marie Walsh,
   'Uncovering the Stories of Seneca Village', Central
   Park Conservancy, 7 February 2019, https://www.
   centralparknyc.org/articles/uncovering-seneca-village

'Gardens were laid out…' and 'In brochures…' Hickman,
   Therapeutic Landscapes, p. 29; p. 31

'What they had in common…' Maximilian Jacobi quoted in
   Hickman, *Therapeutic Landscapes*, p. 2

'Their landscaped parks…' Hickman, *Therapeutic
   Landscapes*, p. 40

'Beliefs in nature's healing properties…' W. A. F. Brown,
   quoted in Hickman, *Therapeutic Landscapes*, p. 34

'I have no doubt…' quoted in Hickman, *Therapeutic
   Landscapes*, p. 3

'He coined the term…' Roger S. Ulrich, 'Aesthetic and
   Affective Response to Natural Environment', in I. Altman
   and J. Wohlwill, eds, *Human Behavior and Environment*,
   New York: Plenum, 1983, pp. 85–125; p. 85

'Ulrich was actually the researcher…' see Roger S. Ulrich,
   'View Through a Window May Influence Recovery',
   Science 224:4647 (1984) pp. 420–2

'In one study, it was photographs…' Roger Ulrich,
   'Visual landscape preference: A model and application',
   Man-Environment Systems 7:5 (1977), pp. 279–93

'In one gloriously circular study…' Roger Ulrich
and M. Zuckerman, 'Preference for landscape
paintings: Differences as a function of sensation-seeking',
Unpublished research, Departments of Geography and
Psychology, University of Delaware, 1981

'But, as Timothy Morton puts it…' Morton, *The Ecological
Thought*, p. 3

'They are also places of contradiction…' Olivette Otele,
Arts and Humanities Research Council, *Reluctant Sites of
Memory*, https://reluctantsitesofmemory.com/

'Many elegantly designed and popular…' D. Seo and Y. Kwon,
'Sustainable Strategies for the Dynamic Equilibrium of
the Urban Stream, Cheonggyecheon', IOP Conference
Series: Earth and Environmental Science 143 (2018)

'It's simply been too popular…' Sven Töpel quoted in
Oliver Wainwright, 'An embarrassment to the city: What
went wrong with the £725m gateway to Cambridge?',
Guardian (13 June 2017), https://www.theguardian.com/
artanddesign/architecture-design-blog/2017/jun/13/
an-embarrassment-to-the-city-what-went-wrong-with-
the-725m-gateway-to-cambridge

'Our children's friends…' quoted in 'Developers accused
of "segregating" children at London playground', BBC
News (26 March 2019), https://www.bbc.co.uk/news/
uk-england-london-47707838

'A 2018–19 monitor…' 'Monitor of Engagement with
the Natural Environment Children's Report', Natural
England, 2019, https://assets.publishing.service.gov.uk/
government/uploads/system/uploads/attachment_data/
file/828838/Monitor_of_Engagement_with_the_Natural_
Environment__MENE__Childrens_Report_2018-2019_
rev.pdf

'The same survey also insists…' 'Monitor of Engagement
with the Natural Environment,' Natural England, 2018.
https://assets.publishing.service.gov.uk/government/
uploads/system/uploads/attachment_data/file/828552/

Monitor_Engagement_Natural_Environment_2018_2019_
v2.pdf

'There was a pond…' and 'I like nature things…'; 'They ran
around…' and 'Sparrers ain't birds…', Beryl Gilroy, *Black
Teacher*, London: Bogle-L'Ouverture Press, 1994 (1976),
pp. 47–8; p.81

'The more stimulating an environment…' see L. J. Wolf et al.,
'Is variety the spice of life? An experimental investigation
into the effects of species richness on self-reported mental
well-being', PLoS ONE, 12:1 (2017), Web.

'I think our job…' Donna Haraway, 'Anthropocene,
Capitalocene, Plantationocene, Chthulucene: Making Kin',
Environmental Humanities 1 (May 2015) pp. 159–65; p.160

Farm

'His shepherds are wrapped up…' Virgil, *Eclogues*, Project
Gutenberg, p. 3

'They are safe places…' Liz Everard, 'Care farming: creating
community in nature', SANE Australia (20 May 2020),
https://www.sane.org/information-stories/the-sane-blog/
wellbeing/care-farming

'Nan Shepherd writes…' Nan Shepherd, *The Living Mountain*,
Edinburgh: Canongate, 2011 (1977), p. 82

'Round on the labourer…' Virgil, *Georgics*, Project
Gutenberg, p. 20

'Only then does he realise…' James Rebanks, *The Shepherd's
Life: A Tale of the Lake District*, London: Penguin, 2015, p. 174

'in nineteenth-century Britain…' Helen Charman, 'Behind
the Poem': On 'In the Pleasure Dairy', the Poetry Society,
Poetry Review (Spring 2020), https://poetrysociety.org.uk/
publications-section/the-poetry-review/behind-the-poem/
helen-charman-on-in-the-pleasure-dairy/

'I never got the chance…' Mozie Fenn quoted in
'Forgotten Stories: hop-picking in the fields of Kent,'
London's Royal Docks, https://londonsroyaldocks.com/
forgotten-stories-hop-picking-fields-kent/

'WWOOF answers the needs…' Sue Coppard, 'History
of WWOOF', WWOOF Independents, https://
wwoofindependents.org/history-wwoof

'It's the "bullshit jobs" phenomenon…' David Graeber,
Bullshit Jobs: A Theory, London: Allen Lane, 2018

'These kinds of activities…' Drew Leder, The Absent Body,
Chicago: University of Chicago Press, 1990

'The Protestant Ethic…' Max Weber, The Protestant Ethic and
the Spirit of Capitalism, London: Penguin, 2002 (1905)

'Whether or not we agree…' Kathi Weeks, The Problem with
Work: Feminism, Marxism, Antiwork Politics and Postwar
Imaginaries, Durham and London: Duke University Press,
2011, p. 46

'I have been taking antidepressants…' Narayani Menon,
'Ishtu', Lecker 1 (2019), pp. 68–70; p. 69

'In Chinese and Ayurvedic systems…' Waltraud
Ernst, ed., Work, Psychiatry and Society 1751–2015,
Manchester: Manchester University Press, 2016, p. 5

'The anthropologist James C. Scott…' James C. Scott,
Against the Grain: A Deep History of the Earliest States, New
Haven: Yale University Press, 2017

'He blamed powerful leaders…' and other quotes, Paul
Lafargue, The Right to Be Lazy, trans. Charles Kerr (1883),
Marxists Internet Archive, https://www.marxists.org/
archive/lafargue/1883/lazy/

'Rerouting and deepening…' Jenny Odell, How to Do
Nothing: Resisting the Attention Economy, Brooklyn and
London: Melville House, 2019, p. xii

'Arriving at Greatford Hall…' quoted in Ernst, 'Introduction',
Work, Psychiatry and Society, pp. 1–30; p. 7

'The twentieth-century philosopher and historian…' Michel
    Foucault, *Discipline and Punish: The Birth of the Prison*,
    London: Penguin, 2019 (1975)
'After emancipation …' Leonard Smith, *Insanity,
    Race and Colonialism: Managing Mental Disorder in
    the Post-Emancipation British Caribbean 1838–1914*,
    Basingstoke: Palgrave Macmillan, 2014
'Many inmate agricultural workers…' 'State and federal
    prison wage policies and sourcing information', Prison
    Policy Initiative (10 April 2017), https://www.prisonpolicy.
    org/reports/wage_policies.html
'One study, the "The Economic Benefits of Ecominds"…'
    Olivier Vardakoulias, 'The Economic Benefits of
    Ecominds: A Case Study', *NEF Consulting*, London: New
    Economics Foundation, 2013
'It's a useful term, but I'm more convinced…' Gregg
    Mitman, 'Reflections on the Plantationocene: A
    Conversation with Donna Haraway and Anna Tsing,'
    Edge Effects 18 June 2019, https://edgeeffects.net/
    haraway-tsing-plantationocene/
'Half of the world's habitable land…' Hannah Ritchie and
    Max Roser, 'Land Use', Our World in Data (September
    2019), https://ourworldindata.org/land-use
'In Australia…' Helen Berry et al., 'Climate Change
    and Farmers' Mental Health: Risks and Responses',
    Asia Pacific Journal of Public Health 23:2 (March
    2011), pp.119–32; Robert Muller, 'Climate Change
    Affecting Farmers' Mental Health', *Psychology Today*
    (December 2017), https://www.psychologytoday.
    com/gb/blog/talking-about-trauma/201712/
    climate-change-affecting-farmers-mental-health
'Drought, fire, flood…' Katerina Bryant, 'Farmers and mental
    distress', *Guardian* (23 December 2018), https://www.
    theguardian.com/society/2018/dec/23/farmers-and-
    mental-distress-im-still-a-bit-ashamed-about-my-story

'Across the drought-prone saddle…' Sam Jones,
'Grapes shrivel as Spanish farmers lament a
relentless drought', *Guardian* (9 July 2017), https://
www.theguardian.com/world/2017/jul/08/
spain-drought-farmers-climate-change-extremadura

'As the Indian scientist and philosopher…' Vandana Shiva,
Stolen Harvest, Boston: South End Press: 1999, p. 8

'The writer Margaret Atwood…' Margaret Atwood, 'Hope
and the "Everything Change"', *Science and the Imagination*
(November 2014), Vimeo, https://vimeo.com/118071435

'Colonisers spread the myth…' Bruce Pascoe, *Dark
Emu: Aboriginal Australia and the Birth of Agriculture*,
London: Scribe, 2019

'It is "the right to healthy…"' Paige Pfleger, 'Detroit's
urban farms: engines of growth, omens of change',
WHYY (11 January 2018), https://whyy.org/segments/
detroits-urban-farms-engines-growth-omens-change/

'That which does encourage us…' Gerrard Winstanley
and the Diggers, The True Levellers' Standard
Advanced, University of Oregon Scholar's Bank, 2002,
https://scholarsbank.uoregon.edu/xmlui/bitstream/
handle/1794/863/levellers.pdf?sequence=1&isAllowed=y

'As Pramesh Pokharel…' Pramesh Pokharel, 'International
day of peasant struggle: Peasant rights and COVID-19',
People's Dispatch (17 April 2020), https://peoplesdispatch.
org/2020/04/17/international-day-of-peasant-struggle-
peasant-rights-and-covid-19/

'The least I can say for myself…' and 'Traumatised and living
as a stateless refugee…' Bessie Head, 'Preface to Witchcraft',
A Woman Alone, Oxford: Heinemann, 1990, p. 28

'She christened it…' Bessie Head, *Serowe: Village of the Rain
Wind*, Oxford: Heinemann, 2008 (1981), p. viii

'But co-operative farming moved…' Head, 'The Boiteko
Project', *Serowe: Village of the Rain Wind*, p. 210

'She wrote about farming as a love letter…' Head, 'Some
notes on novel writing', *A Woman Alone*, p. 64

'In farming, she explained…' Bessie Head, 'Letter to Randolphe Vigne', *A Gesture of Belonging: Letters from Bessie Head 1965–1979*, Oxford: Heinemann, 1991, p. 68

'In A Question of Power…' Bessie Head, *A Question of Power*, Oxford: Heinemann, 1973, pp. 72–3

'It is impossible to become a vegetable gardener…' Head, *A Question of Power*, p. 72

'As she fell asleep…' Head, *A Question of Power*, p. 206

Virtual Nature

'It's not just raising questions…' Rita Felski, 'Critique and the Hermeneutics of Suspicion', *M/C: A Journal of Media and Culture* 15:1 (2012)

'In a landscape of cowboys…' Jean Baudrillard, *America*, London: Verso, 2010 (1986), p. 46

'Hyperreality is a third space…' Jean Baudrillard, *Simulacra and Simulations*, Ann Arbor: University of Michigan Press, 1994 (1981), p. 1

'As the philosopher Kate Soper…' Kate Soper, *What is Nature? Culture, Politics and the Non-Human*, New York: John Wiley, 1998 (1995), p. 196

'Reading Baudrillard's America now…' Baudrillard, *America*, p. 70

'It's best captured in a science-fiction story…' Baudrillard, *America*, p. 45

'Immersion in nature …' Richard Louv, *Last Child in the Woods*, London: Atlantic, 2010 (2005), p. 98; subsequent quotes p. 33; p. 35; p. 65

'In Ancient Greece…' Amy Orben, 'The Sisyphean Cycle of Technology Panics', *Perspectives on Psychological Science* 15:5 (30 June 2020), pp. 1–15

'As her colleague Andrew Przybylski…' Andrew Przybylski in 'Roman: What's Wrong with Screen Time?' produced by Kevin Core, My Name is… *BBC Radio 4* (24 August 2020), https://www.bbc.co.uk/programmes/m000lzjp

'From plastics to electronics…' Tina Costanza, 'The environmental impact of video games', *Silicon Republic* (10 July 2012), https://www.siliconrepublic.com/life/the-environmental-impact-of-video-games-infographic

'In her new media artwork…' J. R. Carpenter, 'Frontispiece', The Gathering Cloud (2016), http://luckysoap.com/thegatheringcloud/frontispiece.html

'Watching the game unfold…' Pete Etchells, *Lost in a Good Game*, London: Icon Books, 2019

'Yes, "there's an undeniable rush…"' Travis Northup, 'No Man's Sky Beyond Review', IGN (15 May 2020), https://www.ign.com/articles/2019/09/14/no-mans-sky-beyond-review

'Knowing another is endless…' Nan Shepherd, *The Living Mountain*, p. 108

'The games critic…' Simon Parkin, *Death by Videogame: Tales of Obsession from the Virtual Frontline*, London: Profile Books, 2015

'Take the Happinss…' see www.happinss.com/en

'In the UK, the company behind the Dream Machine…' Michael Dempsey, 'Training your brain to relax on a virtual island', BBC News (27 July 2020), https://www.bbc.co.uk/news/business-53245567

'Nao begins to meditate…' and other quotes, Ruth Ozeki, *A Tale for the Time Being*, Edinburgh: Canongate, 2013, p. 182; p. 205; p. 238.

'With Synctuition…' 'Review', App Follow (accessed August 2020), https://appfollow.io/android/synctuition-meditation-program/com.synctuition.synctuition

'Digitised mental health services…' Tom Foley and James Woollard, 'The digital future of mental healthcare and its workforce', Topol Review/NHS (February 2019), https://topol.hee.nhs.uk/wp-content/uploads/HEE-Topol-Review-Mental-health-paper.pdf

'More recently, the DARPA-funded...' Albert Rizzo, 'SimSensei', USC Institute for Creative Technologies, https://ict.usc.edu/prototypes/simsensei/

'As Shoshana Zuboff explains...' Shoshana Zuboff, *The Age of Surveillance Capitalism*, London: Profile, 2019, p. 136

'A glossy, glassed cell...' Ginny Battson, 'Glascella – A State of Being', Seasonalight (1 August 2020), https://seasonalight.com/2020/08/01/glascella-a-state-of-being/

'Well, they are gone...' Samuel Taylor Coleridge, 'This Lime-Tree Bower My Prison', 1797

'I lived in the first century of world wars...' Muriel Rukeyser, 'Poem', *The Speed of Darkness*, London: Vintage, 1968, p. 37

'The most anti-capitalist protest...' Johanna Hedva , 'Sick Woman Theory', *Mask* Magazine (January 2016), http://www.maskmagazine.com/not-again/struggle/sick-woman-theory

Lost Places

'After Katrina...' Jean Rhodes et al., 'The impact of hurricane Katrina on the mental and physical health of low-income parents in New Orleans', *The American Journal of Orthopsychiatry* 80:2 (2010), pp. 237–47

'According to the American Psychological Association...' American Psychological Association, Climate for Health and ecoAmerica, Mental Health and our Changing Climate (March 2017), p. 25, https://www.apa.org/news/press/releases/2017/03/mental-health-climate.pdf

'Antipsychotics...' K. Martin-Latry, M. P. Goumy, P. Latry, et al., 'Psychotropic drugs use and risk of heat-related hospitalization', *European Psychiatry* 22 (2007), pp. 335–8

'There's another kind of suffering...' Rob Nixon, *Slow Violence and the Environmentalism of the Poor*, Cambridge, MA: Harvard University Press, 2013 (2011)

'After spending time with miners...' Glenn Albrecht et al., 'Solastalgia: the distress caused by environmental change', *Australasian Psychiatry* 15 (2007), pp. 95–8

'If a person seeks solace...' Glenn Albrecht, *Earth Emotions: New Words for a New World*, Ithaca: Cornell University Press, 2019, p. 38

'One article published...' Kelly Rose-Clarke et al., 'Rethinking research on the social determinants of global mental health', *The Lancet* 7:8 (2020), pp. 659–62

'Climate and health researchers...' Ashlee Cunsolo and Neville Ellis, 'Ecological grief as a mental health response to climate change-related loss', *Nature Climate Change* 8 (2018), pp. 275–81

'The APA has added...' American Psychological Association, *Mental Health and Our Changing Climate*, p. 68; p. 57.

'Are climate grief and solastalgia...' see 'Challenging the Culture of Psychiatric Diagnosis', A Disorder for Everyone, http://www.adisorder4everyone.com/

'Anthropocene disorder...' Timothy Clark, *Ecocriticism on the Edge*, London: Bloomsbury (2015), p. 140

'As Tamás explains...' Rebecca Tamás, *Strangers: Essays on the Human and the Non-Human*, London: Makina Books, 2020, pp. 81–2

'When land is being lost...' Caitlin DeSilvey, Simon Naylor and Colin Sackett, *Anticipatory History*, Axminster: Uniform Books, 2011, pp. 56–7

'As Conrad explains...' and further quotes, CAConrad, 'An Interview with CAConrad', Tripwire 10, Oakland: 2016, pp. 46–68; pp.63–4

'In Hua-Yen Buddhism...' F. Cook, *Hua-Yen Buddhism: The Jewel Net of Indra*, University Park and London: University of Pennsylvania Press, 1977, p. 4

'We are bound together...' Cook, *Hua-Yen Buddhism*, p.16

'When we lose...' Judith Butler, *Precarious Life: The Power of Mourning and Violence*, London: Verso, 2006 (2004), p. 22

'Either we build the islands up…' and other quotes from
  Kiribati, interview with filmmaker Sara Penrhyn
  Jones, *Troubled Waters* (2015), Vimeo, https://vimeo.
  com/130445697

'In the Anishinaabe tradition …' Kyle P. Whyte, 'Indigenous
  Science (Fiction) for the Anthropocene: Ancestral
  Dystopias and Fantasies of Climate Change Crises',
  Environment and Planning 1:1–2 (March 2018), pp. 224–42;
  pp. 228–9

'The goals, for this network and others…' 'About', Climate
  Justice Alliance, https://climatejusticealliance.org/about/

'How do people cope…' Sian Sullivan, '"We are heartbroken
  and furious!" Violence and the (anti-)globalisation
  movement(s)', CSGR Working Paper 133:04 (May
  2004), p. 23

'But as Starhawk insists…' Starhawk, quoted in *Reweaving The
  World: The Emergence of Eco-Feminism*, Irene Diamond and
  Gloria Orenstein, eds., San Francisco: Sierra Club Books,
  1990, p. 79

'Recognise that you are not…' Rhubaba quoted in Angeliki
  Roussou, 'Farewell, Art: Imagining a Hospitable Planetary
  Future', MAP (July 2020), https://mapmagazine.co.uk/
  farewell-art-imagining-a-hospitable-planetary-future

Acknowledgements

Writing a book takes time and a great deal of help. My first thanks are to the Arts and Humanities Research Council for funding my project, Cultures of Nature and Wellbeing: Connecting Health and the Environment Through Literature in 2016. With this support I was able to run and attend many of the events described in this book, and meet the practitioners and people seeking outdoor therapies whose stories I have tried my best to convey. I'm grateful to those people for accepting my presence as a loosely defined 'participant observer' or, rather, someone eager to learn from them and to better understand the true meaning of 'eco-recovery' in our very damaged world.

I'm grateful to Bath Spa University for supporting my research at all stages. Travel to Finland and to many conferences in the UK would not have been possible without seed grant funding from our Research Support Office Interdisciplinary conversations hosted by the Research Centre for Environmental Humanities have helped me extend my thinking and turn a lot of earlier notions upside down. Colleagues and friends at BSU who have attended talks and commented on my work in progress have kindly jostled me in the right direction. Thanks to Owain Jones for encouraging undisciplined research, Sage Brice for introducing me to Aust Cliff, and the artist Antony Lyons, whose extraordinary film *Transgression (Rising Waters)* inspired 'Lost Places' and my interest in the landscape of the Severn Estuary. Kate Rigby, Terry Gifford, Richard Kerridge, Sara Penrhyn Jones and Sian Sullivan deserve particular thanks for sending very good ideas my way, and for all they do to make the environmental humanities a brave and hopeful enterprise.

The Rachel Carson Center at Ludwig-Maximilians-Universität, Munich, will have my eternal gratitude for offering me a Carson Writing Fellowship in 2018–19. This astonishing place has given space and encouragement to so many researchers and creative practitioners, often at that awkward stage in a project when we are trying to turn big ideas into a coherent form. My sincere thanks go to my friend Dr Anna Pilz for being such a generous reader, and to the RCC fellows and students who were kind and clever enough to make sense of an impossibly fragmentary draft of my first chapter, and offer reassurance and very good advice.

My agent, Carrie Plitt at Felicity Bryan Associates, saw the potential in this book in its very earliest form. I am deeply thankful to her for helping transform it in so many ways: in particular for suggesting the structure that enabled me to actually start writing it, and for her detailed editorial guidance as I found my confidence and voice. Thank you to my brilliant editor Angelique Tran Van Sang for giving it a home at Bloomsbury and helping to realise the promise of the proposal, and to

ACKNOWLEDGEMENTS

Jasmine Horsey for her editorial encouragement and vital direction at the final stages of writing. Thanks to Lauren Whybrow and Greg Heinimann for making the book beautiful and to the eagle-eyed Kate Quarry for perfecting the manuscript and cheering it through to publication.

My heartfelt thanks go to all the friends who have shared kindness, walks, swims and stories of what 'nature cures' mean to you, both positive and 'more complicated than that'. My love and endless thanks to my family – Yvonne, Jeff and Caren – for your belief in me and for your insistence we always make the most of good weather and get outside. Thank you to Jo for all the conversations, reading, rereading, jokes, and perfect generosity of love and thought. It would not be possible (or interesting) without you.

Index

A Note on the Type

The text of this book is set in Bembo, which was first used in 1495 by the Venetian printer Aldus Manutius for Cardinal Bembo's *De Aetna*. The original types were cut for Manutius by Francesco Griffo. Bembo was one of the types used by Claude Garamond (1480–1561) as a model for his Romain de l'Université, and so it was a forerunner of what became the standard European type for the following two centuries. Its modern form follows the original types and was designed for Monotype in 1929.

A Note on the Type